D0204229

OFFICIALLY DISCARDED BY
UNIVERSITY OF PITTSBURGH LIBRARY

CORPORATE HEGEMONY

CORPORATE HEGEMONY

William M. Dugger

CONTRIBUTIONS IN ECONOMICS AND ECONOMIC HISTORY,
NUMBER 97

GREENWOOD PRESS
New York • Westport, Connecticut • London

Library of Congress Cataloging-in-Publication Data

Dugger, William M.
   Corporate hegemony / William M. Dugger.
     p. cm. — (Contributions in economics and economic history,
  ISSN 0084–9235 : no. 97)
   Bibliography: p.
   Includes index.
   ISBN 0–313–26711–1 (lib. bdg. : alk. paper)
   1. Corporations—United States. 2. Consolidation and merger of
corporations—United States. 3. Big business—United States.
4. Industrial concentration—United States. I. Title. II. Series.
  HD2785.D84   1989
  338.7'4'0973—dc20   89–2188

British Library Cataloguing in Publication Data is available.

Copyright © 1989 by William M. Dugger

All rights reserved. No portion of this book may be
reproduced, by any process or technique, without the
express written consent of the publisher.

Library of Congress Catalog Card Number: 89–2188
ISBN: 0–313–26711–1
ISSN: 0084–9235

First published in 1989

Greenwood Press, Inc.
88 Post Road West, Westport, Connecticut 06881

Printed in the United States of America

The paper used in this book complies with the
Permanent Paper Standard issued by the National
Information Standards Organization (Z39.48–1984).

10 9 8 7 6 5 4 3 2 1

Copyright Acknowledgments

   Several chapters herein contain previously published material. Sections from the Preface are
reprinted with permission of M. E. Sharpe, Inc., publisher, Armonk, New York 10504, from
the January/February 1987 issue of *Challenge*. Portions of Chapters 1 and 2 are reprinted from
the *Journal of Economic Issues* by special permission of the copyright holder, the Association
for Evolutionary Economics. Part of Chapter 6 first appeared in the *Review of Social Economy*,
and is reprinted with permission.

FOR PAULY

Contents

Preface

THE NATURE OF THE MODERN ECONOMY

The modern economy, whether in Western Europe or North America, is not a competitive market economy but a corporate capitalist economy. The dynamic factor in these capitalist economies is not competition in the market but corporate power in society. The market is merely an arrangement for facilitating the exchange of commodities. Supply and demand in the market are not causes. They are effects. They simply reflect the underlying realities of growing corporate power and of reaction to it. The market does not cause people to act the way they do. It simply registers people's actions. This study will deal with the real power, the real reasons people act, not with supply and demand, not with the market.

In the corporate economies of the contemporary West, the market is a passive institution. The active institution is the corporation. The corporation, not the market, is the prime mover. And the corporation is moving toward consolidation. In the United States, billions of dollars have been diverted from industry and agriculture to finance corporate mergers and acquisitions instead. Even the conservative *Fortune* magazine has estimated that corporate mergers and raids involving public corporations cost $56.7 billion in 1981, $31.5 billion in 1982, $39.5 billion in 1983, and $82.7 billion in 1984. According to the *Statistical Abstract of the United States, 1988*, mergers and acquisitions cost \$179.8 billion in 1985 and \$173.1 billion in 1986. None of that two-year total of \$352.9 billion paid for as much as a single connecting bolt in a new machine or a simple bunsen burner in a new laboratory. Nothing went for an ounce of new fertilizer nor a single seed for a new crop. While U.S. industry needed new, up-to-date machinery and more research and development, it got corporate mergers, leveraged buyouts, shareholder buybacks, junk bonds, insider trading, golden parachutes, and greenmail. And while the American farmer was being bankrupted, we were all treated to more of the same: billions for mergers but only leftovers for the family farm. Even the staid old Federal Reserve System took note of the anomaly. The Fed estimated, in a recent *Federal Reserve Bulletin* article, that mergers, acquisitions, leveraged buyouts, and shareholder buybacks absorbed about \$200 billion in stock of nonfinancial corporations between 1983 and 1985. Not even the Wall Street panic of October 19, 1987, slowed the rising merger and acquisition wave. As reported by the *New York Times* in its January 3, 1989, issue, mergers, acquisitions, and leveraged buyouts completed in 1988 cost a staggering \$266 billion.

The natural and beneficial working of the market is not a reality in most of the industrialized West. The reality is growing corporate power. That growing power has taken some unexpected turns in the United States. In the 1980s, corporate power has moved out of the old, oligopolistic industrial sector. The old industrial behemoths have diversified out of industry. For example, General Motors has bought its way out of the automobile industry by buying the Electronic Data Systems Corporation for \$5 billion and the Hughes Aircraft Corporation for another \$5 billion. U.S. Steel has bought its way out of the steel industry by acquiring Marathon Oil for \$5.9 billion, Texas Oil and Gas Corporation for \$3 billion, and a whole hodgepodge of other companies as well. To reflect its transformation through diversification, U.S. Steel has changed its name to USX. Other formerly industrial behemoths have engaged in their own aggressive pushes to diversify, though not on the same grand scale as General Motors and U.S. Steel. Nevertheless, the trend toward diversification is undeniable. As these industrial behemoths have moved into the new high-technology and service sectors, they have shifted the locus of corporate power into the high-tech sector of the Sunbelt (the military-industrial, southern rim) and into the financial and business services sectors of New York (also the safe haven for flight capital from Third World kleptocracies like Haiti under Duvalier and the Philippines under Marcos). Power is shifting away from the old low-tech, industrial sector of the Frostbelt, leaving rusting plants, crumbling communities, and unemployed workers behind. The Frostbelt is composed primarily of those states that have lost political and economic clout over the past decade, while the Sunbelt is made up of those states that have increased their clout over this same period. The Sunbelt has gained power because its political representatives dominate major military appropriations committees in Congress and because the states in that region are home to a large number of defense contractors. The dominance of Sunbelt politicians has allowed them to channel large streams of Carter–Reagan military spending into their own states. Military spending is the true impetus behind the growth of high tech in the Sunbelt at the expense of the Frostbelt. Furthermore, the federal deficit and the high interest rates paid to finance it are the real reasons for the growth of the financial service sector in New York. These major shifts in the composition of the U.S. economy have little to do with swings in supply and demand in the market.

NEW INTERNATIONAL MARKETPLACE?

In spite of much talk about a new international marketplace, shifts in the composition of the U.S. economy are not natural outcomes of market forces, international or otherwise. True, foreign exchange fluctuations have played havoc with the U.S. trade balance, but those fluctuations were not due to fundamental industrial or agricultural changes. The competition in the allegedly new international marketplace emerged because of a rise in the international value of the dollar, which came about because Paul Volcker, in true monetarist fashion, drove up interest rates while at the Fed and thereby attracted a massive financial inflow that bid up the dollar to ridiculous heights. The high dollar allowed a flood of imports to displace the output of domestic producers. Steel and autos, mainstays of the Frostbelt, were among the hardest hit domestic industries. But the high dollar, which caused the displacement in the first place, was not a natural market phenomenon. Rather than the result of natural market forces, the recent shifts in the U.S. economy are the result of four power processes. These processes are militarization, labor exploitation, the massive federal deficit, and diversification. The processes operate behind supply and demand. That is, they are the prime movers that cause supply or demand to change. Supply and demand react passively to them. Supply and demand are not causal with respect to any of them.

The militarization of the U.S. economy has given rise to massive new investment and employment opportunities in states (the south plus California and parts of New England) with the political power to pull in big defense contracts. So the geographic shift in job opportunities in the United States is not caused by a natural market process. It is the result of the political power of giant defense contractors, and is supported by the members of Congress from certain key states. With the rapid military buildup under the Reagan administration, the geographic shift in employment to the defense-contracting states has speeded up. And, with the emphasis on high-tech, Star Wars projects, the military buildup is stimulating the development of a whole array of new technologies. Hence, the technological shift, represented by the Silicon Valley phenomenon, owes itself to the particular direction of the Reagan military buildup, not to the natural workings of the market. (The military buildup began during the Carter administration but greatly accelerated during the Reagan administration.)

Labor exploitation, just as much as new technology, is the foundation of Silicon Valley. Many of the processes required to turn out the new chips used in high-tech defense systems are contracted out to legal and illegal aliens to perform under substandard conditions for substandard wages. Silicon Valley is a day's ride up the coast from the Mexican border. It is also the final destination for many of the boat people of Southeast Asia, desperate for work of any kind. Much of the work is also outplaced to export platforms such as Hong Kong, Singapore, and South Korea, where repressive governments keep wages low and labor docile. Labor is not the only resource exploited by the high-tech sector. Silicon Valley's water supply, for example, is under serious threat from a whole witch's brew of effluents released in the production of computer chips.

The way the massive military buildup is being financed is also having a strong impact on the shifting center of balance in the U.S. economy. It is being financed with new borrowing, not new taxes. The federal deficit rose from $74 billion in 1980 to $221 billion in 1986 and then dipped to $150 billion in 1987. Net interest paid by the federal government rose from $53 billion a year in 1980 to $139 billion in 1987. The soaring federal deficit, combined with the high interest rate policy of the Federal Reserve, have combined to redistribute a large portion of the national income to the financial service sector. Net interest represented 5 percent of national income in the first half of the 1970s. That doubled to 10 percent of national income in the first half of the 1980s. The financial sector is dominated by the big New York banks, so the way we have financed the military buildup has contributed to the geographical shift of income and jobs out of the industrial Midwest and into the Northeast financial service area. Deficit financing at high interest rates is not a natural market phenomenon but a political program.

Corporate diversification also has had a profound impact on the shifting center of balance of the U.S. economy. Not only have U.S. Steel and General Motors diversified out of manufacturing, but many of the old manufacturing oligopolies have done the same. Their diversification has been financed by milking their core manufacturing businesses for the cash flow needed to buy into high-tech military contracting, services, and other nonmanufacturing businesses. As they let their original manufacturing plants deteriorate without replacing or repairing them, they take the cash flow generated by their neglect and use it to get out of the Rustbelt, the rusting of which they have largely caused in the first place. Some diversifying corporations take one further step—they form a coalition with their former competitors. General Motors is leading the way down this anticompetitive path by forming a joint venture with Toyota and buying into Isuzu. This forming of coalitions is a defensive strategy, not a new investment initiative. It helps cement cooperation between former competitors, which then keeps prices up in the old industry, yielding maximum profit margins and cash flows for use in continued diversification. In sum, militarization, labor exploitation, huge federal deficits, and corporate diversification, not market competition, are causing the deindustrialization of America. Furthermore, monetarism, not the natural market process, has promoted deindustrialization with high interest rates and unstable exchange rates.

RISING CORPORATE POWER

The market is not deindustrializing the United States economy. Natural market forces are not shifting the geographical and sectoral balance of the U.S. economy in a benign adjustment to natural forces of supply and demand. Supply and demand merely reflect the underlying moves of corporate power, new technology, and class conflict. The market is not coordinating economic activity. The market is not monitoring economic activity. The market is not the source of modern technology. Corporate hierarchies, working through collective action, coordinate economic activity. Corporate hierarchies, working with government agencies, monitor economic activity. Corporate hierarchies, working with the joint stock of tools and skills, are applying new technologies to the arms race. Markets only reflect these underlying actions. True enough, supply and demand establish a market price and clear the market. But the real action occurs beyond supply and demand. The real action occurs within the institutions used to organize people for effective collective action. In the West, at the close of the twentieth century, that means one institution in particular—the modern corporation. The capitalist corporation, not the labor union, and not the worker cooperative, dominates the economic process.

Unfortunately, the capitalist corporation is an inherently narrow and short-sighted organization. It has not evolved to serve the public purpose. It has not evolved to monitor and coordinate economic activity for the benefit of society at large. The corporation has evolved to serve the interests of whoever controls it, at the expense of whoever does not. This is a simple but profound truth. The corporation, not the market, is the dominant economic institution in the industrialized West, and it serves the private purpose rather than the public purpose. Furthermore, the recent merger mania has shortened the time horizon and narrowed the scope of the private purpose served by the corporate institution. A corporation that takes the long view of its profits and the broad view of its social responsibilities is in great danger of being acquired by an investor group that can gain financially by taking over the corporation and turning it to the pursuit of more immediate profit. With new financial and organizational tools at their disposal, corporate raiders can now attack even the very largest of corporations.

Junk bonds—corporate bonds of very low quality usually placed directly with large pension or mutual funds—have allowed corporate raiders to tap into vast new reservoirs of finance to fund their raids. M-form organizations—new organizational structures that allow huge commercial empires to be managed by one central staff—provide the managerial tools needed to manage even the largest takeover candidate. So now, no corporation is safe from the threat of a hostile takeover. As a result, corporate managers have rushed to protect themselves from the raiders with golden parachutes and by paying more attention to the immediate bottom line. To pump up their stock's market value and discourage raids, long-term benefits and social responsibility have been sacrificed to short-term profits.

Corporate planning and administration have progressed to a point where a few hundred managers and support staff can run a commercial-industrial empire that spans the globe and employs hundreds of thousands of workers to produce goods and services worth tens of billions of dollars a year. The corporate institution has broken through both organizational and national constraints. So while corporate purpose has narrowed down to the immediate bottom line, corporate planning and administration have expanded. The modern economy has become a global, corporate economy. And the corporate economy is a mindless growth, driven onward by a renegade institution that serves its own narrow and immediate interests and denies its long-term, social responsibilities.

THE CORPORATION IN PERSPECTIVE

Before the rise of the big corporation, economic forces pushed the United States one way, technological forces pushed it another way, and political and other forces pushed different ways as well. The resulting direction of movement was largely haphazard, and the society itself was largely pluralistic. Except for during the Puritan period, no one institution dominated it. But now life in the United States is dominated by the giant, capitalist corporation. The giant corporation is a jealous institution. The values and beliefs it teaches are the purest essence of capitalism. They are also extraordinarily corrosive. Capitalism, Inc. eats away at the alternative lifestyles and institutions that once provided a degree of balance to the society. As a result, the United States is becoming hegemonic rather than pluralistic. The effects are most pronounced in middle-class circles, but are spreading elsewhere.

Careerism is the corrosive personal factor in corporate life. The man and woman on the make in the corporate world must learn to define themselves and their values in terms of their careers. For those not born at the top, the career climb demands sacrificing noncorporate values to the pursuit of corporate ones. Long hours at work and frequent trips to distant cities remove the careerist from kith and kin. The values of the corporate career replace

family values. (corporate values are more rational than the
values learned   they certainly are more enticing ones. Once
lured into purs   the corporate world, the costs of the pursuit
increase steeply.   job turns out to be far more than just a job.
It turns out to be a way of life, an absorbing way of life. In the corporate
fast lane, the images of success, status, and prowess must be pursued and
projected at all times. Ever greater amounts of personal energy and commitment must be given to the corporation by taking them away from the
family, the community, and other spheres of life. The increasing commitment leaves those other spheres of life less and less meaningful and valuable
to the corporate careerist, so that even more personal energy is devoted to
the corporate career and even less to noncareer life. At some point, careerists
become addicts. They become corporadoes. The more they invest in the
corporation, the more they must invest, because it has become the only
thing that gives them a payoff. So at the personal level, the corporate career
pushes many of us into a narrow and addictive channel.

At the institutional level, the core value of corporate life—career success—
corrodes away the values of noncorporate institutions. The main change
here is an accelerated weakening of family and community and a growing
distortion of church, state, and school. These noncorporate institutions used
to provide a rough balance of different values and meanings. But with their
corrosion, a social vacuum has opened up. The social space they once
occupied is being filled by the corporation. The corporation is becoming
more things to more people. It is becoming a total institution.

In the realm of the family, upper- and lower-class families are little affected
by the effects of corporate careers. Poverty, not corporate careerism, tears
the lower-class family apart, while the upper-class family is still able to
insulate itself from the strains suffered by those just below. But the middle-
class family is being eaten away by the strains of corporate careerism.
Through the destructive effects of career, the corporation literally hollows
out the family. The corporation first drew in the father, absenting him from
the family circle as he pursued career values and learned to interpret his life
in career terms. The corporation now lures away the mother too, as more
and more women pursue their own corporate careers. The family of corporate careerists is becoming a hollow shell. It still stands, but it means
much less to us than it used to mean.

Community life in the United States, though honored with much nos-
talgic admiration, was never all that admirable in the first place. The small
town and the ethnic neighborhood were as often as not the main sources
of bigotry, superstition, and intolerance in the United States. Nonetheless,
communal life there may have counterbalanced to some extent the cen-
tralizing forces of the broader society. So as corporate careerism eats away
what communal life there was in the small towns and ethnic neighborhoods,
a counterbalancing institution of sorts is being lost. Progressives will not

miss the small town or the ethnic neighborhood, but that is not the point. The point is that one more counterbalancing influence is being absorbed into the corporate realm.

The school is potentially a stronger and more enlightening counterbalancing institution than the small town or the neighborhood. The college experience has a particularly strong effect on middle-class youth who move away from home for their four years of college life. Unfortunately, the allure of the corporate career has had a profoundly negative impact on U.S. education, from preschool through grad school. Most schools have become mere vocational extensions of the capitalist corporation's need for properly trained and disciplined workers. Schools prepare students for corporate careers and corporate work, not for free inquiry and free life.

In the religious realm, corporate-wrought changes in school, community, and family have left influential church leaders afraid and disoriented. As in other instances of revolutionary institutional change, those who have lost their bearings in the new society are calling for a return to the old values. Many American church officials, particularly the electronic evangelists, attack the schools for teaching so-called secular humanism and the mass media for its alleged liberal bias. Their fear of and anger toward feminism and gay rights reflect the real pain caused by the disintegration of their cherished family and community lifestyles. Nonetheless, their actions will not preserve their lifestyle because they are directed against a series of handy scapegoats, not against the actual agent of change. The real agent of change is the corporation.

In the political realm, the state has become a convenient scapegoat for the disturbing changes unleashed by the corporation's rise to cultural preeminence. With a reactionary wing of Republicans and a conservative wing of Democrats, a one-party system deprives the people of the United States of real political alternatives. Pushed off balance by their one-party system that calls itself a two-party system and by a strangely contradictory kind of antigovernmental patriotism, most people blame the government for what is happening to their family, church, and community. So they attack the government for the harm done by the capitalist corporation. Confused by what is happening to them, Americans are dismantling the welfare state, selling off important government functions to the highest corporate bidders, and deregulating the giant corporations—all of which further strengthen the corporation.

Schools (at least the professional and vocational ones), churches (at least the confused fundamentalist ones), the state (at least under reactionary administrations), and families (particularly those of corporate careerists) are all beginning to reinforce the main drift toward corporate hegemony. Class is important as well, but in an unexplored way. In the United States, a working-class revolt is distinctly not in the offing. But a middle-class counterrevolution, even without the working-class revolution, is occurring at this very moment. The social forces working themselves out as corporate hegemony have their strongest impact on the solid middle class. And it is the middle class that is moving to the extreme right in a counterrevolutionary fashion, even though there is no working-class revolution to counter in the first place. But since most critical intellectuals have more or less ignored the middle class, they have failed to understand the growing right-wing extremism of the middle class in the United States at the close of the twentieth century. The corporation has come to dominate the middle class as never before. But that domination generally has been neglected. So what follows is a badly needed report on the seriously deranged condition of that neglected class. The report is not framed in terms of supply and demand in the market, but in terms of corporate power and corporate hegemony, newer and far more potent factors in the social landscape.

Corporate hegemony, viewed in the large, means that the corporation is coming to dominate other, formerly independent institutions to such an extent that the capitalist corporation is becoming a total institution. The corporation is coming to play a dominant role in all areas of life. The meanings, values, and beliefs of the capitalist corporation have replaced those of the church, the community, the family, and the school. The corporate embrace is becoming total. Corporate hegemony, viewed in the small, means that the corporation is coming to dominate the individuals who perform its tasks. Individual corporadoes are coming to depend on the corporation for the meaning in their lives and for their values and beliefs. As they do, they lose the ability to infuse their lives with their own individual meaning and they lose their own individual values and beliefs. As they lose the individuality of free adults, they gain the conformity of subjects. They become subjects of a totalitarianism as profound as any, even though corporate domination is less coercive and less violent than classical fascism, and even though corporate hegemony provides some of its victims with a large measure of economic abundance.

Acknowledgments

Ken Cochran of the University of North Texas, Warren Samuels of Michigan State University, Rick Tilman of the University of Nevada–Las Vegas, and Marc Tool of California State University–Sacramento each made many penetrating comments on different drafts of the manuscript. Their help is deeply appreciated. Margaret Brezicki, Cynthia Harris, and Todd Adkins of Greenwood Press were very helpful. My mother, Mary G. Dugger, and my father, Charles B. Dugger, still inspire me. I typed the manuscript.

CORPORATE HEGEMONY

Introducing Your Neighbor and Mine:
The Corporate Behemoth

It was among the lower levels of the middle classes, and especially among white-collar employees, that Hitler found his best troops.

—Michel Crozier

A GENERAL THEORY OF HEGEMONY

Pluralism

A culture dominated by the values of one institution contrasts sharply with the pluralist ideal of the Enlightenment. A pluralist culture is composed of the different values and beliefs propagated by several independent institutions; a pluralist society is composed of individuals who hold their own syntheses of different values and beliefs. Obviously, pluralism requires a large degree of tolerance. Without it, the level of strife generated by clashing values and beliefs would be a constantly divisive force. Pluralism also requires a great deal of institutional autonomy. That is, the major institutions that make up a society must be independent enough to be able to propagate their own meaningful values and credible beliefs. Otherwise, one set of values and beliefs dominates the others and pluralism is lost. Pluralist cultures must, by definition, tolerate subcultures and countercultures. The different values and beliefs held by the dissenting social groups cannot be too contradictory, however, lest either the general culture be pulled apart into separate cultures or toleration break down into open conflict. While pluralism may be only an elusive ideal, that fact does not reduce the significance it has played in the West.

Furthermore, pluralism is very fragile—it is always sacrificed during the stress of war. And it is always being threatened by witch hunts, red scares, pogroms, and vigilantism. In spite of all this, pluralism is a profoundly significant ideal. Misused by propagandists, sacrificed during wars, seldom really achieved when peace breaks out, pluralism still lives on as an ideal worthy of the best in us.

The last characteristic of a genuine pluralism is a significant reduction in class differences. Pluralism requires tolerance and openness to alternative values and beliefs. These, in turn, require a high degree of equality, lest the intolerance and closed-mindedness that accompany inequality threaten the independence of alternative institutions and lifestyles. Pluralism and inequality are mutually exclusive. Ideally, a pluralist society would be strictly egalitarian. Historically, pluralism brought about at least a substantial reduction in the class inequalities of feudalism.

Pluralism is worth defending because, whether strictly maintained or only approximated, it is the breeding ground of individual will and of independent, mature character. Strength of will grows only through its exercise. To grow strong, the will must be confronted with real choices to make and defend. We exercise our wills when we choose from a set of competing values and beliefs and then defend our choices. If we have the opportunity to make choices and to defend them from among the different values and beliefs we learn from independent institutions, we can fashion our own unique, individual character from our experiences.[1] But these confrontations and personal choices must be made within a general framework of tolerance, openness, and equality. Otherwise, they result in a reactionary growth, a hardening of false ideals, a reinforcement of racism, sexism, and other rationalizations of exploitation and domination. In a social framework of intolerance, closed-mindedness, and inequality, value confrontations and personal choices result in the development of fascist personalities. Under those circumstances, children develop into little totalitarians. But if we are not confronted with real choices and not forced to defend them against the real alternatives we reject, we never develop much strength of will nor much uniqueness of character. We turn out to be wishy-washy conformists or smiling robots—grist for someone else's mill, subjects of hegemony.

Pluralism is worth fighting for because children in pluralist societies have a chance to grow up within a supportive network of independent institutions that offer individuals meaningful and realistic choices from among the conflicting institutional values and beliefs. Under the right conditions, the individual's maturation interacts with the socialization of alternative groups to produce a free, individualized adult. As the individual grows from infant to child to adolescent to adult, the individual matures within a series of different institutions, each one of which presses its own form of socialization upon the growing individual. The major institutions or socializing groups that most of us pass through are the family, the church, the play group, the school, the gang, the state, the military, the political party, and the corporation or other work group. Not all of these are institutionalized groups whose independence and autonomy are essential to the maintenance of pluralism and the building of human character. In particular, the infantile play group, adolescent gang, and armed service need not be autonomous. In fact, if any of these are autonomous, the resulting disturbances of the peace threaten the tolerance needed to maintain pluralism. A society with a strong and independent military is never a pluralist society.

Assuming the maintenance of pluralism, which means that those groups organized to disturb the peace are kept under control, the growing infant acquires a set of values from her family that almost immediately come in conflict, to some degree, with the values of her play group. Issues are forced, choices are made. An individual with a will of her own begins to emerge. Ideally, she then is confronted with new and to some degree conflicting values and beliefs from her church, if she goes to church, and from her school. If her school is church-affiliated, she loses one important degree of freedom because she loses the challenge of resolving church–school contradictions for herself. If she is lucky, additional issues are forced by her participation in different institutions, more choices are made, and a stronger character emerges. Further encounters with perhaps a gang, a new family, an agency of the state, a corporation, or an armed service also occur as she passes through life. Ideally, each encounter presents new issues and new choices that help her to strengthen her will and to re-form her values and beliefs until there finally emerges the unique individual character of a free adult.[2] Then, her adult experiences and her reactions to them continue the formation and re-formation of her character throughout life.

The ideal maturation process within a pluralist society continuously presents individuals with conflicting values and beliefs promulgated by independent institutions. Resolution of these conflicts is the crucible of individual character. The major institutions must be independent, otherwise they will not be able to present individuals with value conflicts to resolve and synthesize into their own unique character. The significance of pluralism is personal as well as political. Pluralism is important and valuable because of the kind of persons it nurtures, not just because it may also include a multiparty political system and mass media organs owned by private rather than state interests, and certainly not because it may be accompanied by private ownership of the means of production. In fact, U.S. society is not pluralist, though it has privately owned mass media, privately owned means of production, and a privately owned system of political parties. Those are not at the heart of the matter, and never have been. For no matter how many political parties vie for the spoils, unless they represent real alternatives, their numbers make little difference. And no matter who owns the mass media, unless they present persistently critical views on topics of real import, they will not help persons form enlightened opinions on issues of significance. Furthermore, no matter who owns the means of production, if access to them is not available to all, then the ownership system is inadequate.

Character, more than socialism, is the issue. And pluralism, as the term is used here, refers to a society where individuals are free to mold their own character because they participate in many different, independent institutions that force individuals to make choices and to defend their choices within a broad framework of tolerance and equality. The significance of pluralism is in the struggle a person must make within herself to sort out and synthesize her own values and meanings from the conflicting values and meanings that confront her in her daily life as an active participant in different institutional affairs. The personal struggle pluralism forces upon us, as equal participants in conflicting institutions, molds us into free beings. It literally compels us to make real personal choices and to defend them, thereby driving us away from easy conformity and toward individual maturity. Ideally, pluralism makes us question institutionalized authority, and the questioning makes us free.

Of course, the description of pluralism and of how it forms individuals is oversimplified and idealized. Nevertheless, it is sufficient to contrast with hegemony. Hegemony exists in a society where individuals are not free to mold their own characters because they do not participate in numerous different, independent institutions that force them to make and defend real choices within a broad framework of tolerance and equality. Pluralism forces people to develop individual character. Hegemony allows them the ease of conformity and the safety of the anonymous subject. Pluralism degenerates into hegemony whenever any of the major institutions of society comes to dominate the other institutions, making them dependent and taking away their autonomy. Out of all the major institutions, the state is the one that has dominated the others most frequently. So state domination is the typical form taken by a hegemonic society.

The hegemony of Nazi totalitarianism was by far the most brutal and violent ever experienced by the West.[3] The Nazis captured the apparatus of the German state, used it to force millions of men and women to accept the values and beliefs of a single political party, and then murdered millions of innocent people. But the state violence, coercion, and murder of classical fascism are not the essence of hegemony. They are means, not ends. Furthermore, they are also one set of means, and inefficient ones at that. This distinction is far more than a splitting of hairs, for a new kind of domination is evolving that does not use the same means. Nevertheless, though the means differ, the ends do not. Hegemony, regardless of the form, results in the total molding of the shared beliefs and values of men and women. The total conformity of beliefs and values is the essence of hegemony, not the violence and bestiality of state coercion. Personal conformity is the end of hegemony. Political repression is just one of the means, and not a very effective one either.

The Values and Beliefs of Corporate Man

Personal conformity is the most striking characteristic of corporate life. It is an important characteristic obviously shared with classical fascism. People who work for corporations do not just learn certain skills; they learn a set of values and beliefs. The most astute observers of contemporary American culture have commented at length on the conformist values and beliefs of corporate man. David Riesman, C. Wright Mills, William H. Whyte, Jr., and Michael Maccoby have all produced serious studies of the impacts of corporate life on human character.[4] All of the studies find human character to be degraded in some sense by the corporation. Riesman's study of the American middle class encompasses far more than life in corporations, but the imprint of corporate culture is evident throughout his findings. In particular, he found a pervasive loss of individual autonomy and a dramatic rise in "other-directed" human character. His work, *The Lonely Crowd*, was published in 1950, long before business consultants began designing corporate cultures. However, even as early as the Riesman study, the corporation's impact on American values and beliefs was evident, particularly in the middle class.

Shortly after Riesman's book, Mills published his *White Collar*. Middle-class occupations in the twentieth century, Mills pointed out, were predominantly corporate jobs where psychological manipulation had replaced state coercion, and where

the formal aim, implemented by the latest psychological equipment, is to have men internalize what the managerial cadres would have them do, without their knowing their own motives, but nevertheless having them. Many whips are inside men, who do not know how they got there, or indeed that they are there.[5]

The highly manipulative nature of the corporate world had become clear over thirty years ago. In his *Organization Man*, Whyte described how corporate work involved much forced cooperation and going along to get along. The successful organization man typically has had to repress most of the dissenting views he may have held. He has had to learn not to rock the boat and not to incur animosity or acquire notoriety. He has had to adapt to a world of group-think, where creativity and individuality may be particularly risky career strategies. Whyte, an editor of *Fortune* magazine, found that being well rounded, hard working, well adjusted, and a good team player are essential to organizational success, as are conformity and loyalty to the organization. These are the personality characteristics that corporations value in recruits and inculcate in employees. These are also the personality characteristics desired by fascist regimes.

More recently, the psychoanalyst Michael Maccoby studied the character of managers in U.S. high-tech corporations. He was the first of the serious investigators of corporate culture and corporate character to apply the specialized skills of a psychoanalyst to the corporate world. He characterized the successful manager of high-tech corporations as a gamesman who strives for "the exhilaration of running his team and of gaining victories. His main goal is to be known as a winner, and his deepest fear is to be labeled a loser."[6] These managerial players of games learn analytical competence, fairness, and independence—"the values of healthy twelve-year-olds."[7] They also learn to detach themselves, to build "a shell around the heart," to develop an emotional stinginess or even meanness. Idealism, empathy, and compassion are either unlearned or never learned in the first place. (Maccoby seems less concerned about the deleterious effects of the corporation on human character in a later book, *The Leader*.)[8]

In the world of corporate management, particularly in the high-pressure, high-tech corporations, career success is the dominant value. So in the new world of corporate game players, career manipulation has replaced the political repression of classical fascism. A successful career is a relative thing—it is never absolute, never final. One's career is successful only in relation to the careers of those with whom one makes comparisons. Furthermore, the essence of a successful career is reputation—how well one stacks up in the eyes of the other career competitors. In the corporate career game the comparisons never stop, so the career striving never stops either. The racers just keep running. They also keep peering over their shoulders to see who is closing the gap. They do not look straight ahead to see the finish line, because there is no finish line. There is no real objective worthy of enlightened adults.

This competition generates a great deal of anxiety in managers. They value career success so much that many of them are dominated by the fear of failure.[9] The values of these corporate careerists are harmful to mental health and destructive of individual character. They are not the values of a kind, free, adult human being. Real kindness is a hindrance in the corporate career game. If one player were to help a competitor, the competitor could easily use the help to pull ahead of the naive benefactor. Nice guys finish last. Faked kindness, on the other hand, is helpful. If a supervisor, for example, can manage to fake kindness toward his underlings, who then work harder for their "kindly" supervisor, the harder work of the underlings will propel the scheming supervisor ahead in his race against other supervisors. Eventually the manipulative behavior will be found out, but not before it poisons human relations and human hearts. Not only is human kindness poisoned, but faith in others is destroyed as well, because the motivations of others come under constant scrutiny. When a coworker competitor performs a simple act of kindness for you, do you wonder to yourself, "What does she want?" If so, then playing the corporate career game has exacted a heavy price from your heart. It has taken away your faith in others and it has left you open to external manipulation and control.

Real kindness requires faith, and real freedom requires a secure sense of self. Both of these are insurance against manipulation. Neither of these are learned in the corporation. On the contrary, cynicism and insecurity, not faith and security, are learned. The corporate career game is a race with no finish line, with no end in view. It is run against others, and no personal end is sought other than beating out the other guys. A race run against others teaches internal aimlessness and senseless striving for external rewards. A sense of self cannot be acquired because such a sense entails having genuine goals—ends in view that are internally meaningful to one's self. Beating out the other guys does not suffice. It is not a fitting goal for free adults, people free to choose their own goals and secure enough in their sense of self to pursue those goals against opposition.[10]

Although the personal impact of corporate life has been studied and commented upon, social commentators have not drawn the necessary connections between pluralism, hegemony, and corporate capitalism. So, by and large, the possibility that a *new* form of hegemony is evolving before our very eyes has not been seriously investigated. That new form is corporate hegemony.

Types of Hegemony

Hegemony involves a dominant institution, often the state, as was true in Imperial Rome. The Nazis used the state to dominate other institutions, but the state itself was not really dominant. In the case of Nazi Germany, this distinction may seem to be a splitting of hairs. Nevertheless, to understand the different forms hegemony can take, it is essential to note that though the state generally dominates other institutions, the state itself is not necessarily the dominant institution. Rather, it may dominate on behalf of some other institution—it may dominate without being dominant. That this was the case in Nazi Germany became clear toward the close of the Second World War, when the Nazis chose to allow agencies of the German state to be totally destroyed by the advancing Allies rather than give up their vainglorious illusions and sue for peace. Nazi Germany was a specific form of hegemony where a political party, the National Socialists, was the dominant institution, which used the state to dominate the other institutions of Germany. This was classic fascism, to date the most terrifying form of hegemony to evolve. But other forms are possible. Within corporate America another such form is evolving, one more subtle than classic fascism.

Hegemony can take in a variety of forms, depending on which institution is dominant and on how that institution creates and maintains its dominance. In modern times the state is used frequently as the means of domination. This leaves the impression that a dominant state is the essence of hegemony. But that is not so. Any institution can dominate the other institutions in a society. The corporation does so in twentieth-century America. The state is used to dominate, but the state need not be dominant itself. The state is often the means of domination, but the ends of domination are someone else's. In principle, that someone else, so to speak, can be any major institution. It was the church in medieval Europe, for example, and it was the church again, for a short time, in Puritan New England. In a monarchy, unchecked by the church or by other institutions, the dominant institution becomes the royal family. To a large extent, this appears to be the case now in Saudi Arabia and apparently was the case in the Shah's Iran. But in Khomeini's Iran, one form of hegemony, the family-based form, has been replaced by another form, the church-based form. Both forms use the state as the means of domination, but the Ayatollah's church-based hegemony is not the same as the Shah's family-based form because the ends of the two are different. The dominating or hegemonic institution usually uses the state to dominate, but the dominant institution itself can be the political party, the church, the family, the state itself, the military, perhaps the school,[11] or, as in the United States, the corporation.

In fact, the state need not even be the dominating agent. For example, the medieval church in Europe exercised its dominance using nonstate ecclesiastical courts and papal armies as substitutes for the weak agencies of the feudal state. No central feudal state of any substance existed. There was only the Catholic church exercising its universal power and a series of individual feudal fiefs and principalities. Nothing approaching a nation-state existed until after 1485 (the Wars of the Roses) in England. So a strong state is neither necessary nor sufficient for hegemony. A strong state may even resist church-based or party-based, or, in the case of the United States, corporate-based totalitarianism. Nevertheless, an effective and compliant state is extraordinarily useful to hegemony.[12]

In one form or another, hegemony has probably been the general rule in human societies.[13] Although most intellectuals in the United States have come to believe that pluralism is the natural way of life, it is not. To some degree, pluralism has prevailed in Western Europe and her colonies (at least the favored English-speaking ones) for more than three centuries. People have grown used to it, and whatever people grow used to is considered natural. Nevertheless, pluralism in the United States, or the remnants of it, is more the result of historical accident than of natural law. American pluralism had its roots in the confluence of many historical events and trends, which came together by sheer happenstance. For one, the religious Reformation and the secularizing Enlightenment significantly weakened church dominance in Western Europe. Moreover, migrants to the New World (new to Europeans) found themselves far removed from the old institutions that used to bind them. During the migrations, revolutions in England, America, and France further weakened and also rearranged the old institutionalized controls. The Industrial Revolution which sounded the death knell of feudalism, destroyed forever what was left of the old manor in the countryside and the guild in the towns. Meanwhile, the printing press had been spreading heresy and sedition far and wide as more and more lay people learned to read. Market relations broadened as competitive capitalism and the Industrial Revolution completed the destruction of the old institutional order. No single, dominant institution survived intact, save the evolving nation-state. But the early reign of the nation-state, under mercantilism, was short-lived. The rising capitalists, first nurtured by the state, found that the state could also be limiting. Growing in power, the new capitalists would brook no restraints on their pursuit of self-interest. The father of modern economics, Adam Smith, provided them with a rationalization in his theory of the invisible hand. In what he called a "system of natural liberty," each person's pursuit of self-interest was supposed to lead to the benefit of all. The state controls of mercantilism were dismantled.

Buffeted by a whole series of upheavals, the old regime of Europe collapsed and a kind of institutional vacuum ensued. That vacuum gave life to pluralism—a new play ushered onto the stage of history. During the three centuries that the new play has been running in Western Europe and her English-speaking colonies, no single institution—at least not for long and until now—has been able to solidify its dominance over the other institutions that make up the related Western societies. Furthermore, in spite of the rise of capitalism, significant reductions in inequality occurred all across the West. Nevertheless, the impact of that magnificent accident of history is fading. In the first place, pluralism never really spread much beyond Western Europe and her progeny. And now the curtain is closing on pluralism in the West before it even opened in the East. The rising dominance of one institution is closing the play in the West. That institution, the corporation, is the most effective institution in the West, and, except for the state, the most powerful one as well.

CORPORATE CHARACTERISTICS

It's Alive

The corporation is a Frankenstein's monster created by lawyers, politicians, and securities salespeople. But it is far more than just blue sky. It is an artificial person, endowed by law with all the legal attributes of a real human being. It can make binding contracts, sue, or be sued in its own name and on its own behalf. These are things that most real human beings could not do until fairly recently. In particular, blacks in the South and women anywhere in the United States could not make binding contracts in their own names until a few decades ago. Children still cannot do so. A corporation is a formidable institution, with a legal existence separate and distinct from the individuals who create it. A corporation can do anything a real human being can do, and most of those things it can do better. (True, a corporation cannot vote, but it can buy whatever votes it needs through its Political Action Committee.) Corporations can even reproduce themselves by spinning off wholly owned subsidiaries, a mode of asexual reproduction, or by forming joint ventures of several kinds, a mode of sexual reproduction.

Contemporary corporations call sex "merging." Offspring often result from these unions through divestiture. The offspring are often cared for by specialized corporate nannies called holding companies. Corporations can even send their offspring on a vacation (from taxes) to the Caribbean or off to corporate prep school in an enterprise zone. Corporations are notoriously promiscuous. They engage in group sex when the antitrust authorities look the other way. Their orgies were once called consolidations and were arranged by the corporate equivalent of the madame—the investment banker. The house of Morgan organized numerous consolidations at the turn of this century. Morgan's orgies were extremely popular, and the illegitimate offspring of all that consolidating still populate the corporate world. Orgies of the Morgan variety gradually fell into disrepute, however, with the passage of several antitrust blue laws. While these statutes frowned on the old-style "horizontal mergers," a new form of merger has evolved that allows corporations on the make to be as promiscuous as ever.

The hottest new form of merger is the conglomerate merger, and the hottest new house is Drexel Burnham Lambert, Inc. With the "junk bonds" promoted by Michael Milken, financial guru for the new house, and Frederick H. Joseph, its chief executive officer, financing of corporate mergers reached a new high in 1985–86 before the stock market crashed in 1987. The merging quickly recovered in 1988. The junk bonds that have helped to finance all of this merging are corporate bonds considered too risky by bond rating services to be given an investment grade rating, making them difficult to sell in public offerings. But they do pay exceptionally high rates, so huge blocks of them can be sold directly to new-style investment fund managers in search of ever-higher payoffs. With this new source of funding, and with the Reagan–Bush administration's permissiveness in matters of corporate promiscuity, merging has remained very popular for the participants and very profitable for the houses that arrange it. Today's investment banker typically receives an adviser's fee of 1 percent of the value of the deal. The investment banker can also get as much as 4 percent for arranging the financing of the merger, and if he acts on the insider information available to him, even more money can be made. Dennis B. Levine, former managing director of Drexel Burnham Lambert, is typical of the new-style investment banker who is willing to step over the legal line in pursuit of ever-greater profits. Levine used the information he acquired in his fiduciary relationships with clients to buy stock on his own account. He also sold the same information to Ivan F. Boesky, who used it for his own personal gain. Levine made about $12 million; Boesky substantially more. But Gary C. Lynch, head of the Securities and Exchange Commission's enforcement division, made them give (most of) it back. This act of forced contrition has taken a good part of the fun out of arranging corporate trysts.[14]

A voluntary encounter between two amorous corporations is a friendly takeover, while an involuntary encounter (yes, corporations can rape and be raped) is called a hostile takeover. In the event of an attempted rape, usually arranged by pimp-like investment banking houses, the threatened corporation usually calls out for the help of a white knight to save its virtue from the would-be rapist. But if the naive corporation is saved by the white knight, its virtue is lost anyway—to the white knight. The fear of rape has become so widespread that some highly specialized corporations—alleged by their detractors to be impotent—make a practice of threatening young virgin corporations with rape and then accepting a bribe for not doing it to the would-be victim. Called "greenmailers," such corporations often drop out of sight when one of their would-be victims dares them to go ahead and do it. Greenmailers, particularly if proven impotent, are held in very low esteem in corporate circles. The fear of rape has also led to another new practice: corporate virgins of excessive virtue carry poison pills with them at all times, promising to swallow them should anyone threaten them with a fate worse than death. So, in all seriousness, corporations can do *anything* real human beings can do, including the desperate and sordid. Reading the financial pages is as revealing as watching porno movies.

Corporations are alive, just like real people. But, in addition, corporations possess an attribute that even the most powerful real people do not. Corporations, like the gods, possess immortality. The legal existence and functioning of a corporation continues long after the death of the human beings who were its original stockholders, because the corporation is an entity separate from its legal owners. The power of a real person dies with the person, but not so with the corporation. It need never die. Corporate immortality is a very important source of corporate power, for it means that corporate size and power can grow indefinitely. Real human beings can only get so powerful and so large—then they die. But like Frankenstein's monster, a corporation can outlive its creator. Some really powerful corporations may live forever.

Another important legal attribute of a corporation is the limited liability of its human owners. Stockholders are not personally liable for any damages caused or debts incurred by the corporation. If the corporation strikes it rich, the stockholders stand to gain, perhaps a very great deal, as the market value of their shares of stock rise. But if the corporation accidentally wipes out an Indian village (Bhopal) or produces a substance that causes cancer in thousands of workers and consumers (asbestos), the shareholders' loss is limited to the amount they paid for their stock. Corporate insiders do not have to suffer this loss because they can sell their shares before the news becomes public. They can even benefit from corporate disaster by selling the corporation's stock short. So the human stockholders have much more to gain than they have to lose from reckless or short-sighted corporate actions.

Organized Irresponsibility

The financial relation of stockholders to the corporation amounts to a kind of organized irresponsibility. That is, the corporation is organized in such a way that the humans who stand to gain from its actions are not responsible for those actions should they go awry. The limited liability of stockholders evolved out of a legal ambiguity encountered by the seventeenth-century English joint-stock company (essentially a joint partnership), the direct ancestor of the modern corporation. Creditors of an early joint-stock company that defaulted on its debt found it difficult to collect from the stockholders, particularly from those who did not own the stock at the time the debt was incurred. So the legal position of corporate creditors relative to some stockholders was quite ambiguous. On the other hand, the legal position of some stockholders was also ambiguous. Potential stockholder investors, particularly very wealthy ones, often were reluctant to invest in stock for fear of being sued for the company's subsequent debts. By the early nineteenth century these legal ambiguities had been cleared up once and for all, in favor of the stockholders, by the establishment of strictly limited liability for all stockholders.[15] That is, the individual stockholder was no longer personally (financially) responsible for any harm the corporation might cause. Thus the organized irresponsibility of corporate life was institutionalized.

Organized irresponsibility has been further institutionalized into the corporation through gradual changes in its board of directors. The board is elected by the shareholders, with each share of common stock generally carrying one vote. The board is supposed to represent the interests of the shareholders by selecting the appropriate managerial team and overseeing its performance. However, in today's mature corporation, most members of the board are actually chosen by the managerial team, making the board beholden to management, even though the board is supposed to oversee management. This incestuous relationship between the board and management is not the whole story of organized irresponsibility. In addition, most large corporations now carry directors' and officers' insurance policies that offer protection against personal liability owing to their negligence. So at least to some extent, directors and officers do not have to be responsible; they merely have to be insured. But in 1986 it became prohibitively expensive for many corporations to get director and officer liability insurance because the large insurance companies pushed up their rates very aggressively. To meet this growing corporate problem—the possibility that directors and officers might become personally responsible for their actions—the little state of Delaware, home to many of the largest corporations in the world, passed a new law. This new law makes it possible for corporations incorporated in Delaware to adopt a provision in their charter that eliminates the directors' personal liability for not exercising their duty of due care as directors. The stockholders of the corporation wishing to free the directors from their responsibility to act with care have to vote for the new provision before it takes effect. But the stockholders are unlikely to object to such irresponsibility, since they are essentially irresponsible as well. Nor is the board likely to be overly diligent in its oversight of management, since management now picks the board. Stockholders in large mature corporations merely send in their proxies, rubber-stamping managements' candidates for the board and proposals for amending the corporate charter.[16]

If the stockholders are not really liable and, therefore, not really responsible, and if the same applies to the board of directors, then is any real person responsible for the actions of this artificial person—this immortal corporation? The answer is no. The corporation is a true Frankenstein's monster—an artificial person run amok, responsible only to its own soulless self. Some fascinating possibilities present themselves. Corporations have already begun to buy up their own stock, holding it in their treasury. Taken to the logical conclusion, when 100 percent of the stock is treasury stock, the corporation will own itself. It will have dispensed entirely with shareholders from the species homo sapiens. To whom or to what would it then be responsible? Take these speculations about organized irresponsibility a bit further. Corporations are automating their operations as quickly as possible, accepting little or no responsibility to the displaced workers and managers. Could a corporation entirely dispense with not only human ownership but also human workers and managers? It would then have no need for us at all and no responsibility to us either. What would it be then? Its physical existence is not at all hard to imagine. It would exist physically as a network of machines that buy, process, and sell commodities, monitored by a network of computers. Its purposes would be to grow ever larger through acquiring more machines and to become ever more powerful through acquiring more computers to monitor the new machines. It would be responsible to no one but itself in its mechanical drive for power and profit. It would represent capitalism at its very purest, completely unconcerned with anything save profit and power.

Management is, or at least should be, responsible for corporate actions.

But management, particularly of large, mature corporations, has become increasingly bureaucratic.[17] The bureaucratization of corporate management has reinforced the irresponsibility of the corporate institution. In theory, a bureaucracy is an organization in which responsibility is carefully and formally assigned to identifiable and accountable individuals—real persons. So, in theory, bureaucrats are responsible. In actual practice, however, a bureaucracy often degenerates into an organization in which responsibility becomes so diffused among so many different individuals that each of the individuals is able to avoid personal responsibility for harmful actions taken by the organization. In the degenerated bureaucracy, no one is responsible because the bureaucracy has become an organized irresponsibility. More than a few federal agencies have deteriorated into organized irresponsibility—the newspapers are frequently full of the latest scandals in the Pentagon and the National Aeronautics and Space Administration, for example. But analogous scandals are found in private, corporate bureaucracies as well. The newspapers are simply much more hesitant about printing corporate scandals because corporations can and do withdraw advertisements from offending papers or even sue for libel. In spite of the appearance to the contrary, then, corporate irresponsibility is just as rampant as government irresponsibility.[18] And just as few corporate officials as government officials ever get punishments commensurate with their misdeeds. Bureaucracy is their cover. Both state and corporate bureaucracy can deteriorate into organized irresponsibility to such an extent that even though we know that wrongs have been committed, we cannot find out who did them, and even if we could, we cannot hold them personally responsible. When bureaucracy comes to contradict personal responsibility, as it widely does in both the public and private spheres of life, it is easy for those who would abuse their power for personal gain to do so with impunity. The impunity is greatest in the private realm of the giant corporation. In the public realm of the government agency, a really aroused congressional or executive investigation can lay bare the wrongdoing, and newspapers will publish all the embarrassing details. But the private affairs of corporations are less easily penetrated and less readily publicized. Hence, the organized irresponsibility of the private, corporate sphere is more entrenched and protected than that of the public agency.

The degree and frequency of corporate illegality and impunity is staggering. A few examples may suffice: a major stockbroker, E. F. Hutton, pled guilty to two thousand counts of mail and wire fraud in a check-kiting scheme; a major defense contractor, General Dynamics, flagrantly overcharged the Pentagon on defense contracts; and a major drug maker, Eli Lilly, failed to inform the proper authorities of the death of patients who took its Oraflex. Even though these crimes cost several lives and many millions of dollars, so far no one has spent even a day in custody as a result. The pattern of corporate illegality and irresponsibility has become so pronounced that federal legislation originally aimed at punishing organized crime figures is actually punishing established corporations engaged in allegedly legitimate business. The law in question is the Racketeer Influenced and Corrupt Organizations Act, commonly known as RICO. The civil provisions of RICO give private parties the right to sue for treble damages if the defendant was involved in "racketeering," or a pattern of illegal activities. RICO was passed in the early 1970s during the Nixon law-and-order crusade. But RICO catches and holds responsible the wrong people. It has been used against so many legitimate corporations, that the corporate establishment is calling for a drastic change in the law. The National Association of Manufacturers and the U.S. Chamber of Commerce both oppose the law.

Organized irresponsibility, then, is a major characteristic of the giant corporation. To repeat the other characteristics, the modern corporation is a unique legal entity that can do everything a real person can do, and better. Not only can it grow and reproduce without limit, but it can divide like an amoeba. The corporation can also live forever. Powerful real persons are equal to the rest of us in the end, for the grave gets us all. Not so with powerful corporations. They can continue amassing power indefinitely. As we shall see later on, the powerful corporation can even create and inculcate its own values and beliefs in its human servants. It can create its own culture, using the lens of career to focus corporate culture on profit, size, and power.[19]

Corporate Contradictions

One more characteristic of the modern corporation is of major significance. The corporation is profoundly contradictory, in that it contradicts itself and the quasi–pluralist society within which it has grown to maturity. It contradicts pluralism because pluralism produces creative and responsible individuals. The creativity and responsibility of the individual are fundamental values of the Enlightenment and are basic characteristics of individuals born and raised within a pluralistic society. But when such individuals enter the corporate world, the corporation must change them to make them fit. Since individuals striving for career success in the corporate world are anxious to fit in, the corporate rules easily come to replace personal responsibilities, and the norms of corporate culture quickly replace individual creativity. But the corporation needs responsible and creative individuals to keep it profiting and growing. The corporation is a system of organized irresponsibility that needs responsible servants. It is a tight hierarchy that needs creative rebels for innovation. It feeds on creativity and responsibility but produces conformity and irresponsibility.

These contradictions are the push behind the corporate drive for more power and size. Corporations must grow, for size yields power. Power, in turn, can be used to overcome the intensifying internal contradictions. Through their growing brute strength, corporations can continue to prosper even though they undermine the human traits on which they depend.

THE DRIVE FOR ECONOMIC POWER

Corporate Size and Concentration

The internal contradictions of the corporate institution are being transcended through a drive for more power: large U.S. corporations are getting much larger, economic concentration is increasing, and corporate power is growing apace.[20] The U.S. economy continues to evolve from a power-dispersed system into a power-concentrated system, but the evolution goes on unnoticed by most mainstream economists.[21] The evolution has been marked by three major merger waves. The first wave which involved primarily horizontal mergers, crested at the turn of this century. The second wave swept over the economy in the 1920s and left behind it a structure of vertically integrated, oligopolistic corporations dominating the economy's industrial center. This structure, John Kenneth Galbraith's planned sector, has been in place now for over half a century.[22] An investigator familiar with the evolution of this structure would expect concentration ratios to have remained relatively stable since the Great Depression because the concentrated, planned sector was already largely in place by then. But investigators with a laissez-faire predisposition downplay the extent and significance of corporate power by pointing out that average Census Bureau concentration ratios have not risen dramatically over the past several decades. This relative stability in concentration ratios does not prove that there is a healthy level of market competition in the industrial economy. Rather it is evidence that the planned corporate core has maintained its dominance for half a century.[23]

The third merger wave, which swept over the economy in the 1960s and again in the 1980s, has added to this measurement problem. Increasing conglomeration rather than vertical or horizontal integration has characterized this merger wave. The resulting conglomerate corporations possess new sources of power and put their power to new uses. Since the official Census Bureau market concentration ratios do not reflect changes in corporate power owing to conglomerate mergers, most observers have been lulled into complacency about the rising power of conglomerate corporations. They also misdiagnose the cause of cumulating industrial weakness in the United States, blaming it on high taxes and government regulation.

Concentration ratios measure the combined market shares of the largest 4, 8, 20, and 50 firms operating in defined markets or product areas. The Bureau of the Census computes the ratios, generally every five years. Extreme conceptual and empirical difficulties in defining and redefining markets and product areas are frequently encountered, so it is very hard to make meaningful comparisons of changing concentration ratios over long periods of time. Furthermore, the data that do exist show no real trend in concentration ratios over the past few years in the United States. Nevertheless, with the help of Jim Carpenter, I compared the concentration ratios for 4-digit product groups from the 1958 and 1972 census data. The comparison yielded the following ambiguous results: the 4-firm ratio fell in 83 groups, rose in 83 groups, and remained the same in 14 groups. Data limitations precluded comparing the 1958 and 1972 ratios in 130 groups.[24] I also compared concentration ratios for 4-digit product groups from the 1972 and 1977 Census of Manufactures and found that the 4-firm ratio fell in 210 groups, rose in 189, was unchanged in 43, and could not be compared for the rest of the groups.[25]

The overall level of market concentration has changed very little, giving critics of corporate power no support for claims that corporate power is rising. Nevertheless, concentration ratios do not pick up the effects of conglomerate mergers. Furthermore, concentration ratios miss a very important dimension of economic concentration and power—aggregate concentration. Aggregate concentration can be measured in several ways. For example, corporations with total assets of $250 million or more represented only one-tenth of one percent of all corporate income tax returns in 1981. And yet that tiny number of giant corporations accounted for more than two-thirds of corporate net income.[26] In manufacturing alone, the largest 200 corporations increased their share of held assets from 53 percent in 1955 to 61 percent in 1983. The same 200 largest manufacturers increased their share of total value added by manufacturing from 30 percent in 1947 to 44 percent in 1977, an increase of about half.[27] Concentration continues to rise in the corporate world, even though the official market concentration ratios do not show this.

A far more striking trend is the rise of conglomerate concentration. Simply stated, a conglomerate is a firm that operates in more than one industry. The Census Bureau's "multiple-industry company" is the closest statistical definition we have for such a firm.[28] These multiple-industry companies are truly giants. In 1977 they represented slightly more than one-half of one percent of all companies surveyed by the Census Bureau, but they hired 49 percent of all employees, paid 57 percent of total payroll, and pocketed 52 percent of total sales and receipts for the entire U.S. economy. Compared to the 1963 survey data for multiple- and single-industry companies, the number of employees in 1977 had grown by 60 percent in multiple-industry companies but by only 40 percent in single-industry companies; the payroll for multiple-industry companies had grown by 249 percent but by 211 percent for single-industry companies; and sales and receipts for multiple-industry companies had grown by 324 percent but by only 201 percent for single-industry companies.[29] So the multiple-industry, conglomerate-type companies have consistently outgrown the single-industry companies since at least 1963. Willard Mueller, a long-time student of corporate developments, was correct when he stated: "Now, in much of the economy, conglomerate enterprise is no longer the exception but the rule."[30] Actually, conglomerate enterprise and the problems of power it creates are not new. A few very powerful conglomerates had formed in the United States by the end of the First World War.[31] Nevertheless, the conglomerate used to be the exception, not the rule. As the conglomerate form of corporate enterprise becomes ever more important, the market concentration ratios watched by most economists become increasingly less relevant as measures of corporate power. Economic power comes less and less from control of a single market and is instead more and more conglomerate in origin.

Conglomerate Power

Control of a specific industrial market used to be the major source of corporate power—witness the rise to power of General Motors, U.S. Steel, Alcoa, DuPont, and the other corporate behemoths of their generation. But their power was tenuous because it was power over a specific market that was tied to the fate of the industry serving that one market. As that industry declined, so too did the old industrial oligopoly that remained dependent upon that one industry. Many of the old giants have been running a race between the speed at which their industry is declining and the speed at which they can learn to run diversified, conglomerate empires. If they remain single-industry companies, no matter how powerful they are in that one industry, they will die when it does. This would not necessarily be the case for the conglomerate.

Conglomerates fall into two broad groups: go-go conglomerates and imperial conglomerates. The go-go conglomerate is the result of financial speculation. Its power is ephemeral, even though it blazes its way through Wall Street as everybody's darling. Many go-go conglomerates rose to temporary prominence during the 1960s. ITT, Litton, LTV, and Gulf + Western were originally of the go-go variety. By taking over numerous smaller corporations, the management of a go-go conglomerate can generate paper profits with which to impress its stockholders. Some of the paper profits can also find their way into management's pocket. But the go-go conglomerate soon either disappears or reorganizes on firmer grounds after the original speculators lose control. A reorganized go-go conglomerate sometimes evolves into an imperial conglomerate. The imperial conglomerate is regal in shape and power. It is not a temporary phenomenon of speculative hype and moonglow, but a formidable and permanent institution. General Electric, General Motors, DuPont, and U.S. Steel are imperial conglomerates. They are not above a bit of speculative razzle-dazzle when it suits their purpose, but they are composed of far more stern stuff. This is what confuses some observers of conglomerates. They mistake imperial conglomerates for go–go conglomerates, thereby grossly underestimating conglomerate power in general. Go–go conglomerates come and go, often accumulating little real power. But imperial conglomerates are permanent institutions of immense power. They have tended to evolve out of old one-industry oligopolies.

Conglomerate power is not tied to any single industry or market. It is completely fluid—fungible, if you will. There are four major sources of conglomerate power: reciprocal dealing, cross-subsidizing, mutual forbearance, and fungibility. None of these are possessed to the same degree by single-industry firms, even if the firms are complete monopolists.[32] We shall briefly examine each of these sources.

A conglomerate has infinite opportunities to engage in reciprocal dealing—the polite term used for a corporation's ability to twist the arms of its upstream suppliers, its downstream distributors, or its otherwise totally unrelated firms by promising to engage in reciprocal buying or threatening to discontinue such buying. "You buy my product or I won't buy yours." A corporation's power to twist arms in this fashion directly relates to its size and to the number of products it buys and sells. Holding size constant, the more diversified the firm, the greater its power, regardless of its market share in any one market. General Motors' apparent use of its huge shipping business to pressure railroads into buying diesel locomotives made by a GM division is an excellent example of reciprocal dealing.[33] John F. Winslow, former counsel to the Antitrust Subcommittee of the House Committee on the Judiciary, has documented many of the uses of reciprocity by conglomerates in his *Conglomerates Unlimited*.[34] Reciprocity is an economic power possessed to much greater extent by multiple-industry, conglomerate corporations than by single-industry, nonconglomerated ones.

A conglomerate is said to have "deep pockets." That is, it can undertake very costly offensive or defensive campaigns in one market because of its revenues from other markets. For example, to discipline a price-cutter in one geographic market, a corporation operating in several geographic markets can undercut the chiseler in the one market and recoup the resulting losses from other market revenues. This is sometimes interpreted as a subsidy to consumers in the price-cut market. But it is more like picking the pockets of consumers in the other markets, for as soon as the price-chiseling ends, the temporarily "subsidized" consumers in the price-cut market will find out how fleeting corporate philanthropy is when the price they pay is pushed back up to what the traffic will bear.[35] It then becomes clear that the corporation has not been drawing on its own "deep pockets," but on the pockets of its customers. And the more customers it has in different markets, the more power it has. Many small pockets, spread all over the economy, are better than one single, deep pocket. A conglomerate that operates not only in geographically separate markets but also in markets for completely different products has far more pockets to pick, and thus more power, than a single-industry company.

When large corporations meet in a contested field, their responses are fairly predictable. Corwin Edwards explains:

There is an awareness that if competition against the large rival goes so far as to be seriously troublesome, the logic of the situation may call for conversion of the warfare into total war. Hence, there is an incentive to live and let live, to cultivate a cooperative spirit, and to recognize priorities of interest in the hope of reciprocal recognition.[36]

General Motors, for example, has avoided total war with a large rival—Toyota—by forming an alliance with it, the new United Motor Corporation. Rather than fight, at great cost to each, the two giants have joined forces in a joint venture producing cars for the U.S. market. Such joint ventures between giants have become commonplace. However, when a giant corporation meets a small one in a contested field, the response is different. The giant predictably attacks its small rival, for as Edwards explains: "The large company is in a position to hurt without being hurt."[37] To the extent that the small firm is limited to one market while the large firm is not, the large firm can squeeze the small firm in that one market, and the small firm cannot retaliate in the other markets served by the large firm. Mutual forbearance toward other behemoths keeps the large corporation's flanks secure and allows it to press the attack against weaker rivals more vigorously. In its relations with other behemoths, the more points of contact between them, the more opportunities exist for securing tacit mutual-forbearance agreements. Such opportunities and the economic power they yield are directly related to the number of different markets served by the corporation. So a corporation can increase its power of mutual forbearance by diversifying into many markets, even if its market share in the various markets does not rise.

The fourth power, possessed to a far greater degree by a conglomerate than by a single-industry firm, is the higher degree of fungibility given the conglomerate by its diversification into many different markets and industries. A conglomerate has access to the liquid working capital generated by a number of different firms in unrelated areas of the economy. This makes the conglomerate's aggregate or overall cash flow more predictable and more easily transferable to other uses than the cash flow of a single-industry firm. Hence a conglomerate—an imperial conglomerate, in particular—can plan the movement of its financial resources far more effectively than can a nonconglomerate. This ability must not be underestimated, for it makes corporate immortality a reality for the conglomerate. The ability to appropriate capital from many different sources and then move it quickly to other uses frees the conglomerate from the fate of any one source or use of its capital. If one industry dies the conglomerate lives on, unaffected. So whole industries can come and go, whole regions may rise or fall, but the conglomerate can continue to grow in size and power. This ability has lent a whole new thrust to office technology. The head offices of conglomerates are becoming increasingly more sophisticated in employing technologies to monitor the uses and sources of capital. Mainframe computers, linked peripherals, whole libraries of software programs, leased phone lines and satellite dishes, and myriad connected bank accounts and corporate subsidiaries are the new tools of the trade in the "information economy." And the imperial conglomerates have mastered the new tools better than any other institution.

Corwin Edwards sums up the imperial conglomerate's different sources of power in one simple statement: "It can spend money in large amounts."[38] In the capitalist system, if you can control the sources and uses of capital, you can control the system. Reciprocal dealing, cross-subsidizing, mutual forbearance, and fungibility are ultimately financial powers, which are possessed to a much larger extent by diversified corporations than by single industry ones. And these financial powers have risen dramatically in recent years because of the latest round of conglomerate mergers and the rapid development of new information-processing technology. When large, diversified corporations come into contact in more and more areas, they increasingly go beyond mere mutual forbearance to numerous reciprocal arrangements, both formal and informal. The most important of the informal arrangements are joint ventures[39] and direct or indirect ties between boards of directors.[40] The most formal arrangement between behemoths is, of course, merger. Mergers between very large corporations used to be fairly rare. Most mergers in the 1960s were the result of a large conglomerate taking over a smaller, single-industry firm. In the 1980s that has changed significantly. Now giants are merging with other giants, and through the first half of 1984, *The New York Times* estimated, 27 mergers involving acquired companies each worth $400 million or more were announced or completed. The total acquisition value of these giant mergers was $58.6 billion.[41] *Fortune* magazine estimated that mergers and raids involving publicly held corporations cost $56.7 billion in 1981, $31.5 billion in 1982, $39.5 billion in 1983, and a whopping $82.7 billion in 1984.[42] So the main drift in the 1980s is toward more mergers between very large companies and more conglomerate concentration, and is strongly tending toward what Thorstein Veblen called "One Big Union of Financial Interests."[43] The trend is toward a coalescence of conglomerated corporate power and a sophisticated, computerized use of that power, not to dominate a particular market or another conglomerate, but to dominate the public at large. Extensive economic power is being amassed in imperial conglomerates.

The New Dispensation

Under the evolving new dispensation, a new line of demarcation can be discerned. This line runs between imperial conglomerates on one side, and the public at large on the other. As the giants slowly learn to live and let live among themselves, they are turning toward us. Business is still very much a competitive game, but the composition of the teams is changing. Independent business used to compete against independent business, though, of course, not in a perfect world of pure competition. Now the businesses are all on the same team, and we—the rag-tag consumers—are on the other one. On the side of the corporation, Thorstein Veblen argued,

the traffic runs on the same general lines of reserved and evasive rivalry within and of sturdy solidarity toward the outside, toward the underlying population; very much as the local community of retailers carries on the business traffic of a typical country town.... [T]he cost of it falls on the underlying population.... [I]t is an enterprise in usufruct carried on under a loosely defined code of Live and Let Live, designed to safeguard the joint advantage of the usufructuaries.[44]

Veblen was saying, in his unique way, that the higher circles of the corporate world were learning not to exploit each other, but to exploit us instead. As corporate enterprise becomes ever more concentrated, not so much into market monopolies but into conglomerate empires, corporate competition is directed less and less at other corporations—which are learning to live and let live. Instead, corporate competition is turning more and more toward the consumer and the unorganized or unprotected worker. Conglomerate concentration is increasingly making corporations very formidable prey, so rivalry between behemoths becomes mutual forbearance. But small investors, consumers, workers, and communities have not grown in power as imperial conglomerates have. In the resulting imbalance, the predatory attention of conglomerate enterprises is turning toward the weaker prey. The plane of competition, or line of cleavage, is rotating.[45]

Much of the criticism of conglomerates focuses on the detrimental effects of conglomerate mergers on smaller business rivals. The search for arguments to support antitrust action against such mergers causes this focus. Trust busters can find ample support, of course. The conglomerate's powers make it an awesome business rival and anticompetitive force. However, the trust-busting tradition in the United States has directed attention away from the rotating plane of competition, which is slowly rotating away from other large business rivals toward the small business, the small investor, the consumer, the worker, the managerial cadres, and the community. The imperial conglomerate is playing the central role in this new "competition" against whoever can be forced to bear the costs of corporate contradictions. This new competition has nothing to do with changes in market concentration ratios, so those ratios do not indicate what is evolving.

Nevertheless, some of the effects of that evolution have become obvious: the "natural" rate of unemployment has risen from the 3 to 4 percent range of the 1960s to the 5 to 6 percent range of the 1980s. The rise has been caused by the conglomerate-directed deindustrialization of the U.S. heartland. The industrial center of the economy is shrinking because conglomerates use formerly free-standing industrial companies as cash cows to finance the conglomerates' drive for power in other, higher-growth areas of the economy.[46] The conglomerates use their power over fungible capital to disinvest in basic industry in order to invest in the new high-tech, information-processing services and in the lucrative government areas of defense-contracting and space-exploration. By allowing plant and equipment to wear out without replacing it, the conglomerates use the huge cash flow of their captive industrial companies to finance their moves into new service companies. Hence the old industrial belt of the United States has been turned into the Rust belt, and many industrial workers have become permanently unemployed. Employment opportunities, economic dynamism, and power have all moved from the industrial heartland, home of the old industrial oligopoly, to overseas locations and to the service centers— the new homes of the conglomerate.

The acquisition and use of new kinds of economic power have compensated, to some extent, for the growing lack of personal responsibility and creativity within the corporate institution. Some U.S. corporations have decentralized their organizations in an attempt to open up their managerial bureaucracies to entrepreneurial initiatives from within. But far more U.S. corporations have turned outward in a search for the power needed to sustain their top-heavy, bureaucratic systems of organized irresponsibility.[47] This turning outward has given additional impetus to the growing giantism of American corporations because it has taken the form of conglomeration. With conglomeration also have come new forms of economic power, making the conglomerate a formidable locus of economic power and forestalling, perhaps indefinitely, the coming to a head of the economic contradictions contained in corporate enterprise.

Corporations have gained major economic powers through conglomeration. But their most significant power is a product of their sheer size. Unlike the rest of us, the corporate giants do not have to take the world the way they find it. They have become so large, they can change the rules of the game. Their size has given them the clout to force government to write new laws or waive existing laws, alter tax schedules, impose trade restrictions, and guarantee loans. They are able to reshape the social and legal environment in their own favor. Because they are so enormous, they can organize PACs (Political Action Committees) all over the country. Because they are so enormous, they can give money to *both* political candidates running for the same office; so no matter who wins, you lose. Because they are so enormous, they can mobilize national campaigns against allegedly unfair foreign competition in their bailiwick. And because they are so enormous, when they claim that they will have to close their plants and lay off their workers unless they get what they want, politicians listen. Because they are so enormous, they are creating a new dispensation.

Examples of the political power that comes with sheer size are easy to come by: giant insurance companies can force states to write new laws limiting their liability. The giants can simply threaten not to insure anyone in the state unless the state obliges with new, more favorable liability limits. Giant auto companies can force the federal government to waive existing laws regarding fuel economy. The oil giants can force favorable tax treatment of their industry. Big steel can force government to impose trade restrictions on Japanese steel imports. The big three U.S. auto companies can do the same with Japanese autos. Lockheed, and then Chrysler, by threatening their own bankruptcy, forced the federal government to guarantee huge loans to them. ITT apparently helped bring down the Allende government in Chile and convinced the Nixon administration not to press an antitrust action against its acquisition of Hartford Insurance.[48] In sum, their sheer size has given giant corporations political power to match their economic power, and they use it to change the rules of the game in their favor.

The growing economic and political power of the giant, conglomerated corporation is the base from which corporate power is spreading into all spheres of life. As the corporation spreads its dominance, its corporate hegemony, the curtain is closing on pluralism in the West. A new play is opening. However, the play's theme is an old one—hegemony. Only the principal player is new—the modern, conglomerate corporation.

None of this is to say that the U.S. corporation has become all powerful, for it obviously has not. And none of this is to say that its organized irresponsibility has gone unchallenged, for it obviously has not. On occasion, its power is successfully overcome and justice is served. A notable example of this occurred on June 14, 1985, in a Cook County, Illinois, Circuit Court, when Judge Ronald J. P. Banks convicted three officials of the Film Recovery Systems Corporation of murdering Stefan Golab. Golab had worked for Film Recovery Systems in a plant that used a cyanide solution in open vats to reclaim silver from used film. He died from cyanide poisoning, and the judge found the co-owner of the corporation, the plant manager, and the foreman all guilty of his murder. The other co-owner of the corporation, however, has remained outside the law. He convinced the state of Utah not to extradite him to Illinois.[49] Even if one of them got away, this is the first time that corporate officials have been held personally responsible by a U.S. court for such a serious act. But it does not represent a turning back of corporate power in general. The case involved a small, privately held corporation, not a giant, public one. In the typical giant corporation, numerous layers of bureaucrats and labyrinthine channels of authority protect individual managers from personal responsibility. Foremen may be at more risk for their deeds after the Film Recovery System Case, but the higher circles of real corporate power have nothing to fear. Corporate power at the higher levels is not threatened.

The broad outlines of corporate hegemony are just becoming visible, if we look carefully and fearlessly. Corporate irresponsibility, immortality, dynamism, and power have not yet overcome all barriers to complete hegemony. The corporation has not become the sole fountainhead of meaning and value in American life, but the other fountainheads are drying up, and the drive for more corporate power seems irresistible. The future is not predestined. It is ours to make. Nevertheless, current trends and social forces indicate that the new dispensation is, or soon will be, corporate hegemony. The shape of things to come is most obvious in the world of the middle-class, white-collar, corporate employee. That world itself has been shaped by the sustained corporate drive for power.

Social Power

For where envying and strife is, there is confusion and every evil work.
—James 3:16

UNLIMITED CORPORATE SIZE

Uncontrolled Growth

In addition to diversification into conglomerates, the drive for power has continued to push up the size of corporate enterprises. The growth in size of U.S. corporations is described in Table 1. The table includes data from corporations filing tax returns with the Internal Revenue Service. The very largest corporations classified by the IRS are those with assets of $250 million or more. They accounted for only 0.06 percent of all filing corporations in 1965 and 0.11 percent in 1982, the latest year for which the IRS has published the data. The table begins with the year 1965 because in that year the total assets and the net income of the very largest corporations were just one-half of the assets and income of all filing corporations. Since 1965, however, the scales have tipped increasingly toward the side of the very large corporation. No matter which IRS measurement of corporate size is used—

Table 1
Total Assets, Total Receipts, and Net Income (Less Deficit) of All Reporting Corporations and of the Largest Corporations with Assets of $250 Million or More, 1965–82 (in Billions of Dollars)

Year	Total Assets		Total Receipts		Net Income	
	All Units	Largest Units	All Units	Largest Units	All Units	Largest Units
1965	1,724	862 (50%)	1,195	374 (31%)	74	37 (50%)
1966	1,845	945 (51%)	1,307	420 (32%)	81	41 (51%)
1973	3,649	2,275 (62%)	2,558	1,056 (41%)	120	69 (58%)
1974	4,016	2,586 (64%)	3,090	1,426 (46%)	146	93 (64%)
1975	4,287	2,790 (65%)	3,199	1,451 (45%)	143	90 (63%)
1976	4,721	3,105 (66%)	3,635	1,679 (46%)	185	122 (66%)
1977	5,326	3,544 (67%)	4,128	1,926 (47%)	219	141 (64%)
1978	6,014	4,078 (68%)	4,715	2,210 (47%)	247	157 (64%)
1979	6,835	4,748 (69%)	5,599	2,743 (49%)	285	192 (67%)
1980	7,617	5,358 (70%)	6,361	3,229 (51%)	239	158 (66%)
1981	8,547	6,165 (72%)	7,026	3,675 (52%)	213	147 (69%)
1982	9,358	6,881 (74%)	7,025	3,647 (52%)	154	113 (73%)

Source: Internal Revenue Service, *Statistics of Income, Corporate Income Tax Returns* (Washington, D.C.: Government Printing Office, various years).

assets, receipts, or income—the very largest corporations have grown to dominate all the measurements. The giant corporation now dominates the U.S. economy to an extent undreamed of in earlier years. They account for nearly three-fourths of all corporate assets, over one-half of all corporate receipts, and almost three-fourths of all corporate income. They comprise a powerful world wherein a relatively small number of giant corporations compete against a relatively large number of small enterprises, and against the rest of us. The small enterprises may be more flexible and innovative, but the large ones have been able to more than make up for it with their sheer size and power. To continue growing, the very large corporation has had to adopt a new structure, and the new structure has been forcing a new kind of adjustment of its own—a cultural adjustment. Power and size interact with each other in a cumulative fashion. The drive for power leads to a growth in size while the growth in size causes a need for more power to hold the larger organization together and make it manageable. In a reinforcing spiral toward corporate hegemony, more corporate power leads to larger corporate size, and larger size leads to more power. Walter Adams and James W. Brock, in their book *The Bigness Complex*, provide ample evidence of the circularity of power and size.[1]

The Corporate Need for Control

Continued growth has forced the large corporation to experiment with a new, more powerful organizational structure, a structure more capable of dealing with the problems brought on by its increased size and diversification. Some of the very early attempts at restructuring occurred at DuPont and General Motors in the 1920s. These pioneers in corporate restructuring began with what business managers call U-form organizations and turned them into so-called M-form organizations. (U-form stands for "unitary form," while M-form stands for "multiple-division form.") Top managers at GM became famous in managerial circles for their pioneering work in corporate restructuring.

The early U-form corporation was divided into "unitary" departments. Each department performed only one (unitary) function of the organization. The functional units of the pre–First-World War corporation were usually finance, production, and marketing. All managers involved with the finance function were grouped together into one (unitary) finance department. So all finance people were united administratively, and they all ultimately reported to the same finance head. Likewise, all marketing people were united administratively, and all of them ultimately reported to the same marketing head. So too with all the production people. Each functional group was united, hence the name, "U-form." At least in principle, the U-form held managers strictly accountable. Those responsible for production were accountable to the head of the production department. Those responsible for marketing were accountable to the marketing head, and so on for each function performed by the organization. But as these U-form corporations grew during and after the First World War, their functionally united groups became large and cumbersome with many layers of management. The larger the U-form grew, the harder it became to hold any single manager responsible for the profitability of a particular product, because the financing, producing, and marketing of each product were the responsibilities of different functional departments.

If something went wrong in a particular product line, marketing would blame production for inadequate quality control. But production would blame marketing for poor sales performance. And finance would blame everybody else for lack of cost control. So the department heads struggled against each other, either to avoid responsibility for failure or to claim responsibility for success. As a result, in the early years of GM and DuPont, the top managers and owners were increasingly frustrated in their attempt to make the two giant corporations more profitable. Other corporations that grew into very large, diversified organizations, usually through consolidation and merger, ran into the same organized irresponsibility problems with their U-form organizations.[2] That is, the organization itself seemed to build in a lack of managerial responsibility. Business organization had become a hindrance to further corporate growth. The U-form had become obsolete.

The more advanced M-form structure, on the other hand, separates its functions into multiple divisions. Ideally, each of these multiple divisions is a more-or-less autonomous operating group responsible for the production and distribution of a particular product or product line. Each autonomous division performs its own operating functions, so that the head of each division can be held responsible for all of the functions contributing to the profitability of his or her group. These M-form organizations are more flexible and more decentralized than the old U-form structures, which have largely been replaced in the contemporary world of giant corporations. The M-form organizations also are more responsible, in the sense that each autonomous division is a profit center, a single group, performing all of the operating functions itself, and therefore directly responsible for the profitability of a particular product. Profit responsibility is built into the organization, replacing the organized irresponsibility of earlier corporate organizations. The financial performance of each of the multiple divisions or profit centers is monitored by a centralized corporate office, usually headed by the chief financial officer of the parent corporation. The financial data gathering and number crunching at the corporate office greatly focuses and enhances the control of upper management over what now matters most—the money. The General Motors Corporation pioneered the development of the new U-form organization during the period between the two world wars. It was only after the Second World War that other large corporations began following GM's lead.

As Figure 1 illustrates, changing from the old U-form structure to the new M-form structure has greatly simplified the reporting responsibilities of managers at the product level (PRODUCT A, PRODUCT B, PRODUCT C in Figure 1). The change has made the product-line managers directly responsible for the profits made by their product. Each product-line manager in each of the multiple divisions now has direct control over the functions—production and marketing—that determine the profits earned in each prod-

Figure 1
Organizational Forms

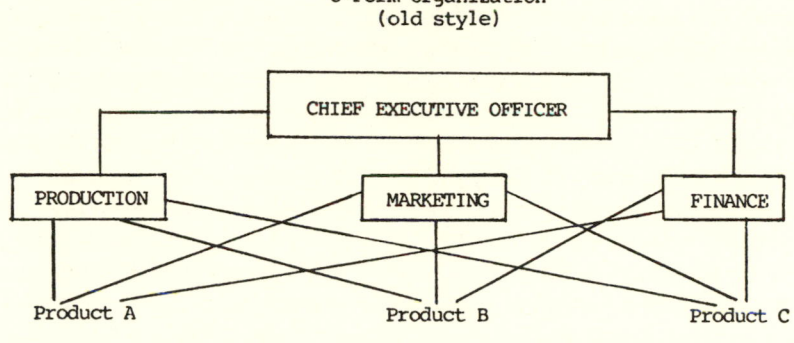

U-Form Organization
(old style)

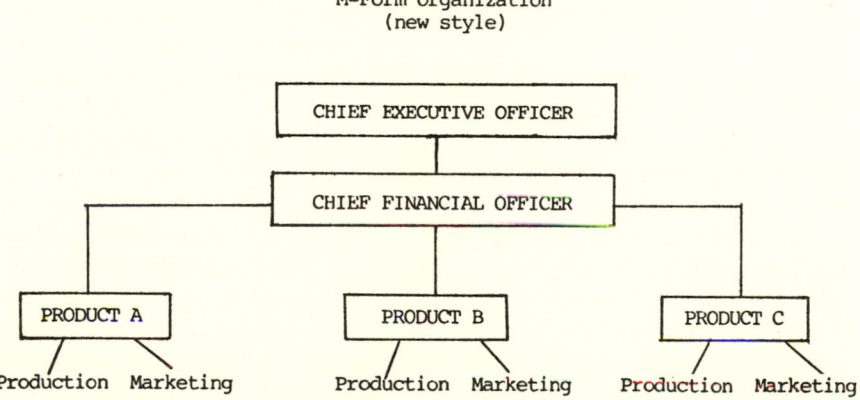

M-Form Organization
(new style)

uct line. Furthermore, the M-form structure centralizes the finance function into a new corporate head office, run by a powerful new corporate official—the chief financial officer. The M-form can be expanded almost infintely to include additional product lines, as new products or new companies are added to the organization. The new M-form also maintains much tighter control over the financial flows within the organization.

The corporate offices of conglomerated corporations have become so powerful that they now serve as substitutes for the capital market of old. Most of the autonomous divisions of conglomerates used to be free-standing corporations with their own independent corporate officials and stockholders. They became divisions of a conglomerate only after they were taken over in a merger. As dependent subsidiaries of the acquiring conglomerate, they no longer pay out their surplus capital funds to shareholders who used to reinvest the funds in the financial market. Nor do they acquire new capital funds, when needed, from the financial market. Instead, the central corporate office of the conglomerate controls the funds of the dependent subsidiaries, who have been turned into operating divisions. The old independent corporations with excess funds used to pay out dividends to their shareholders. Then their shareholders would reinvest the funds in the stock or bond market. The old independent corporation with a need for new funds used to acquire the new finance by issuing stocks or bonds to investors in the market. But now the corporate head office allocates capital funds to the divisions it decides need them, and it appropriates capital funds from the divisions it decides should supply them. In this way, the new corporate office, with its own administrative decisions of central managers, replaces the old capital market, with its supply-and-demand haggling of independent corporations and investors. In this way, the corporate head office also replaces the top layer of managers who used to run the formerly free-standing, independent corporations that have been merged into the conglomerate.

The very large corporation has adopted a more sophisticated structure that allows for decentralizing operational decisions and for clarifying profit responsibilities, but the new structure itself creates a new kind of problem similar to that encountered by large holding companies. (A holding company is a paper corporation, a hollow shell designed simply to own other corporations.) At their weakest, holding companies are unable to plan or coordinate the activities of their operating companies. The operating companies are little more than investments in a financial portfolio. Such holding companies are really not organizations at all. They are financial funnels and ownership depositories, the tools of nineteenth-century swashbucklers.[3] But the imperial conglomerate is the tool of the twenty-first-century swashbuckler. It is a full-fledged, powerful organization that is managed as a whole. It is more than the sum of its parts. The corporate office plans and coordinates the different divisions, forging them into a commercial empire capable of perpetually running any number of different industries of any size, anywhere on the earth or in the heavens. The essence of an imperial conglomerate is its lack of limits and its synergy. Being more than the sum of its parts, the limitations of any of its parts do not bind it. So its power is more than that of a commercial entity. It is more than a monopoly of any one market. It is an empire.

Herein lies the challenge of M-form conglomerate organizations, the dominant type of American corporation today. To operate as a whole, to benefit from the synergy between the parts, the parts must be coordinated and the movement of the whole must be planned. The huge corporation has become so large that it has had to be broken down into its parts—hence the M-form structure composed of autonomous divisions. Breaking the organization down into parts, each one of which can be held accountable for its own operation as a profit center, has meant that corporations can now grow to unlimited, infinite size, and still be manageable. And yet breaking the corporation down into its parts also threatens the synergy between the parts. Overall coordination and long-term planning at the central corporate level are now more important than ever. They require far more information-processing capacity than ever before, hence the proliferation of new information-based technologies and jobs.

The corporate world is going through a true technological revolution. The technology involved, however, has little to do with the production of goods or services. It has to do with the organization and control of people. The technological revolution is in organization and information rather than in production and distribution.[4] The M-form structure is just the first stage of the organization-information revolution, but it is clearly forcing the corporate world into the next stage. Since corporations can live forever, they can, theoretically, grow forever as well. Until recently their size was technologically limited by their primitive form of organization, the old U-form. However, the invention of the M-form lifted the limit on size; computer technology and communications advances also helped. Nevertheless, with continued growth, new problems relating to size are being encountered. The operations of multiple, autonomous divisions can be planned by the corporate office, but plans must be implemented. The divisions must follow the general direction of the plan. They must not work at cross-purposes, lest the synergy between them be lost. The divisions must pursue some common purpose, hold some common values, and share some basic beliefs. In short, they must be united into a whole by something that is larger than the sum of the parts. They must develop a common, corporate culture.[5]

A corporate culture is a set of shared beliefs and values inculcated in the corporation's employees. The corporate culture reinforces and reshapes the employee's general desire to do well into a compulsion to get ahead, through loyalty to and hard work for the corporation. Corporate culture is an internalization of corporate control. So it is a tool of social control. The huge and ever-growing corporate conglomerate needs a corporate culture to unify its autonomous divisions. In *The Reckoning*, David Halberstam shows that Nissan and several other Japanese corporations have already developed some excellent cultural models, ripe for export to the United States along with their cars.[6] William G. Ouchi, in his *Theory Z*, shows that leading U.S. corporations are borrowing and building their own unifying corporate cultures along Japanese and other lines.[7] Regardless of the source, U.S. corporations are acquiring the unifying control tool they need to continue growing while maintaining control over the employees of their far-flung empires.[8]

The leaders in corporate culture building in the United States usually have been less diversified corporations, rather than imperial conglomerates. Among the better-known U.S. corporations to have developed strong cultures are Caterpillar Tractor, General Electric, DuPont, 3M, Digital Equipment Corporation, IBM, Dana, Procter and Gamble, Hewlett-Packard, Johnson and Johnson, Tandem Computer, and Continental Bank.[9] Only a few of them, like GE, DuPont, and 3M, are full-blown, imperial conglomerates. However, this is not to say that most full-blown conglomerates do not need strong corporate cultures. Quite to the contrary, the imperial conglomerate's need for a strong culture is very pressing. In a recent *Fortune* article, business consultant Morty Lefkoe even claimed that most merger attempts that fail do so because of the lack of a common corporate culture.[10] Since most large conglomerates have grown through fairly recent takeovers of diverse, formerly free-standing corporations, many of which had cultures of their own, forging their diverse cultures into one common conglomerate culture has not been easy. Although the cultures of different U.S. corporations have many similarities, the personnel of captured corporations generally enter into their new conglomerate environment with considerable misgiving and even overt hostility, particularly in hostile takeovers. These attitudes make the inculcation of the new conglomerate's culture a slow and difficult process. So new conglomerates would be expected to have relatively weak cultures. On the other hand, GE, DuPont, and 3M are older imperial conglomerates that have had more time to inculcate the shared beliefs and values of their cultures into successive generations of managers. Although most new conglomerates do not yet have really strong cultures, if they follow the pioneers, they will soon enough.

Forging the new conglomerate corporation into an imperial conglomerate, into a unified whole, has become a growth industry. It has spawned the new high-tech, information economy. Furthermore, along with the investment bankers and corporate lawyers who have been arranging new mergers and restructurings as fast as possible, business consultants specializing in the problems of conglomerate management have been doing a very brisk business in the sale of advice.[11] The most influential pioneers in conglomerate consulting were in the Boston Consulting Group. They rose to prominence in the late 1970s with their so-called product portfolio approach to conglomerate management. In their approach, the corporate office of the conglomerate was advised to classify its subsidiary corporations or divisions into four basic types: (1) *Cash cows*, or subsidiaries that possessed a large market share of a stable or declining industry (formerly powerful old industrial oligopolies made excellent cash cows); (2) *Stars* possessed a large market share of a growing industry (new high-tech, information-based service companies made excellent stars); (3) *Dogs* possessed a small market share of a stable or declining industry; (4) *Cats*, or question marks, possessed the potential for acquiring a large market share of a growing industry.

Once the corporate office determined the nature of its subsidiaries or divisions, it could then integrate them into an overall growth strategy for the conglomerate as a whole. With the help of its investment banker, the corporate office sold off the dogs for the best obtainable price. Such subsidiaries were of little use to the corporate office. Their weak market position offered little opportunity for a higher profit margin in the short run, and their stable or declining industry offered little growth opportunity for the long run.

After selling off its dogs, the corporate office tried to achieve an overall balance in its holdings of cash cows and stars. The cash cows, with their strong market positions, offered high profit margins in the short run. Also, since cash cows operated in stable or declining industries, they required little new investment in plant and equipment. Their large depreciation allowances were greater than their investment requirements, particularly if their existing plant and equipment were allowed to deteriorate. This left them with an accumulation of surplus funds for investing elsewhere. They were literally cash cows ready for vigorous milking. Cash cow subsidiaries provided the short-run funds for investing in the long-run growth of star subsidiaries. The stars, with their market power in growing industries, could grow very rapidly in output and profit if they could acquire the large flow of funds they needed to expand their plant and equipment. So the conglomerate's corporate office matched the cash flow provided by its cash cows in the short run with the cash needs of its stars for expansion in the long run. It is no coincidence that most cash cows were manufacturing subsidiaries with high capital–output ratios, because the higher the ratio, the higher the depreciation allowances available for milking. Such manufacturing subsidiaries were located principally in the Midwest and were in stable or declining industries. Their vigorous milking by conglomerates speeded up or precipitated their decline and turned the old industrial heartland of the American economy into the Rustbelt. But their milking financed conglomerate stars who, also by no coincidence, were generally high-tech companies located in the Sunbelt or in low-wage, underdeveloped countries. Barry Bluestone and Bennett Harrison provide further discussion and empirical evidence in their *The Deindustrialization of America.*[12]

Conglomerate offices, once they had sold off their dogs and matched the need for funds of their stars with the flow of funds milked from their cash cows, had to decide which of its cats or question marks could be developed into new stars. Those that could were retained; the others were sold off, divested. Conglomerate divestiture of unwanted cats and dogs occurs quite frequently as a matter of course. Such divestitures do not represent a change in practice, just a housecleaning. Conglomerates are not moving back to single-industry status. Census data show just the reverse—more instead of less diversification. Nevertheless, many financial analysts and business jour-

Figure 2
Financial Flows

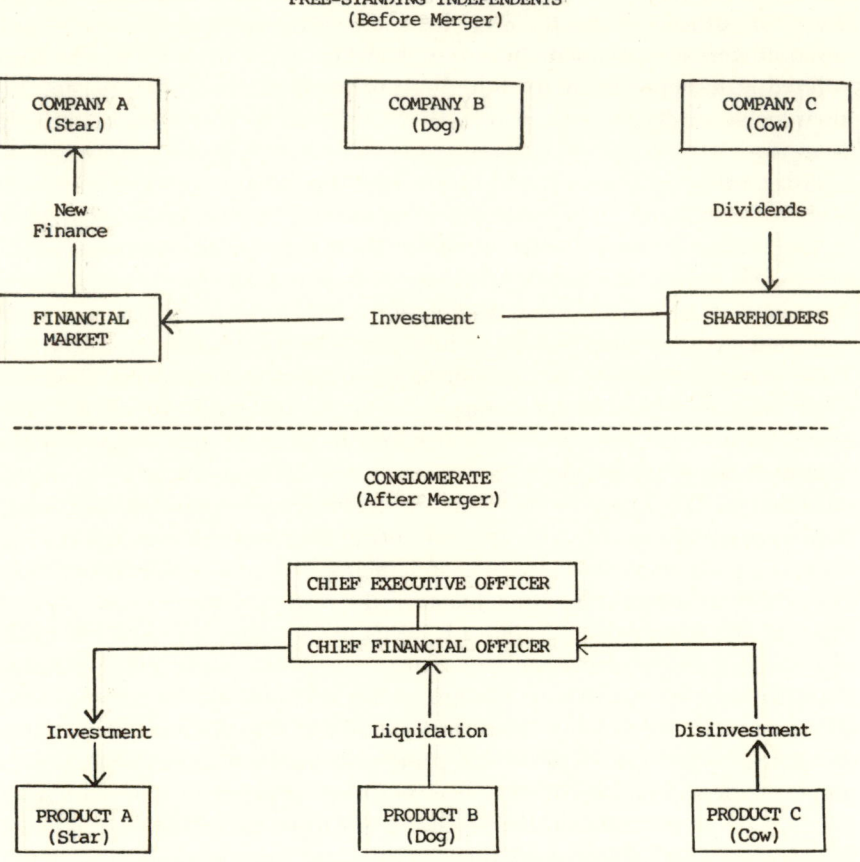

FREE–STANDING INDEPENDENTS
(Before Merger)

| COMPANY A (Star) | COMPANY B (Dog) | COMPANY C (Cow) |

New Finance

Dividends

FINANCIAL MARKET ← Investment → SHAREHOLDERS

CONGLOMERATE
(After Merger)

CHIEF EXECUTIVE OFFICER

CHIEF FINANCIAL OFFICER

Investment   Liquidation   Disinvestment

| PRODUCT A (Star) | PRODUCT B (Dog) | PRODUCT C (Cow) |

nalists continue to misinterpret conglomerate housecleaning as a return to single-industry operation. Such interpretations simply are not supported by the broad empirical evidence.[13]

Another diagram will be useful here. Figure 2 illustrates how the financial flows, principally between stars and cash cows, are arranged before and after merger into a giant conglomerate. As Figure 2 shows, cats are gotten rid of as quickly as possible. If they cannot be turned into stars, they simply disappear through divestiture. Dogs, on the other hand, remain in the conglomerate menagerie, but only long enough to be liquidated. The cows are milked vigorously, through disinvestment, to provide the cash flow needed for investment in stars. Figure 2 also shows the drastic reduction in the roles played by shareholders and the financial market. The powerful imperial conglomerate can largely dispense with the nuisance of shareholders and financial markets; they are simply bypassed. Neither the pesky share-holders nor the risky financial market need be relied on for a regular flow of funds. The conglomerate's menagerie now provides it with a regular flow of funds instead. The market does not really disappear, but its social control function does.

The Boston Consulting Group's menagerie approach to managing the conglomerate did rationalize it into a kind of whole that was more than the mere sum of its parts. Nevertheless, the approach dealt only with the financial dimension of the conglomerate enterprise, creating a financial synergy between the parts, but nothing more. The Boston Consulting Group's aproach was a halfway house on the road to full unification, a kind of financial expedient that kept the conglomerates of the 1970s going until the corporate culture of the 1980s developed.

Corporate culture unifies not just the financial dimensions, but all of the dimensions of conglomerate enterprise.[14] Overemphasizing the financial results of subsidiaries or divisions to the exclusion of other performance dimensions can quickly lead to managerial neglect at best, and to rampant opportunism at worst. That is, subsidiary managers can meet their quantified financial objectives at the expense of their other, nonquantified duties. They can save expenses and make themselves look good financially by not performing costly functions in the short run, the slighting of which will not be felt until the long run. Of course, by the time the effect of this managerial neglect is felt, it will be the responsibility of someone else; the original perpetrator will have been rewarded with a promotion to a larger division or an important post at the corporate office before the bottom line of his or her former division is finally affected. By then, it is someone else's problem. Such managerial neglect, under a system that overemphasizes immediate financial results, naturally leads to rampant opportunism. Division heads learn to concentrate on meeting their own financial targets at the expense of other objectives, and certainly at the expense of any non-quantified, nonrewarded objectives.

Opportunistic division heads quickly learned how to maximize the return to themselves from their corporate position. They began to do a bit of milking on their own behalf. They also became cynical opportunists who maximized their own salaries, perquisites, bonuses, and insider profits. They could do so at the expense of whoever was foolish or weak enough to bear the cost, be it another manager, another investor, the conglomerate, or the society at large. Even ignoring the personal and social costs of managerial opportunism, the costs to the conglomerate can become large. Under the circumstances, synergy between the different parts of the conglomerate whole becomes extremely difficult to create. A system of control far stronger than that devised by the Boston Consulting Group is required to teach the lower level managers to work together for the higher good. The continued growth in corporate size and diversification allowed for a rise in managerial slack at the divisional level that has to be taken up. A surprising majority of executives agree that more controls are necessary. In a fascinating survey of executives from thirteen representative U.S. corporations, Allan Cox learned:

Most executives believe controls within the corporation are necessary. Fifty-one percent top executives and 56 percent middle agree such controls are needed to curb corruption—or at least indiscretion. Their thinking is that the size and complexity of their management structure is an invitation for unchecked indiscretions or outright dishonesty available to a random few.[15]

LEARNING TO WORK FOR THE HIGHER GOOD

Whose Good?

Managers are well paid. The Administrative Management Society estimates that in 1984 U.S. managers in lower- to middle-level corporate positions were paid an average annual salary of $32,270, up 7.7 percent from 1983. These managers also received various packages of pension and insurance plans, profit sharing, and other fringe benefits.[16] Top management is paid much better, particularly in large corporations. The Dartnell Institute of Financial Research estimates that chief executive officers of U.S. corporations with yearly sales of $1–10 billion received an average annual base salary of $138,000 in 1981 and an average total annual compensation of $221,000.[17] In that same year, 31.8 million Americans lived below the poverty level of income ($9,287 for a family of four).[18]

Relative to many millions of Americans, corporate managers are doing very well. Nevertheless, the corporate liberality toward its managerial class does not mean that the corporation exists for the good of its middle managers. It does not. Rather, the corporation exists for the good of its higher order—its CEOs and major stockholders. The potential opportunism and avarice of its middle managers (the lower good) runs counter to the higher good. Although middle managers are paid well, they are corporate employees, not autonomous agents free to trade for their own account. And the conscious purpose of corporate culture is to keep a tight reign on the pursuit of personal interests, particularly when those interests detract from the higher corporate interest. For no matter how well they are paid and how closely they are watched, some middle managers can still misbehave; some can still pursue their own interest. Exploiting the corporation financially is the obvious misbehavior. But managers might also devote their energies to empire building, to family matters, to friends, or to other superfluities. Corporate culture is designed to control such misbehavior.

Narrowly defined, corporate culture is the internalized control of managerial behavior. External control is also applied. The M-form organizational structure is a major advance in the technology of external control; so too is the whole range of computer storage, processing, and monitoring technologies applied in the computerized office. But they are all insufficient because they are all external. Internal controls are also needed to stimulate and monitor managers. Up to now it has not been possible (legally) to physically insert computer-activated electrodes into the managerial brain. Although it cannot be done physically, at least not yet, it can be done culturally, particularly to those obsessed with career success.

How Values Change: Coercion and Career

The most secure and effective form of control over others is the power to alter their values. Control over others can be based on coercion—others can be forced to do as they are told. Such is the nature of the slaveowner's control of the slave. But control based on coercion is tenuous. Slaves resist and revolt because control based on coercion creates resentment and duplicity in the coerced. Slaves learn to walk with a shuffle around their masters, even while burning with resentment. Slaves can be forced to give lip service to the master's values, but it is far more difficult to force the internal acceptance of those values. When the force is removed, so is the social control, because it was not willingly accepted. Social control through coercion is temporary. More permanent social control is based on the ability to alter the internal values of others to gain their willing acceptance of the control. Then the control becomes legitimate. It is deemed right and good by those over whom it is exercised. It no longer requires the whip.

Ambition is a far more powerful social control mechanism than coercion. Based on fear, the power of coercion fades when the coercion is removed. But the power of ambition has its tap root sunk deeply into shared values and beliefs, into culture itself. Ambition is sunk particularly deep into the culture of the self-made individual—into American culture, that is. In the nineteenth century that ambition manifested itself in the exuberance of the pioneer on the moving frontier. It bubbled over in the form of gold rushes and land booms. In the twentieth century that ambition manifests itself in the rampant careerism of U.S. managerial strata and has become anchored even more deeply in the cultural reservoir of values and beliefs shared by the broad American middle class. Now it takes on the form of dual career couples and suburban sprawl. But personal ambition is the same powerful motivator, whether pursued on the frontier or in the career.

Thorstein Veblen came to know better than any other social observer how American ambition distorts values and beliefs. Cultural change and value distortion in the United States can be understood best in terms of four invaluation processes—contamination, subordination, emulation, and mystification—which were first sketched out by Veblen.[19] These four power processes change the motives for action and the meanings of action. They are the ways and means of manipulation because they determine why we act and what our actions mean. Contamination replaces one set of meanings and motives with another set. The contaminating motives and meanings invade the social space once occupied by a declining institution. Subordination raises one set of motives and meanings over a declining set. The rising set of motives and meanings comes from a dominating institution and pushes down those of a declining institution. Emulation mimics one set of motives and meanings. Emulation is a push for status and power through imitation of the high and mighty. Mystification confuses one set of meanings and motives with another set. Mystification is a push for symbolic dominance.

All of these processes, of course, work through the medium of the individual human will, and are intimately related to ambition and social control. Numerous recent observers have studied the relations between ambition and social control. Their insights and evidence are drawn upon here.

Invaluation Processes—Contamination

The first of the four invaluation processes of interest to us is contamination. The values of others can be altered and one's own values reinforced if their values can be contaminated with your own. Then their emotional attachment to their own original value can be turned to your account. Contamination is a powerful way for those in positions of high status and authority to alter values into strings that can be pulled and buttons that can be pushed to get underlings to want to do what is desired by the person or institution that is doing the manipulating. Most of us want to be good at what we do. We usually take pride in our artisanship, in the general serviceability of our skills. This pride, when uncontaminated, makes most of us try to be dexterous at our crafts. Whether househusbands, typists, cleaning women, sculptors, truck drivers, or nuclear physicists, we value doing our crafts well. But this value we place on a task well done, for its own sake, can be contaminated by another value. It can be turned into something else and used as a button by someone else. Then someone can push our button, for their sake. This is precisely what happens when technical craft becomes corporate career.

The value we place on our craft is a value that is inherent in the craft itself. We value our craft because we find it of intrinsic worth. As artisans, we are craft-directed and self-directed.[20] Nevertheless, through contamination, our craft becomes our career. Both artisans and careerists value the tasks they perform, but for very different reasons. The artisan's values are intrinsic and internal, while the careerist's are extrinsic and external. The careerist is a contaminated artisan, an artisan on the make. The careerist performs tasks to advance his career, rather than to advance his craft. The careerist values a task performance because it gets him an external reward, because it gains the approval of others, particularly the approval of superiors rather than the approval of fellow artisans. The careerist and the artisan may perform the same task, but since the careerist does it to curry favor, the careerist can be manipulated far more readily than the artisan. From the point of view of the organization that needs to control its employees, the careerist is an asset. He comes to the organization fully equipped with buttons that can be pushed and strings that can be pulled. He is useful. The artisan, on the other hand, is a problem to the organization. She lacks buttons and strings. She must have them installed before she is fully operational. Installation (contamination) can be time-consuming and expensive; better that it be done at school and at public expense than at work and at corporate expense. So the process of contamination usually begins in school where youthful explorers who learn for the fun of it are turned into obedient students who learn for the external rewards of grades. Regardless of where it is done and at whose expense, it is essential to the maintenance of organizational control. She must be taught career values to replace craft values. To get a handle on her performance, the internal and intrinsic must be contaminated with the external and extrinsic so that the emotional charge of the craft can be activated by pulling on the strings of the career. Michael Maccoby, in *The Gamesman*, described how the desire for success affects managers, contaminating the craft of getting things done with the career of getting ahead. Maccoby's findings show that the power of contamination is considerable.[21]

Invaluation Processes—Subordination

Closely related to contamination is a second way to alter or even implant values in those to be controlled. If their values resist contamination, the values of others can still be altered or at least overcome if their (lower) values can be subordinated to your (higher) values. A familiar illustration will help. As commander in chief, the president of the United States values young men as soldiers, sailors, and fliers. On the other hand, the women of the United States value the same young men as brothers, sons, and husbands. Military value conflicts with family value. If the military value is to prevail, then the president must be able to exercise power over the potential pacifists, the potentially insubordinate women. This can be done by subordinating their "womanly" family values to higher, "manly" values. In large measure, the male-dominated culture has already done it for the president. Just for good measure though, the women constantly should be taught the higher value of patriotism.

The subordination of others' values is never direct. An ambitious national leader, for example, never asks others to subordinate the value they place on their life to the value the leader places on defeating a national rival. Instead, such a leader calls upon some higher order of values such as national honor, as did Napoleon and Hitler. In economic conflicts, when subordinating community values to their own, corporate leaders never directly ask the community to give them more profit. Instead, corporate leaders refer indirectly to higher values or natural laws. "Free enterprise" sells very well in the United States as a higher value, and "the market" sells very well as a natural law. The high values afforded science and experts are also effective. Never is a community directly asked to sacrifice clean air and clean water to corporate profit. Instead, the market needs deregulating, and free enterprise needs defending. Furthermore, scientific experts, on corporate retainers, impress the community with cost-benefit ratios, statistical analysis, and other scientific talismans of great power. Corporations appear almost philanthropic in these matters, for they never argue to the public that regulation cuts their profits, though corporations will often point out that they may be forced to close their plants and lay off their workers because of the economic burdens imposed upon them by environmental controls.

Careerism and ambition play important roles in subordination as well as in contamination. As a manager learns to elevate his career to a higher-order value, he subordinates his other values to his career values. Male careerists are more prone to do so than female careerists, particularly when it comes to subordinating family to career. So from the point of view of the organization seeking to control the managerial worker, men are more useful because they are more willing than women to subordinate their family to their career. Furthermore, men may more readily than women downgrade their family because men are more able to do so. Patriarchical family relations that raise the man above the woman make it possible for men to shirk their family duties by pushing them onto their wives. Jacqueline B. Stanfield shows that this is the general case even in dual-career families, where wives who take up a career frequently continue contributing far more time and effort to the family's welfare than do their career husbands. Many women in that situation are pushed into trying to be a superwoman, attempting to perform two wholly absorbing roles simultaneously and feeling guilty for not being able to do the impossible. Their husbands offer little help around the home, so being unable to subordinate one set of conflicting values to another, they are trapped.[22] Although men too are trapped by career values through subordination, most of them are able to subordinate their wives' values to their own. Career men have it easier because they usually can push their home duties off on their wife, leaving the men with a clear conscience when their family values are subordinated to their career values. Ralph Nader and William Taylor studied at length nine male corporate leaders in the United States. In nearly all of those leaders, family and community values were subordinated to the values of corporate career.[23]

Invaluation Processes—Emulation

Another way to change the values of others is to get them to emulate you. Emulation is the most powerful invaluation process. It is the tap root of career and conformity. At bottom, a careerist is an emulator, a mimic of those who are highly respected (envied) in their fields. Emulation occurs when people learn to envy (respect) the values of higher-status individuals and to mimic or duplicate them in a competition for personal status and invidious distinction. Emulation is a complex form of personal attack on another person or persons to whom the attacker is actually attracted. It is based on attraction, not repulsion. It is an attempt to be like the other person or persons, only more so. It is raising one's standing in a group of status-ranked strivers, all of whom are constantly trying to inflate their own status while simultaneously deflating the status of their competitors.

Successful emulation requires constant self-aggrandizement through the conspicuous display of excellence in conventionally approved channels. It requires far more, however, than the ability to show off one's status. Merely showing off makes it all too obvious that the show-offs are not satisfied with their own status because it is lower than the status of their competitors. Merely showing off creates distinction, but of the wrong kind. The right kind is invidious distinction, a distinction that creates envy in the minds of one's competitors but at the same time demonstrates complacency in the mind of the perpetrator. Successful emulators can become quite brutal toward those they have surpassed. In *Showing Off in America*, John Brooks described the qualities of the toughest top executives in the United States: "The qualities that distinguish these men are arrogance, gratuitous cruelty, self-centeredness, lack of consideration of others, pettiness, fickleness, schoolyard bullying—a catalogue of predatory-invidious traits."[24]

An emulator does not rock the boat. He does not want to destroy the values held by those whose status he attacks. He wants to possess them, but to a greater extent. This makes the emulator profoundly conventional, and it makes the process of emulation an extraordinarily powerful mechanism of social control. Thorstein Veblen's study of emulation is a major contribution to the study of values.[25] He showed how emulation transformed a potentially revolutionary situation in America into a very conservative era. The way Veblen saw it, by the close of the nineteenth century, American farmers and workers were clearly at odds with the growing power of big business. The frontier escape hatch had closed, and the traditional path to a better life in America had closed with it. It was in their purely rational, economic interest for the farmers and workers to throw the robber barons out of power. But the farmers and workers, Veblen's "common man," did not want to revolt against the robber barons. Instead, the common man wanted to become more like the robber barons. According to Veblen, the power of emulation overcame the economic interest of the common man, turning him into a highly conventional and conservative defender of the status quo rather than a revolutionary. As the frontier closed and as career ladders proliferated in the professional and managerial ranks of the growing corporate world, the man on the make eagerly tried his hand at the new corporate career game. Pushing his way into the growing middle class of kept men, the common man became sucked into the petty rivalries and invidious distinctions of middle-class life and the white-collar career.

Within a few decades, interrupted by a glorious but short revolt of youth (the 1960s), the rivalries and invidious distinctions of corporate career had so raised the acceptable standards of life that the "common man" had to be aided in the rat race by the "common woman." By the 1970s, one salary had becone insufficient to finance the ever-rising level of conspicuous consumption. A house in the suburbs with two cars in the garage and two college-educated kids are impressively expensive, but no longer enough to keep up with the competition. The kids now need M.B.A.s from prestigious private universities, and to get into them it is becoming almost mandatory that they attend the proper prep school. Furthermore, the level of living must not only be quite vast in terms of quantity, but also quite refined in terms of quality. All of this requires more money. Two or three cars are not enough. At least one of them must be a Mercedes or some other suitably refined make. Summer vacations at a second home are also needed, but are not enough. Winter vacations, with tans to verify them, must be added. And so it has gone throughout the twentieth century; the relentless pressure of emulation has pushed the acceptable standard of living ever higher and has pushed down ever lower the self-esteem of those who do not keep up. The pressure of emulation has placed the heavy hand of competitive conformity on everyone's shoulder.

The emulative pressures of middle-class life and white-collar corporate career in America have created the widespread insecurity required by corporate cultures. Make no mistake, the system is working. Their insecurity make managerial personnel highly susceptible to indoctrination by the values and beliefs of specific corporations. Most lower-level workers also come to the corporation, ready-made for the deskilled and degraded tasks that need doing there. Their self-esteem properly lowered by emulative pressure, and their traditional jobs squeezed out by the fight against inflation, millions of unorganized working-class whites and dispirited minorities are grist for the corporate mill.

The force of emulation also explains why the egalitarian drives of the civil rights movement and of women's liberation are being lost. In spite of the real successes of the Reverend Jesse Jackson's Rainbow Coalition and Operation PUSH, the flight of the black middle class from the urban ghetto and from black small business—following the earlier move of the white middle class into suburbia and white-collar careerism—is depriving most blacks of the money and leadership that fueled their movement. The women's liberation movement also is being deformed. The old egalitarian drive of the sisterhood is being transformed by emulation into a drive for more career opportunity in the corporate world. Rather than trying to replace the emulation of careerism with a more egalitarian and humanitarian way of organizing work, the rage among women on the make is "networking." This networking merely replaces, or at least supplements, the old–boy system of status enhancement in the corporate world with an old–girl system. It is still emulative, inegalitarian, and careerist. That is, networking still involves status seeking, self-aggrandizement, and the sacrifice of all other values to career values, whether or not the network of opportunists is male or female.[26]

A financial indication of the strength of emulation and conspicuous consumption is the distribution of financial and liquid-asset holdings of American families. According to an authoritative study published in the *Federal Reserve Bulletin*, only 10 percent of all families had been able to build up $50,000 or more in financial and liquid assets in 1983, and fully 61 percent of all families held less than $5,000 in such assets.[27] This means that the vast majority of U.S. families have little slack in their budgets for building up a readily-available financial reserve. Even fairly affluent families, with annual incomes of $25,000–$29,999, had a median holding of only $5,147 in financial and liquid assets in 1983.[28]

Home ownership boosts the net worth of many affluent families, but the boost is largely illusory. If they sold their homes to get their net equity, they would have no place to live. Their equity would then be eaten up by rent payments, making their gain a temporary one. Furthermore, 40 percent of fairly affluent families (income from $20,000 to $29,999 a year) do not own their own homes in the first place.[29] Nevertheless, the net worth of affluent families (measured as the median net worth of families with incomes of $25,000 to $29,999) was only $28,876 in 1983.[30] That net worth includes the net equity in homes. Under the pressure of competitive spending for conspicuous consumption, even the fairly affluent are unable to build their net worth much above a mere pittance. In fact, half of all U.S. families had a net worth of less than $25,000 in 1983.[31] This is a profound indication of the strength of emulation in a society originally based on Puritan frugality.

Emulation occurs not only in the realm of consumption spending, but in all dimensions of life where personal status plays a role, as it does in a career. Emulation is similar to subordination in that it also involves the lowering of the prestige or significance of one set of values and the raising of another set—conspicuous consumption over Puritan parsimony, for example. For another relevant example, consider the case of a young man raised in a tight-knit, ethnic mill community who enters on a corporate career. Through emulating high-status corporate executives, he can be induced to denigrate the values and hopes of his boyhood friends and elevate the values and career struggles of his corporate peers and corporate bosses. The former community member will then feel only slight pangs of conscience if, in his career climb, he finds it expedient to close the plant that provides employment for his former community or if he finds it necessary to mount a decertification campaign against the union that represents his old buddies. Emulation is the most effective method of cooptation and is the process that has turned some of the radical yippies into the self-centered yuppies of the American pop scene.

Invaluation Processes—Mystification

A fourth way to change the values held by others is to mystify them, to confuse them into supporting your values instead of theirs. Mystification requires the manipulation of valued symbols. If motherhood and apple pie, for example, can be mystified and confused with national honor and war, the values of nurturing within the family can be drawn upon to support war between the nation-states. Likewise, if workers value the right to earn a living, mystification can get them to value the right to work. Furthermore, values symbolized by "private property" and "individual initiative" can be manipulated to protect corporations from collective bargaining and state regulation. Widely shared, communal values can be distorted or stretched to cover a multitude of actions, from polluting the air to exploiting the work force. Mystification is strongly akin to "newspeak." It allows the War Department to be the Defense Department, the MX missile to be the Peacekeeper missile, the economic surplus to be the cost of capital, and it allows conglomerate profit to be the higher good. Mystification is done by linking a negatively charged value to a positively charged value. This positive linkage reduces the repulsion felt by others to things that you value. So if you value war, multiple warheads, and surplus income (profit), while others do not, you should link them with things that others do value, such as defense, peace, and earned income. The importance of confusion in the shaping of human values cannot be overestimated.

To serve one's employer, to pursue the higher corporate good, frequently requires managers and professionals to be absent from their families until late at night or to be away on distant assignments for extended periods. It also frequently requires the psyche's complete energy and attention, whether at home or on the road. From his extensive survey of U.S. executives, Allan Cox concluded, "While a good many executives may be appreciative of their families' needs and of their presence and support, some obviously view their homelife disdainfully. Many spend excessive hours at the office, and travel extensively even when they may not need to, in order to avoid a less than happy home."[32] Nevertheless, most corporate managers and professionals have very negative feelings about family neglect and emotional detachment from loved ones. If they neglected their families and became emotionally detached from their loved ones, the guilt from doing so would be devastating. Corporate managers do not neglect or detach. Instead, they work hard into the night on their careers and pursue challenging new opportunities out of town. This is not neglecting the family—a negatively charged value. This is advancing the career—a positively charged value.

They do not bring their work home in their briefcases to remain detached from the family circle of emotions. Instead, they bring their work home in their briefcases to get a promotion. Or so they have learned to believe. So they feel pride, not guilt. But if their wives divorce them or their children rebel against them, they are mystified and feel betrayed. They did not neglect their families out of malice. They did not emotionally detach out of frigidity. Nevertheless, they still neglected their families, even if it was to get a promotion. They still emotionally detached from their loved ones, even if it was to pursue their career.

Corporate Culture

A culture is a set of shared values and beliefs. Spurred on by careerism, the four invaluation processes are changing pluralist U.S. culture into hegemonic corporate culture. The values and beliefs of the corporate world are coming to replace the values and beliefs of the old frontier world. Just like success on the frontier required a certain set of values and beliefs, so too does success in the corporation. But a pluralist culture's shared beliefs and values come from many independent institutions—church, state, family, school, union—while a hegemonic culture's shared beliefs and values come from a single dominant institution. Human character in a pluralist culture is created by each person through a painful internal reconciliation and synthesis of conflicting values and beliefs. Human character in a hegemonic culture, on the other hand, is molded through an external inculcation of supporting values and beliefs. U.S. culture and character are already far more hegemonic than pluralist, particularly among the corporate middle class. It is within this social stratum that hegemony is evolving. Critical intellectuals seldom study the white-collar middle-class world. We either study the abuses of the upper class or the struggle for a decent life of the working class. As a result, we are being blindsided by the development of hegemony in the United States.[33]

SPEEDING UP THE MANAGERIAL CLASS

A Precarious Position

The position of the managerial class is now a very precarious one. The working class in the United States is at least partially organized to defend its economic interests. But middle managers almost never organize into unions or any other collectivity to defend themselves. Instead, they pursue their own personal interests as individual careerists. Divided by their individualism and blinded by their careerism, middle managers are easy prey for the organized interest of big, conglomerated capital. Members of the working class feel solidarity with other workers. But a manager has no solidarity with other managers. So when a manager is fired or abused, his colleagues do not come to his aid. Instead, they scramble for his job. He is on his own, and if he loses out in the career climb, then he alone is blamed for it and he alone must deal with it. His mates offer little solace, lest they become associated with a loser.

The managerial careerist, though individualistic in his climb, does not serve his own interests with his corporate work. Instead, blinded by his careerism, he serves the interests of the controlling corporate ownership. He is as alienated as any member of the working class, but he does not know it. His values are so contaminated that, when he works for someone else's profit, he never realizes that he is being manipulated. His buttons are pushed and his strings are pulled by someone else. He works for them, not himself. All the while, the managerial careerist remains unaware of his buttons and strings and of the sacrifice he is making of himself. Unaware of being manipulated, the careerist sacrifices not only himself but also his family and friends to his career. Separated from family and friends, the managerial careerist emulates other, higher managerial careerists who, in turn, emulate those of even higher status. The emulation and accompanying invidious distinction extend all the way up the ladder to the top rung. The top rung is occupied by big capital, by the controlling interest of the conglomerate that employs the careerists.

Although the managerial class is well paid, its class position is precarious, even more so than its financial position. Denied an organized defense of its own interests by its careerism, and impregnated with values from above, the managerial class is not really a class at all. The power exercised by managers is not their power. The corporate purpose that managers pursue is not their purpose. The wealth they manage is not their wealth. In truth, the managerial class is a dependent class, a kept class. It possesses no power, no status, no substantial wealth of its own. Even its culture is not of its own making.

Separation of Ownership from Control

Nevertheless, the managerial function is essential in our highly organized corporate world. Without managers, corporate organizations would collapse. Because they are essential, and because of what was once a separation of ownership from control, many observers have argued that managers comprise an independent class. From Adolf A. Berle and Gardiner C. Means through John Kenneth Galbraith, institutionalist students of the U.S. corporation have attributed independent motives to corporate managers.[34] These independent managerial motives are claimed to run counter to the profit motive of ownership. Berle and Means, in their pioneering study *The Modern Corporation and Private Property*, argued that more and more mature corporations were controlled by the management rather than by the stockholders. As the original corporate owners died off, the ownership of stock was diffused; as the number of shareholders rose, no single shareholder owned enough stock to control the corporation. Stock ownership became a passive form of ownership. It became ownership without control, according to Berle and Means.

The separation of stock ownership from control and the continued growth of the corporation allowed for a broad range of managerial discretion relative to the stockholders. As long as the immediate profits that flowed to stockholders were satisfactory, the management was free to pursue its own objectives. Those objectives could run along two very different lines: personal or organizational. If management used its discretion to pursue personal objectives, then instead of earning the maximum profit for the distant stockholders, managers could puff up their own salaries and perks, invent new incentive plans and retirement benefits, and grant themselves lucrative stock options. They could hire more and more subordinates to elevate their own status. They could farm out lucrative contracts to friends and relatives and waste stockholder resources on their own pet projects and grandiose schemes. Or they could just take it easy and live the good life, playing golf, drinking scotch, and enjoying their secretaries.

But if management pursued objectives along a different line, they could do such things as sacrifice immediate stockholder profit for higher long-term corporate growth. They could even pursue technological advances (craft) instead of profit (career) by allocating resources to research and development instead of to dividends. They could, in general, take the long-run point of view for their organization and try to ensure its continued growth and prosperity, instead of constantly going after the short-run profits that look good to stockholders. Management could pursue these organizational objectives so long as enough profits were earned to keep the distant shareholders satisfied. So not only was a running margin of managerial malfeasance opened up by the separation of ownership from control and by the continued growth in corporate size, but a margin of managerial diplomacy was also made possible by the lifting of the stockholder's obsession with short-run results. Exactly how management used its range of discretion depended on the circumstances of each case.

John Kenneth Galbraith, in his *New Industrial State*, argued that the opening up of the managerial range of discretion had a somewhat benign effect on corporate behavior. Corporate bureaucracies, originally organized for the single-minded pursuit of profit, evolved into "technostructures," according to Galbraith. Within these technostructures, the drive for more profit was softened to some extent by the goals of managerial "technocrats" (artisans). Galbraith saw corporate management as essentially technocratic rather than bureaucratic. That is, managers valued technological advance and expanding output for their division's organization rather than maximum profit for their conglomerate shareholder/employers. Whether or not the

resulting behavior of organizations under this so-called managerial capitalism would be a single-minded pursuit of shareholder profits has been the
focus of a long controversy.[35]

Nevertheless, in the 1980s, the old, broad range of managerial discretion
is being narrowed in three related ways. First, the conglomerate itself, with
its new M-form organizational structure and its profit centers, is becoming
a more effective system of external control of management performance.
The sharp-penciled auditors and hard-nosed strategists of the conglomerate's corporate office are far more effective at forcing division heads to
pursue the bottom line than the far-removed shareholders of the free-
standing corporation of old. The information revolution has been crucial
in improving corporate control over managerial performance. Conglomerate headquarters are now the centers of a vast flow of timely and accurate
information about the performance, particularly financial, of the conglomerate's far-flung empire. Second, the corporate culture itself is providing a
growing system of internal, culture-based control to supplement the external, information-based control of the conglomerate's corporate office.
Third, the growing threat of a hostile takeover, even of large corporations,
keeps the managerial nose much closer to the proverbial grindstone. As a
result, managers are being sped up. The speedup means that they are being
made to work harder and longer for the more narrowly drawn benefit of
the corporate bottom line. Their short-lived discretion, originally opened
up by the separation of ownership from control in the large corporation,
is being taken away by the conglomerate, with its ability to take over even
the largest corporations and control even the most independent of CEOs.
However, the conglomerate is eliminating not only the running margin of
managerial malfeasance but also the longer-term objectives and the slight
softening of the immediate profit motive that had been experienced under
independent managements.

In a recent study, Edward S. Herman of the Wharton School has thrown
considerable doubt on the proposition that the profit motive was ever softened by the rise of a so-called managerial class, possessed of a wide margin
of discretion. Herman concludes:

In sum, the triumph of management control in many large corporations has not
left them in the hands of neutral technocrats. . . . The frequently assumed decline in
managerial interest in profits, which supposedly should result from the decreased
importance of direct owner control, has not, in fact, been proved.[36]

A closer control of managerial discretion is being achieved through new
corporate culture, new organizational structure, new information technology, and the growing threat of takeover. This tightening up will not lead
to improvement in long-term corporate performance, however. Short-run
profits may very well rise as a result of the tightening up, but long-run

performance could deteriorate. Marc R. Tool explains: "The more complete and meticulous the control of subordinates, the *lower* one would expect the volume and quality of economic performance to be in the shop, the foundry, the office, the classroom, or even the board room."[37]

The speedup means that the U.S. managerial class is being sucked into the same vicious circle that sucked in the working class nearly eighty years earlier. That vicious circle was first called the speedup by labor radicals. The industrial workers of the United States, around the turn of this century, were subjected to Frederick Taylor's "scientific management."[38] So-called scientific management involved first finding the fastest way to perform each task in a particular manufacturing process. The fastest way was determined by managerial experts, by time-and-motion specialists, not by the workers themselves. In the next step of the speedup, all workers were held to the faster pace of work by an elaborate piecework system of payment. Higher output and profit were the results; so too, sometimes, was higher income for the workers. Worker alienation and industrial strife, of course, were frequent side effects. But gradually a third step evolved in the speedup. This step was a response to the side effects encountered in the second step. In the third step, the recalcitrant workers were taught to like the sped-up pace of work, or were at least taught to tolerate it. The "human relations management" movement, also known by a number of other names, involved showing the workers that the corporation really cared about them. A few dollars spent on bulletin boards, lunchrooms, bowling teams, better lights, personnel directors, newsletters, and the like, paid big dividends in reduced strife and easier worker cooptation.[39]

Of course, some workers were more difficult than others. Particular difficulty was encountered with workers who were organizing into industrial unions. The steelworkers and autoworkers took more than lunchrooms and bowling teams. Pensions, health insurance, large wage hikes, and more, were required in these more difficult cases. And even then, militant workers never learned to like the speedup. But they tolerated it, more or less.[40] Furthermore, even if some unions could not be coopted, they could be induced to shift the formal area of conflict away from the organization of the labor process. Collective bargaining dealt more and more with wages and fringe benefits, and less and less with how work was organized and managed. This more crucial question was increasingly held to be a managerial prerogative. So management was left free to continue the speedup.

Continuing the speedup, however, required ever-closer control of the worker, and tighter control caused more worker alienation and strife. This, in turn, called for tighter controls and more effective cooptation. But the more coopted and controlled the worker, the harder it was to speed her up and appeal to her sense of artisanship. A vicious circle had begun: more control and more cooptation meant less artisanship, which called for even more control. The fundamental contradiction between managerial control and worker spontaneity greatly intensified the other contradictions of corporate enterprise because it slowed down or halted productivity improvement, making it harder and harder to get more profit out of the workers. So more profit must come from the consumers and from the community at large. And now, at last, the hungry eye has also turned inward, looking for ways to squeeze more profit from the managers themselves. The temporary slack given them by the separation of ownership from control is being taken up.

The separation of ownership from control that occurred in many mature corporations gave management a large degree of control, but management quickly lost its control to the conglomerate. Management still controls daily operations and makes the big policy decisions, but within a new, highly restrictive institutional framework and a system of institutionalized greed. That institutionalized greed takes concrete form not in the flimsy old conspiracies of a few wealthy capitalists, but in the powerful form of a new institution—the imperial conglomerate.

The Worm Turns, on Itself

The new conglomerate has gained control over the managers just as the managers earlier had gained control over the workers. So now it is management's turn to be sped up. The managerial class, as it begins to speed itself up, has none of the defenses possessed by the working class. Managers feel no solidarity and have no unions to join, nor would they join them if they existed.[41] Devotion to individual career success precludes any collective resistance, and the ambition of careerists also precludes any personal resistance. Ambitious members of the managerial class stand completely exposed and alone.

Speeding up the managers first involved the construction of M-form organizations composed of profit centers. Then the output of each profit center could be measured and the head of that profit center held responsible. Harold Geneen's management of ITT illustrates the point. ITT was probably the most aggressive of the conglomerates to sweep over the corporate world in the 1960s, and Geneen was the driving force behind it. Every year, year after year, each and every one of his acquired subsidiaries was expected to increase its earnings by at least 10 percent. No matter what, the bottom-line objective had to be met. Upon taking over a company, Geneen wrote,

we would talk about our goal of at least 10 percent annual growth. It did not make any difference if times were good or bad. When they were good, we should be able to make our goal easily; when they were bad, we had to work harder. But we had to make our goal each and every year. That was the message. And the new company managements believed us, because they knew we meant what we were saying.[42]

This single-minded pursuit of short-run profit, this obsession with the immediate bottom line described so frankly by Geneen, has become characteristic of American management. Geneen's single-mindedness is archetypal of the higher-level executives of conglomerated corporations. He is the major shaper of postwar managerial practice in America. To see how much current practice differs from earlier managerial practice, contrast Geneen's postwar book *Managing* with Chester Barnard's prewar classic *Functions of the Executive.*[43] Both of the men are experienced executives from major corporations; Geneen from ITT, and Barnard from the Bell family of AT&T. Both are archetypes and both wrote their books out of their own experience. But while Barnard stressed the systemwide, cooperative behavior needed in large corporations, Geneen stresses the need to meet immediate profit targets. The difference in emphasis between the two is indicative of a profound shift in how American corporations are managed. That shift has involved a narrowing of focus, a shortening of horizon, and the intrusion of corporate interest into other spheres of life.

As the focus has narrowed to an obsession with profit, the time horizon has been reduced to short-run, annual, or even quarterly profit targets. (Geneen once absolutely forbade long-range planning at ITT.)[44] And, paradoxically, this narrowing and shortening of corporate purpose has necessitated a broadening of corporate control over the lives of corporate employees and the general environment within which the tightly controlled employees attempt to meet the corporate purpose. (Geneen's ITT was accused of not only trying to bring down the elected government of Chile, but also of trying to tamper with the political and judicial processes of the United States.)[45]

In the American corporation of the 1980s, the increased focus on short-run profit has placed nearly irresistible pressure on middle-level managers to use any means required to meet their assigned objectives. Geneen explains this Machiavellian management with characteristic candor in what he calls his minicourse on management: "A THREE-SENTENCE COURSE ON BUSINESS MANAGEMENT: *You read a book from the beginning to end. You run a business the opposite way. You start with the end, and then you do everything you must to reach it.*"[46] In short, once you are given your end, it justifies whatever means you have to use to reach it. Geneen is remarkably candid about the general principles of management and should be commended for it. On the other hand, he is silent when it comes to particulars. He says nothing about the difficulties encountered by ITT after his departure. After having to slash its dividend in 1984, the once high-flying conglomerate had to fight off dissident stockholders in 1985 and 1986 with a massive, $1.7 billion divestiture program. Also, Geneen says nothing about the details of ITT's involvement in the ouster of Chile's elected government, and nothing about the interesting activities of Dita Beard, ITT's chief lobbyist during the most controversial part of Geneen's reign.[47] Although

Geneen's account of his archetypal management may be self-serving, it does provide excellent insight into conglomerate ends and the dominance of ends over means in the conglomerate's world.

The M-form profit-center structure pioneered by General Motors, the cash cows, cats, dogs, and stars of the Boston Consulting Group, and the Harold Geneen–style obsession with the bottom line have been widely adopted by conglomerates, who are now adding a new element to unify their organizations even further. This new element is the corporate culture, a set of shared beliefs and values that welds the conglomerate's disparate parts into a unified social whole, not just a financial whole. The creation and inculcation of this corporate culture—the brainwashing of the conglomerate's managerial cadres—is the most recent step in the speedup of the managerial class. Corporate culture teaches middle-level managers to value being sped up by the likes of Harold Geneen. Aided by their corporate culture, managers have learned cheerfully to work harder and faster as a team for the higher good. Managers also gladly give their conglomerate employers their evening time and weekends. This surplus time is given with no overtime pay. After all, managers are career personnel, not mere hourly workers. Managers do not punch a clock. They do not have to, because they voluntarily exploit themselves for the higher good. They voluntarily intensify their efforts and extend their workdays into the night and weekend.

Of course, this exploitation, this rich source of profit, is not seen as such by the managerial class. Unlike the working class, which originally saw the speedup for what it really was, the managerial class is far more sophisticated.[48] (Or so the managers think, when they have time.) Their sophistication is a product of their culture—their corporate culture. They never give a second thought to the institutionalized greed that they serve so tirelessly. Obviously, they have not read Marx or Veblen.

3

Education and Career

To believe that they are unhappy would probably be un-American. For if they are not happy, then the very terms of success in America, the very aspirations of all sound men, lead to ashes rather than to fruit.

—C. Wright Mills

THE UNIQUE POSITION OF U.S. EDUCATIONAL INSTITUTIONS

The Enlightenment Ideal, à la John Dewey

The "sophistication" of corporate managers, which has primed them for the corporate speedup, was learned, or at least reinforced, in school. This is not the American educational ideal, but it is the reality for many of us. Upton Sinclair remarked: "And I thought to myself: that is what modern education is—a league of the old men to make the young what the old want them to be."[1] To understand this reality, described so starkly by Sinclair, we must first understand the American educational ideal. Our beliefs about what education should be are rooted in the Enlightenment—that optimistic period in Europe when the feudal chains of rank and superstition were, at last, broken and when the effects of pluralism were grasped by the likes of

Voltaire, Hume, and Locke. Although expressed and fleshed out differently by each Enlightenment philosopher, the goal for education was to turn out citizens capable of thinking for and supporting themselves, and to pursue their own enlightened self-interest within a tolerant framework of civic virtue and public order.[2] Nevertheless, educating the poor was considered a risky endeavor, for it was thought that they might become discontented with their lot. For enlightenment exposes exploitation, whether it be of poor serfs by rich lords under feudalism or of unorganized workers under deregulated capitalism. Enlightenment can even expose middle-class exploitation—the self-exploitation for the bottom line practiced by the managerial class of twentieth-century America. In any case, education as enlightenment is inherently subversive of the status quo. Hence, the reality of education contradicts the ideal.

No one understood that contradiction better than John Dewey. As the premier twentieth-century spokesman for U.S. educators, Dewey explained both the Enlightenment ideal and the contradictory reality of U.S. education.[3] In a democracy, Dewey argued, the primary responsibility of schools is "to send out young men and women who will stand actively and aggressively for the cause of free intelligence in meeting social problems and attaining the goal of freedom." That was the ideal, but the reality was different. Dewey mused about his students, "what assurance is there in the existing system that there will be opportunity to use their gifts and the education they have obtained?"[4] And he knew the answer to his question—precious little, under the current dispensation. To make his educational ideal the reality required

securing greater industrial autonomy, that is to say, greater ability on the part of the workers in any particular trade or occupation to control that industry, instead of working under these conditions of external control where they have no interest, no insight into what they are doing, and no social outlook upon the consequences and meaning of what they are doing.[5]

Half a century has passed since Dewey called for "greater industrial autonomy," and it has not come to pass. The main drift has been in the opposite direction, making our educational ideal even harder to realize in practice. Dewey's arguments implied that the failure of American education to live up to Enlightenment ideals was due to the inability to apply those ideals, once they were learned, to the working world.

Another astute critic of education, Thorstein Veblen, argued that those ideals could not be taught in the first place. With the exception of a brief period of transition, major educational institutions in the United States had never been free from outside domination, Veblen argued. This outside domination even included our finest colleges and universities and made it very difficult to inquire freely into the way society really worked because such inquiry was inevitably embarrassing to the powers that be. Those powers then moved to discourage the inquiry and/or remove the inquirers. Nevertheless, from roughly the 1870s up to the First World War, the U.S. academy enjoyed a period of relative freedom caused by the fading dominance of clergy and the rising dominance of businessmen on the academy's governing bodies. Before the clergy could be completely pushed out by the businessmen, the struggle between them left a kind of power vacuum. During the interregnum, higher education in the United States was left more or less free to pursue its own goals. At roughly the same time, a flood of returning European-educated, American academics filled U.S. universities and colleges with idealistic young men, largely of nonbusiness and nonreligious orientation. Temporarily freed from the sectarian constraints of the clergy and not yet under the free enterprise thumb of the businessmen, professors and their students pursued enlightenment, not salvation or the dollar. The higher learning was autonomous, a microcosm of pluralism. Even such an iconoclast as Veblen could survive there, though not for long. Soon the businessmen solidified their power over the "higher learning in America," and the Russian Revolution sent a shudder through them from which they have never recovered. Educational autonomy was brought to an end. Veblen, along with many other bright academics, spent their remaining days outside the academy.[6] In the social sciences, little has changed since then, particularly in economics. To this day, critical and creative minds find little room to exercise their abilities in the academy. For criticism and creativity still lead to a break with timid colleagues and conflict with school authorities. Only if the break or the conflict occurs after the dissident has gained tenure, or its equivalent, can she survive in the academy. So great care is usually exercised to weed out the critical and creative mind before tenure is granted. And in some educational institutions, the practice of tenuring the educational staff is not followed. Such is often the case in public schools below the college level and outside the large cities. Teachers there are subject to dismissal for any number of reasons, or for no reason at all. Low pay certainly contributes to the lack of creative and critical minds in the American academy, but far more important, particularly in the social sciences, is the fact that critical, creative thought is inherently antagonistic toward the status quo. In the United States, a teacher who criticizes the status quo can still draw heavy fire from administrators and parents.[7] Under these circumstances, self-censorship becomes standard operating procedure for all those teachers who want to avoid difficulties.

This lack of autonomy in U.S. educational institutions and the resulting lack of truly creative minds in them is due to two structural shortcomings in the U.S. educational system, which make American educators and academics peculiarly subject to pressures from outside the educational system itself. Even if they were better paid, educators and academics would still be limited by outside pressure in their critical and creative work.

The first peculiar structural shortcoming of education in the United States is found in the lower learning. The lower learning, meaning everything below the college level (no invidious distinction intended) is hindered by excessive fragmentation. The private schools and public schools are separate and distinct, but that is not the truly peculiar element. The truly peculiar structural element is in the public school system, where the schools are divided up into thousands of often tiny independent school districts. Each independent school district has its own school board, its own set of officials, and its own curriculum. The redundancy is obviously very inefficient, plaguing us with far too many school boards and school officials as well as with conflicting or overlapping curriculums. Unlike our major competitor, Japan, this redundancy and fragmentation is a basic characteristic of our educational system. In Japan, a considerable degree of centralization, standardization, and consolidation of the lower learning is a basic characteristic of the system. In the United States, what centralization, standardization, and consolidation that does occur is done at the state level. At the federal level, some funding and guidance are offered, but federal participation in education has declined significantly through the first half of the 1980s. Earlier federal participation had been directed at reducing racial and economic inequities, not at reducing fragmentation. Important as inequity and inefficiency are, the most important effect of fragmentation is the weakening of resistance to outside pressures. In the lower learning, professional educators are divided up into thousands of different administrative units. Each unit, because of its small size and lack of solidarity with other units, is quite dependent upon its own local school board. In a vital democracy, this tie to the grassroots would be invigorating. In a degenerate democracy, it is debilitating to the students and the teachers who pursue Enlightenment educational ideals, because their pursuit of those ideals puts them in conflict with the material interests of the locals who control the school board and use their control to protect their interests.[8] If given their heads, at least a few students invariably want to know why some people have plenty to eat while other people go hungry—and will not settle for rationalizations and stereotypes. Trouble is the inevitable result for the teacher who gives them their heads. For such teachers, working in fragmented little independent school districts run by dictatorial school boards beholden to the locals, the fragmentation leaves them with nowhere to go for support. Their union might help, if it can, and if they have a union. But a strong, centralized, national institution is needed to overcome the reactionary power of the "independent" school boards, particularly those outside the large cities. Several attempts have been made to construct a national institution to further Enlightenment ideals in the lower learning, and many courageous educators have sacrificed a great deal for the enlightenment of their students, but precious little headway has been made. Fragmentation has contributed to a divide-and-conquer result in the American lower learning, one which is not found to the same degree in most other educational systems. (15,821 school districts existed in 1984.)[9]

The second peculiar structural shortcoming in U.S. education is in the higher learning. The peculiarity of the higher learning here involves the governing boards of colleges and universities. The European model, from which the U.S. system borrowed heavily, is based on governing boards composed of academics. But the U.S. version has governing boards of nonacademics, a crucial variation. Up to the 1870s, college governing boards (the United States had no universities until then) were dominated by clergy. Then businessmen replaced them, even on the governing boards of newly created universities. The academics themselves have never controlled a major college or university in the United States, in striking contrast with colleges and universities in most other countries. This peculiarity has given a district tone to the higher learning in the United States. Although the physical plants of most U.S. institutions of higher learning are very impressive, and though the noncontroversial sciences are very well funded, the dependent faculties are often underpaid and far less impressive than the buildings. This peculiarity has made the higher learning in the United States more a thing of expensive brick and mortar than of free mind and spirit. In the nineteenth century, the governing boards of clergy worked much sectarian mischief in the higher learning. Nevertheless, their academic rule was far less distorting of Enlightenment ideals than the contemporary rule of corporate businessmen. Even C. Wright Mills, who was never fond of what he called "men with their collars on backwards," was more or less approving of their academic rule:

The most fundamental question to ask of any educational system is what kind of a product do its administrators expect to turn out? And for what kind of society? In the nineteenth century, the answer was "the good citizen" in a "democratic republic." In the middle of the twentieth century, it is "the successful man" in a "society of specialists with secure jobs."[10]

Abject Dependence

The structural deformities of U.S. educational institutions—fragmentation of the lower learning and nonacademic governance of the higher learning—make them far less able to resist outside pressures than their counterparts elsewhere. And those pressures now are tightly focused on the career. From would-be students and their parents, the schools are pressured to specialize in preparing students for successful careers, primarily in the corporate world. The corporate world itself also puts pressure on the schools to prepare students for successful careers. In the lower learning, the federal government has pressured school districts to end racial segregation so that black and brown children can compete more directly with white children in the career race. Integration is desirable in and of itself, but what are people being integrated into? Is it integration into a life fit for kind, free human beings, or is it integration into a rat race? These are the kinds of questions students and teachers should be asking about careerism. However, precious few of them are doing so.

Troubling questions are seldom asked in U.S. schools because of the abject dependence of schools on outside support. If the public schools do not deliver the kind of career preparation demanded by parents, those who can afford it put their children in private schools that do deliver. Those parents who cannot, or who prefer public to private schools, put pressure on their public schools to supply what is demanded. This parental pressure is reinforced by corporate pressure, particularly in school districts where businesses have been encouraged to "adopt a school," as is done in the Chicago public schools. So to prepare their little charges for their future careers, schools test them endlessly for skills and direct them into all kinds of tracking schemes where each track is designed to match the skills of the child with some appropriate path of career development. Except in a few Montessori schools, which allow children to learn through exploring and doing, the free development and curiosity of the child do not really determine the educational path of the child. Instead, the career demands of parents, the testing of schools, and the needs of employers determine the child's path through the school system.

Rube Goldberg Lives

Imagine, if you will, a huge jerry-built network of pipes, funnels, and filters that resembles an immense Rube Goldberg device. Millions of students are stuffed into the bottom of the device by their anxious parents, and the device begins sorting them through a set of funnels that connect upward with pipes that lead up to other funnels connected to other pipes leading to more funnels. The entrance to the device is at the bottom, where a tiny funnel siphons off a small number of students before they have to mix with the others. Their parents seem particularly pleased with themselves, as the tiny funnel separates their children from all the rest. Upon closer inspection, these parents can be seen stuffing envelopes marked "tuition" and "donation" into two slots in the huge mechanism. The slots are marked "student fees" and "endowment," respectively. Some of the parents whose children seem too fat to squeeze through the tiny funnel can be seen placing envelopes as fat as their children in the slot marked "endowment," whereupon their children slide right through. The fix is in, from the very start. But then, surprisingly enough, some of these fat "endowment" children seem to pull a few very thin children through the tiny funnel with them. (The whole mechanism seems to work on the suction principle.) These thinner children are "scholarship" children. Their parents have nothing to put in the slots, but the device is fooled into letting a few of them squeeze up into the preferred funnel by the tremendous suction created by the "endowment" children as they pass through. The reason parents try so hard to stuff their children into the tiny funnel, in spite of the fact that many of the children are too fat to get through without being greased with donations to the endowment, is easy to discern. The tiny funnel is connected to a pipe that leads up to several other funnels that lead to pipes that lead to funnels marked "Yale," and "Harvard." These last two funnels lead, in turn, up to the "prime careers." The tiny funnel, you see, is the entry to the subsystem of the larger system that leads into the desired prep schools, and they, in turn, lead up to the Ivy League. Upward from the Ivy League leads the very tiniest funnel of all. It appears to be of solid gold and leads to the highest levels of management in the most powerful corporations.

But only a very few children get through the first tiny funnel that leads into the prep school. The vast majority can only fit into three other funnels at the bottom of the Rube Goldberg device. The smallest of these three is marked "Christian Academy." The next, in terms of size, is marked "Catholic." The largest of the three, much larger than all the rest combined, is marked "public." All of the children passing through the "Christian Academy" are white and their parents look quite concerned, not about anything in particular, just concerned in general. Most of the children passing through the Catholic funnel are also white, but large numbers of brown ones and a significant number of black ones pass through the Catholic funnel along with the white children. Through the largest funnel pass many black and brown children, along with white children and even children with handicaps. The parents of these public school children seem to be of all persuasions, except for very rich. Many of the children passing through this largest funnel could not get through the others, particularly the tiny one leading to prep school and the one marked "Christian Academy." This is the case even though Christ, after whom the Christian funnel is named, was reported to have loved all children. But then hypocrisy seems to permeate the whole device.

While the prep school funnel leads upward, the Christian academy funnel leads sideways, away from the rest of the system into a southern zone of numerous little funnels where only white children are allowed. The prep school and Christian academy subsystems share a definite insular quality—they are both more or less closed off from the public subsystem and they are both predominantly white. The Christian academy serves the children of a marginalized slice of native-born Americana. This sector is marginalized in that it lives largely in the old South where the segregated, rural way of life is being squeezed harder and harder by urbanization, integration, and migration. The prep school, on the other hand, serves mainline, old money, which is sure of itself and of its honored place in American society. The young Christians who are able to find their way through their subsystem of pipes and funnels, guarding all the while against contamination by something called secular humanism, emerge from their end of the Rube Goldberg device to settle down as plant managers and low-level managerials at runaway plants owned and controlled by the emerging preppies.

The prep school, Christian academy, and Catholic school are all called private schools, meaning that they are financed by private sources. Tuition pays the bills for the Christian academies. The endowment helps pay for the prep school. And the low pay of women (called "sisters" to make them feel better about being exploited?) or the house take from gambling (bingo) helps meet the Catholic school's expenses. The private schools claim superiority over the public schools and maintain a degree of insularity of subject matter and homogeneity of student body, which significantly narrow the educational and social range of their students. The Christian academics (this category includes both the marginalized southerners and traditional Catholics) insulate themselves from secular humanism, however each concerned group defines it, and from whatever else they consider undesirable. The traditional Catholic school student was a white, urban ethnic. However, over the past two decades the traditional Catholic students have been moving to the suburbs and many brown and even black students have been pushing into the vacancies left in urban Catholic schools. This has considerably reduced the racial homogeneity of the urban Catholic school. Legally speaking, it is still a private school. Nevertheless, it has become more like the public school than the other private schools. Although still pugnaciously sectarian in perspective, even the majority of teachers in most Catholic schools are now laypersons rather than sisters. This has improved instruction and reduced insularity in Catholic schools, but it has also greatly pushed up costs. Deprived of a steady flow of easily exploitable sisters, Catholics now have to pay decent salaries for teachers. The resulting financial strain has made Catholic educators very keen on educational vouchers, so keen that they are willing to ignore sectarian differences and form alliances with the Christian academies in order to push for this form of state-funding. The prep schools, because they are endowed, are not as keen on vouchers as the others, but they are bent on attracting the right kind of scholarship students. Life among the preppies can become overpoweringly stuffy and boring, so a few lively and appreciative scholarship students are recruited to brighten things up in the ivy halls. These scholarship students provide the diversity in the insulated and homogeneous world of the preppy.

From the largest funnel, the one marked "public school," the youthful initiates are marched through a pipe into grade school, where they are taught not to wet their pants in class, not to talk in class, not to speak without raising their hands, and not to be impertinent. They also learn how to walk through the pipes in single file, how to add, subtract, multiply, and divide— unless the school is afflicted with computers, in which case they skip the math and try to learn how to read instead. But above all else, they learn how to compete—for grades, for teacher's approval, and for status among their little peers. That is, the successful ones learn how to compete. The others learn how to fail—how to get Fs, how to get disapproval, and how to lose status among their peers. Preppies do not learn these latter skills in their schools, but at least a good portion of the Christians and the Catholics do. From the bottom of the Rube Goldberg, career-priming machine, the public school funnel leads up through the grade school to the middle school and then the high school. Added on to the system as an afterthought is the junior college, which is stuck on to the pipe leading from the high school. The junior college serves as a consolation prize for those who did okay in high school but are not continuing on to the next funnels, marked "large state university."

These large state universities are usually located in out-of-the-way places like Champaign-Urbana, Illinois; Bloomington, Indiana; and Austin, Texas. If nothing else, their location does keep the older youth who attend them out of the big cities where they might get into serious trouble. In spite of their geographic isolation and definite hayseed flavor, they are integral parts of the Rube Goldberg, career-priming machine. While polishing off large quantities of beer and recreational drugs, it is here where the students themselves are polished off. That is, they are given their final career preparation at the state university. From here, the young upwardly mobile professionals enter the legal profession, the medical profession, or the middle levels of the corporate world. Then they quickly flee from the rural setting to take their rightful places in the career world of the big cities as true yuppies. However, they find that the preppies have slipped in ahead of them on the career ladder—the fix was in all along. The state universities were never intended as pipelines to the highest level of the corporate world. The Ivy League has been supplying that career level from the very beginning. The need for middle-level managers is very great though, and the state university supplies the large body count needed there.

Some of the students never leave the Rube Goldberg contraption, because they mistake it for a real educational system. Most of them stay in it in order to become a part of the thing, to make it work. Some of them stay in it because they are sadists. Regardless of their motives, the stay-ins become professors in the colleges and universities only if they can stand remaining students for four to six more years after finishing college. It takes that much longer to get the Ph.D. degree, and the Ph.D. is required of professors. Or if they simply finish college, they can become elementary or secondary school teachers. Those teachers who cannot teach become administrators—they tell the others how to teach. The professors who cannot do research do likewise—they become deans and tell others how to do research. The teachers who can teach and want to do so struggle throughout their working lives to bring a touch of enlightenment to their students, in spite of all the obstacles put in their way. Many even succeed as educators, even though they are pressured from all directions to stop rattling the pipes of the Rube Goldberg, career-priming machine. Be grateful if some of them taught you. It probably cost them dearly, for they were not supposed to be teachers. They were supposed to be machine tenders, career boosters, and patriotism primers. One even rode a space shuttle to glory.

Lest my Rube Goldberg analogy stretch your credulity, an authoritative statement from Robert M. Hutchins is in order. Hutchins served as dean of the Yale Law School and as president, then chancellor, of the University of Chicago. Hutchins states:

This is the position of the higher learning in America. The universities are dependent upon the people. The people love money and think that education is a way of getting it. They think too that democracy means that every child should be permitted to acquire the educational insignia that will be helpful in making money. They do not believe in the cultivation of the intellect for its own sake.[11]

The Fate of the Teacher

In the lower learning, the teacher in any of the social sciences who really tries to help students with their questions about class, race, poverty, wealth, power, or war skates out on very thin ice.[12] Young people inevitably raise such questions at some point in their lives, and teachers who pursue those questions courageously with their young charges inevitably raise issues that enlighten, enrage, and radicalize some of their students. If the wrong thing happens to the wrong student, that teacher is finished in that school district. It has happened innumerable times. The little tragedy plays itself out something like this: A student asks why he saw striking workers picketing a local factory. The teacher, noticeably upset because she is from a working-class family and knows full well why, and because the student is from a well-to-do local family and knows why too, evades the questioning provocateur. But soon the other students are curious as well. So she gives it to them—she tells her young charges what it is like to claw your way up from the working-class poverty she knew. She tells them about the strikes her father was caught up in. Several of the students inevitably go home and tell their parents. If they are the wrong parents, an angry call is made to friends on the local school board. Her contract will not be renewed next year. She can fight her unfair dismissal, but in most school districts it would be an uphill battle, and the battle itself would forever brand her as a trouble maker.[13] The fate of free-thinking teachers is not as bleak in inner-city public schools, which serve the black and brown lower class, as it is in suburban and rural schools. This is because in the inner-city school, teachers are usually organized. Their union contracts provide considerable protection against arbitrary dismissals. Also, though the working conditions may be harsh and the duty hazardous, in the inner-city school the students and parents relate to the teachers differently. The teachers are often looked up to by their impoverished charges. In the affluent school, however, the teacher is viewed as a quasi-servant by her students and their parents because the teacher is usually from a lower socioeconomic class than them. So, the affluent, higher-status students and parents feel less hesitant about putting troublesome teachers in their place than the poor, lower-status students and parents do.

Professors in colleges and universities generally have considerably more freedom of speech inside and outside the classroom than do teachers in the lower learning. However, free thinking and enlightenment are almost as rare in the higher learning as in the lower. The processes of repression differ, but the results are about the same. In the lower learning, the process of repression is blunt and direct. In the higher learning, it is sophisticated and indirect. The fact that would-be professors must remain students for four to six years longer than would-be teachers is of profound significance. So too is the fact that professors eventually are either granted tenure or fired, while the practice of granting tenure or firing is less widespread in the lower learning.

After four years of college, the would-be professor must go on to graduate school to earn a Ph.D. degree. It is a requirement—new faculty simply are not hired without it. The degree takes from four to six years of additional work, two or three years of classroom study and then two or three years of work on a dissertation. Depending on the graduate school attended, tuition and fees alone will cost from $10,000 to $80,000. In addition, the would-be professor must be able to afford the four to six years of very low income and tolerate the extended period of subservience as a student. These conditions generally discourage most of the adult population, since most cannot go very long without a full income and since most self-respecting adults find it difficult to remain in the subordinate student role much past their teens. Those who try for the Ph.D. but then drop out along the way are usually granted consolation prizes in the form of a master's degree. However, many persevere, at least through the two or three years of class-room study known as course work. During the graduate student's course work, significant differences begin to emerge between the successful students in the social sciences and the successful students in other disciplines. The critical, inquisitive minds approaching the social sciences ask questions about class, race, poverty, war, and social justice. Inevitably, Marx is read, as are other radical thinkers. But these are highly unorthodox questions and highly inappropriate readings. If they are not dropped, the course work suffers: disagreements with instructors surface, "scenes" occur, and grades fall. So critical, inquisitive minds drop out of the social sciences at a much faster rate than in the other disciplines. The questions raised by critical minds in the other disciplines do not cut as close to the bone as social questions do.

So in the social sciences in particular, the course work weeds out large numbers of free thinkers, giving an increasingly conformist hue to the social science graduate students who stay in the system past the consolation-prize stage. After completing their course work, these students must pass a set of comprehensive examinations over the body of orthodox theory in their discipline that they studied in the classroom—no matter that they already passed thorough examinations in those classes in the first place. They are examined again anyway, just to make doubly sure. If they pass their "comps," they go on to the dissertation stage of acquiring the Ph.D. If they fail, the consolation prizes are their reward. By the dissertation stage, the winnowing-out process has significantly reduced both the number of continuing students and the diversity of their group.

Writing the dissertation and defending it comprise the last stage of their formal education. To complete this stage, the graduate student must write a piece of original research, something that contributes to the fund of academic knowledge in her discipline. Doing that is not so hard, particularly in the social sciences, because so little is really understood by academics about the social world anyway. What is hard though, at least potentially, is defending the research to the dissertation committee. The dissertation committee is usually composed of from four to six established professors, most of whom come from the Ph.D. candidate's own discipline and have strong vested interests in defending the orthodoxies of that discipline. Real trouble is encountered in the defense if the research comes to unorthodox (radical) results or uses unorthodox methods. Usually, each member of the dissertation committee must accept the dissertation or the candidate does not get the degree. This trial by committee generally weeds out any remaining unorthodoxy or free thinking among the graduate students. The survivors then get their degrees.

Much to their surprise, their ordeal is not over. Now they must get an academic department somewhere to hire them. And, once hired, they must endure a seven-year apprenticeship as assistant professors before either being granted tenure or being fired. The seven-year period is not really an apprenticeship, as assistant professors are free to teach classes and do research on their own. Nevertheless, during the seven years they must prove to their colleagues, their dean, vice president, president, and board of trustees that they are fit to be granted tenure. At the end of the period, if a candidate has not been weeded out earlier with a "terminal contract," a committee of her older departmental colleagues decides whether she should be recommended to the dean for tenure. This is her second trial by committee. To win the committee's approval, she must have published a sufficient quantity and quality of research in refereed journals and have demonstrated sufficient teaching ability to warrant the approval of this august assembly. Once again, the unorthodox and the free thinking are weeded out by established professors with vested interests in defending the existing orthodoxy in their discipline. If the departmental committee looks with favor on the candidate for tenure, they pass their blessing on to the dean. The dean can and often does go against their recommendation for tenure, however. Then the candidate must fight for it and end up being fired in most cases anyway. If the dean bestows her blessing, the decision goes to the vice president for academic affairs for his blessing, then on to the president and finally to the board of trustees. At any of these higher levels, the candidate's tenure can still be denied, which means that the candidate is fired. If granted tenure, the candidate is usually promoted to associate and then to full professor. They possess academic freedom, to a remarkable degree, after that.

But after enduring all that, precious few of them actually exercise their academic freedom. They have no reason to do so. After all, they are as orthodox as they can be—otherwise, they would not have survived the weeding-out process. Nevertheless, a few of them go through personal experiences, after they have been tenured, that radicalize or vitalize them. People do change. Also, a few free thinkers and radicals do slip through the long and arduous years of weeding out. So a saving remnant does exist. Its impact is significant but contradictory.

On one hand, free thinkers and radicals do help students enlighten themselves. Unorthodox social theory and social history can be learned at some American colleges and universities. The ability to engage in critical inquiry can be acquired at such institutions. I have been fortunate to be a teacher at some of those remarkable places. Unfortunately, the saving remnant is usually too scattered across hundreds of geographically isolated campuses to have a major impact on any single college or university. This scattering of radicals and free thinkers, this diaspora of the American mind and conscience, does not still their voices. Here and there a student or two is awakened to the existence of social injustice, of class inequality, and of the insanity of war. The scattered remnants can come together once or twice a year at professional meetings, ostensibly to present papers to each other, but more importantly, to give each other the support and encouragement needed to carry on.

On the other hand, the scattered remnant of inquiring intellect and critical conscience have another, contradictory impact on the higher learning. Members of the scattered remnant serve to legitimize the institutions that tolerate them. Most colleges and universities of any status seek to maintain a reputation for academic freedom, lest their stodginess become too well known. So within these colleges and universities, at least some of the departments need a token free thinker or radical, but only one. Often left with little choice in the matter, the free thinker or radical serves the purpose of preserving the institution's reputation for academic freedom. She is in the same kind of position as the token black employee, hired by a corporate employer to prove that the corporation does not practice racial discrimination. To have more than a minimal, isolated impact, the free thinker must transcend the token role she is being forced to play by bringing into the department more free thinkers. Though quite difficult to achieve, sometimes three or four of the remnant can gain a foothold in the same department. When they do, things begin to happen. Students wake up and begin to read and to argue. Class meetings become lively arenas of free inquiry. People get excited. They take a stand. Clubs are formed and statements are made. Rebuttals are formulated. Enduring friendships and disagreements are formed. Life begins to flow through the once stodgy halls. Voices are raised; but so too are eyebrows.

A classic, oft-repeated cycle is set in motion. The cycle has run its course in a good number of social science departments—economics and political science departments are the most prone. It runs like this: the mini-renaissance gathers momentum as a few more free-thinking, radical types join the faculty and as similar students are attracted as well. Angela Davis, W.E.B. DuBois, Betty Friedan, Charlotte Perkins Gilman, Karl Marx, and Thorstein Veblen are names that come up more frequently in the discussions both in the classrooms and the halls. Orthodox feelings are hurt as a result, and orthodox reputations are threatened. Letters are sent to deans. More eyebrows are raised. Then one of the new, free-thinking faculty comes up for tenure and the battle lines are quickly drawn. The free thinker, being a survivor, has learned how to play the game very well, otherwise, she would have never gotten this far. So she has taken great care to publish articles widely. She is an excellent teacher with high student evaluations—students really do appreciate honesty and free inquiry. She has also known that she must serve on faculty committees to demonstrate her service to the university. In short, she has covered all the bases very well. After a struggle, involving much hard work, envy, and spite, she is tenured. But the struggle brought attention to the department. Now the administration knows what is going on. The struggle was also costly to her supporters. They had to spend whatever political capital they had accumulated to back her. They called in all their credits with faculty and administration for use in the defense. And now they are depleted. Her detractors, however, have been strengthened by the struggle. Now they are united in moral outrage, and now the administration owes them one. Furthermore, in the inevitable petitioning and demonstrating on her behalf, a few students went beyond the bounds of polite academic discourse. Youth naturally tend to do that sort of thing. Nevertheless, the trustees are incensed and the alarmed administration is forewarned. The peak of the cycle has been reached. It is all downhill from there. No more radical free thinkers will be tenured. No matter how well they cover all their bases, and no matter that their department recommends them with flying colors for tenure, they will not get through the administration. If the dean comes down with a sudden case of academic principle and okays her, the vice president will nail her, or the president, or the trustees. Appeals are made, the American Association of University Professors is called in. Legal action is taken. But regardless of its outcome, which is often favorable, morale in the department is broken. Resignations are submitted. Students drift away. People begin playing it safe once again. The nadir of the cycle has been reached. And the department may stay there a very long time. The remnant is dispersed again and again, life leaves the place to its former denizens—the machine tenders and the budding careerists.

Repression of free thinkers and radicals in the higher learning seldom requires the direct intervention of corporate businesspeople who make up the majority of the trustees on the boards of trustees. Radical tenure cases seldom reach the board level since radicals are weeded out long before. If not weeded out in the prolonged period of graduate study, they are dispersed across the country to labor alone, with little support from those around them. If temporarily gathered together in one department—an infrequent but exciting experience—they are soon dispersed again by pressure from their peers or from their administration. Only as a last resort do the trustees have to step in to straighten things out. With repression more direct in the lower learning, the educational system as a whole is more or less free from critical thinking and enlightenment. So it has come to resemble the Rube Goldberg career-priming machine described above, a far cry from the Enlightenment ideal espoused by John Dewey.

Nevertheless, the career-priming machine can be mistaken for an educational system. Many people make that mistake and act upon it. They are the heroes and heroines that many of us have been fortunate enough to encounter along our way through the machine. Rather than encouraging us to work for the external rewards of grades, rather than punishing us when we do not, they try to teach us. They know that teaching is a marvelous, even magical thing. They know that you cannot teach anyone anything of value. Instead, you can only help them to learn it for themselves. They know that learning cannot be forced upon someone else, but that minds can be warped and stunted by trying to do so. They know that learning is an internal thing—a kind of miracle that transforms us from the inside out, and they help us to let it happen. They do not force us to make it happen. But they are few and far between. Others force us, cajole us, warp us. They install strings deep inside us. They put buttons on our guts. And now, people above us can pull those strings. They can make us dance to their tune. They can push our buttons, buttons that churn up our bile and make us look at our friends with envy. With their help, we can become careerists, primed for the climb up the ladder and lusting for success. It must be noted, in all fairness, that most teachers do not really get personal pleasure out of what they do to us, and to our children. Most teachers are simply doing what they are told to do by the school boards, trustees, parents, and future employers.

LITTLE CAREERISTS: THE FATE OF MIDDLE-CLASS YOUTH

An Aside

Radical theoreticians and commentators investigate the working class and the poverty stricken. That is all well and good, but a whole realm of social experience lies largely uninvestigated by the free thinkers. Only a few have turned their attention to the middle class. The upper class and the power elite have been investigated quite well. Not so with the middle class.[14] Hence, the heavy emphasis here on middle-class experience. The middle class has been ignored at great cost by radical theoreticians. As a result, critics are blindsided. They seldom foresee the great waves of repression and regression that have emerged out of middle-class experience. The United States is in the midst of such an upswell, and it is going largely unanalyzed. So bear with me a while longer as I trace out the career of the middle-class youngster as he emerges from our Rube Goldberg career-priming machine.

Speeding Up the Kids

Our kids are being sped up, and not just by drugs. They have to work harder and longer just to keep up with other kids. They enter the rat race sooner, and they run faster than we did. To get a good job requires more degress than we needed. What used to take a high school degree now takes a college degree. What once took a college degree now requires an M.B.A. All these degrees do not really get them ahead; the extra degrees just keep them up with the competition—which is the essence of the speedup. You have to work harder and longer just to stay where you are. The speedup, which began with the working class and was cheerfully administered by the managerials of the middle class then spread to the managerials themselves. Now it is spreading even farther and penetrating deeper into the social fabric. It is infecting the children of the managerials. But the infection has taken some time to spread. It was interrupted in the 1960s by an outbreak of free thinking among the youth, primarily those attending colleges and universities during the height of the public revulsion against the war in Southeast Asia. This period of public revulsion also coincided with a brief period of war-induced full employment, which temporarily freed the youth of the country from the disciplining effect of a slack labor market. The war wound down in the early 1970s. So too did the public revulsion, as well as the number of new jobs for young people. The unemployment rate moved steadily upward, and a slack labor market reemerged. The youth revolt in education died out, to be replaced by careerism. Careerism, in the 1980s, is the form taken by the speedup of middle-class youth—they are pushed harder, and at an earlier age, to secure for themselves a lucrative career. For them, the speedup has taken an educational form.

As capitalism began to spread in the West two centuries ago, workers found the length of the workday getting longer and longer. Now as the speedup is spreading into middle-class youth, they find the period of schooling getting longer and longer. Schooling starts at an earlier age and lasts until an older age. At the starting end, this stretching out is indicated by the rise in enrollment in preprimary school by children who were formerly free of all school. In 1970, 37.5 percent of all children in the age bracket 3 to 5 years were enrolled in preprimary schools. By 1986, 55 percent of all such children were enrolled. Little of the rise in enrollment was due to the rise in female employment, as is often presumed. In 1986, among children whose mothers were not in the labor force, 50.0 percent were enrolled in preprimary schools. For children with mothers in the labor force, 58.9 percent were enrolled. Surprisingly little difference, then, is found between the enrollment of children with mothers in the labor force and of those with mothers out of the labor force. Their mothers' relation to the work force is not the determining factor. The determining factor is the ambition parents have for their child's future career. It is very significant that children with the highest rate of enrollment in preprimary school are the children of college-educated women; nearly three-fourths of these children are enrolled.[15] In the most prestigious preprimary schools, those with the best track record of getting their little graduates into the best prep schools, the parental competition to get their little careerists accepted has become extreme. The Trinity or Dalton schools are generally considered the best preprimary schools in New York, and in those schools about 900 applicants compete for every single opening.[16]

Not only is the educational competition starting at an earlier age, but it is continuing until a later age. Children barely have time to be children. They work longer at school than ever before. Although the speedup has been most pronounced at the early stage, as indicated by the dramatic rise in preprimary school enrollment rates, it is also showing up at the later stage. In 1970, 14.9 percent of all young adults in the age bracket 22 to 24 years were still in school. By 1986, the enrollment rate for the same age bracket had increased to 17.9 percent.[17] The M.B.A. degree is becoming almost a requirement for those competing for the higher levels of corporate management. Only a limited number of positions of real power exist at the higher levels, and a rising number of college-educated corporate careerists are competing for them. In 1970, only 10.7 percent of the population possessed a college degree. By 1986, 19.4 percent possessed them.[18] As a result, the educational ante needed to play the game has been upped to include an M.B.A., and preferably not just any M.B.A., but one from an Ivy League school. After all, in the late 1980s some 60,000 M.B.A.s are being passed out annually.

The speedup of our youth cannot be directly measured other than with enrollment figures. It certainly does not show up on educational achievement tests. Over the past several years, SAT and ACT scores have slowly declined and now are stabilizing. What the slight declines mean exactly is anybody's guess, but they do not reflect higher educational achievement. Indirect indicators of the educational speedup are available, however. One indication of increased pressure on young people is the rise in their suicide rates. Looking just at suicide among white males, the rate rose from 94 per million in 1970 to 173 per million in 1985 for youths 15 to 19 years old.[19] The speedup of our youth is taking its toll. Their speedup has two sources: emulative and economic.

Parents of middle-class youth want the best for the children, as do parents of all youth in all times and of all classes. But the best means different things to different classes and in different times. In this time and for this class—the middle class—the best in education means the Ivy League, the gateway or pipeline to the higher levels of corporate management and control. So the standards to emulate are set by the Ivy League, most prominently by the Harvard Business School. Those aspiring youth unable to get into Harvard or one of its sister Ivy Leaguers try to get into schools that are as close to being like Harvard as they can. This is because Harvard graduates are greatly overrepresented at the highest corporate levels. About one in ten of the Fortune 500 are headed by a Harvard graduate.[20]

Peter Cohen, himself a Harvard man, muses about the Harvard M.B.A.:

> What is this fellow but an oversized gadget, the sad result of an educational process that mistakes efficiency for the end toward which it should have been a means. A piece of equipment produced on that assembly line leading from Sunday school to high school, from high school to college, from college to graduate school, from graduate school to the corporation.[21]

By emulating the Harvard Business School to the best of their abilities—limited by the extent of their endowment, of course—colleges and universities try to turn out a highly valued product for a competitive market rather than a thoroughly educated human for a pluralistic society. The demand for their product must be continually puffed up with corporate recruiters, while the supply of their product must not be allowed to expand to the point of ruining the market. To maintain demand, the school carefully structures its curriculum to meet the needs of corporate recruiters (not the needs of educated humans). To limit supply, tuition rates and standards are kept as high as the prospective student body can stand. To maintain demand and limit supply at the same time, schools that truly are competitors with Harvard also force their students to compete savagely for grades and class rank. The tremendous stress placed on student competition, even at Harvard, which could afford to cut the students a little slack, "alienates its

Table 2
The Rising Economic Pressure from the 1960s to the 1980s

Years	Average Unemployment Rate	Average Poverty Rate	Median Family Income
1965–69	3.7	14.2	26
1970–74	5.3	11.9	29
1975–79	6.9	11.8	29
1980–84	8.2	14.3	27
1985–87	6.7	13.8*	28*

*For 1985–86 only.

Note: Unemployment and poverty rates are in percent. Median family income is in thousands of 1986 dollars.

Source: Council of Economic Advisers, *Economic Report of the President, 1988* (Washington, D.C.: Government Printing Office, 1988).

students from one another, driving them to the destructive selfishness, the 'rugged individualism' that, for too long, has been mistaken for a mainspring of progress."[22] The effects on supply and demand are quite salubrious, but the effects on human beings are not. "You learn in school not to give a shit if the people you climb over are weak or sick or small or blind."[23] At least that is what Peter Cohen claims to have learned getting his M.B.A. from Harvard, the business school most emulated by all the others.

The speedup of students has an economic source as well as an emulative source. The economic source of the speedup is obvious—hard times. The unemployment rate is up, the poverty rate is up, and family income is down. The economic pressure to get more educational credentials, to work harder, and to try to earn more has been mounting, unevenly, since the boom years of the 1960s. Table 2 gives the grim details in half-decade averages for unemployment, poverty, and family income. Since the 1960s, the unemployment rate over the business cycle has risen, making it more difficult for young people to get their first jobs in the 1980s. Jobs are available in the service sector, at the minimum wage, and in the white suburbs. But to get jobs with a future, the rising unemployment rate has forced most middle-class youth to get more educational credentials before they enter the labor market. If one youth gets more credentials before entering the labor market, her individual chances of getting a good job improve. But if all youth get more credentials before entering the labor market, none of their chances improve. Instead, the number or quality of credentials needed to get a start in a particular job just goes up. Old labor radicals understand this "fallacy of composition" as the essence of the speedup. That is, when one worker increased his output, he might get a bonus. But when all workers increased their output, the required output would go up for everyone. Everyone would have to work harder, and usually for the same old pay.

For today's middle-class students competing for a limited number of good jobs, the rising unemployment rate and rising level of educational attainment have forced them to get more credentials just to have the same chance at a good job. Among today's generation, everyone has to work harder (get more credentials) for the same old jobs. The race has sped up, so the push to get credentials has intensified. The recent rise in the poverty rate has served as an object lesson in what happens to those who fall behind. They fall into poverty. And the flat behavior of median family income shows that even though we are getting more educated and more women are working outside the home, as far as the typical family is concerned, real income has risen very little in two decades. We have been working harder and smarter but, as a whole, getting nowhere—another object lesson to those who ease up in their own efforts. We must continue working harder and smarter just to keep from falling behind.

Perhaps, in addition to emulative and economic pressures, a third source of educational speedup has emerged in recent years. Unlike the first two sources, both centered in mainstream, middle-class life, this emerging third source is from those who are being pushed to the margins of American life. During the youth revolt of the 1960s and 1970s, a backlash against permissiveness in the schools began gathering force. Although it was neither dormant nor numerically superior at the time, Vice President Spiro Agnew called it the silent majority. The backlash has since re-organized as the Moral Majority and the Eagle Forum and is led by the likes of Jerry Falwell and Phyllis Schlafly. The parents in these groups are genuinely concerned about the education and welfare of their children. Yet such groups oppose open discussion of human sexuality, human evolution, nationalism, nuclear war, and social criticism, and they strongly support more classroom discipline and classroom prayer. The latter will not help children deal with sex, war, and moral decay unless combined with open discussion of these problems.

All this strife and striving in the American school does not appear to signify that the schools have actually increased social mobility in America. For some decades now, social mobility in America has been real, but of a very modest degree. Peter Blau and Otis Dudley Duncan, in a classic study of social mobility in the middle of the twentieth century, found only a moderate amount of upward occupational mobility among American men (women were not studied). The upward movement that did take place was only a short distance. Furthermore, such upward movement was primarily due to three factors that are unrelated to any fundamental improvement in the existing structure of opportunity in America: (1) the number of white-collar jobs have been growing faster than the number of blue-collar ones; (2) upper classes have lower birthrates than lower classes and are failing to fill all the upper-class slots with upper-class children; and (3) immigration from farms and other parts of the world into the bottom of the American job hierarchy has pushed the urban, native-born up the ladder.[24] Increasing education has had little impact on the relatively fixed structure of opportunity. More white-collar jobs are opening up, but they generally are not in high-status, high-pay occupations. The Blau and Duncan study, though a classic, is somewhat outdated. But more recent studies by Christopher Jencks and his associates reconfirm the minimal effect of increasing education on the structure of opportunity in America. According to Jencks and associates, even radical school reform would have little impact on economic and social inequality.[25] Although the fix as to who gets what is clearly there, it goes much deeper than just the educational system.

LITTLE BUSINESSMEN AND LITTLE BUSINESSWOMEN

Their Introduction to the Corporate Culture

Once they emerge from the Rube Goldberg career-priming machine, with their M.B.A.s in hand, the little businessmen and little businesswomen are usually placed in the middle levels of the managerial world, unless they come from Harvard, in which case they are placed somewhat higher, or unless their family controls the corporation, in which case they often are placed somewhat lower, but only temporarily and only to avoid the winks and smirks of those in the know. With their first corporate job after the M.B.A., the career competition proper begins in earnest. Through the formal corporate culture, elaborate steps are increasingly taken to keep the new hopefuls from finding out the true nature of the competition. The founder of the corporation is depicted as a man or woman from humble beginnings, who rose to unheard of heights of success through his or her hard work and ingenuity. (The more typical fate of men or women who really do rise rapidly from humble beginnings—such as John DeLorean of General Motors or Steve Jobs of Apple Computer—is that they are muscled out of power.) The new hopefuls, if still unsophisticated, attempt to model themselves after the mythical founder. They hope that their own hard work, long training, and intelligence will win them rapid promotion on the basis of their own merit. As long as they believe it, they contribute a great deal to the corporate purpose. But they do not rise a great distance up the corporate ladder. For, you see, the fix is still in.

The corporate career game is not one of "contest mobility." Rather, it is a competitive game of what the sociologists like to call "sponsored mobility." As they gain in sophistication, the little businessmen and businesswomen learn to call the game they play "networking" and "mentoring." They learn that what really counts is who they know, not what they do. Some of the corporate hopefuls learned this lesson long ago in prep school. In particular, if their parents, usually the father, made large contributions to the endowment of their prep school and served on the school's board of trustees, they learned quite early about having connections and friends in the right places. The corporate hopefuls from less-enriching backgrounds usually have to learn this lesson the hard way.

Businessmen, male corporate hopefuls, have been networking for years. They just never called it that. The word entered the business vocabulary with the sophistication of the women's lib movement. Pioneering businesswomen, female corporate hopefuls, quickly learned that competence and hard work were just not enough. Connections were needed. Men had them; women wanted them. The women called the men's system of connections "the old boy system." When the women began constructing their own systems, they called them "networks." The less pejorative name has stuck. Now even the men use it to describe what they had been doing all along—namely, building a network of trustworthy associates in potentially useful places, or at least a network of associates in positions of influence who are willing to trade favors. Once constructed, the network can then be drawn upon for influence like a bank account can be drawn upon for money. Networks, like bank accounts, can be depleted if not constantly replenished. A bank account is replenished by depositing more money. A network is replenished by doing more favors for the associates in it or by adding new associates when the old ones have outlived their usefulness. Networks are based on reciprocity—you scratch my back and I scratch yours—not on friendship. Of course, enemies make very poor network associates, but a network is not a community of friends. It is a bank account composed of influential associates who owe the depositor. Neophytes at networking often err. They either keep on depositing and never withdraw, or they overdraft. Network deposits and withdrawals are not made in money, however. They are made in personal favors that further the corporate careers of the participants against the nonparticipants. When an influential position opens up in the corporate hierarchy, the hopefuls draw on their networks to put in the fix in their favor. The successful bidder will owe a favor of roughly equal value to those responsible for her success. Until she can pay off, her network associates stand in the same relation to her as the investment bankers stand to a successful venture capitalist—they own a piece of her. This is the point at which neophytes can go wrong by mistaking network associates for friends. Friendship, which is actually quite rare in our corporate culture, does not require strict reciprocity to be main-

4

The Family

Family life, is life in and of itself.

—Ferdinand Tönnies

EVOLUTION OF THE TWO-CAREER FAMILY

Introduction: Hollowing Out

The family has not died out in America. Men and women continue to cohabitate and they still have children and try to raise them as best they can. It's true that about a third of American children will go through divorce. But what divorce does today, death did a few decades ago. Today, many children say good-bye to one of their parents at the courthouse. Yesterday, they said good-bye at the gravesite. The family is undergoing profound changes. It is hollowing out, rather than dying out. A hollowed-out institution or individual is one that has lost its meaning. The hollowed-out institution still operates, but it no longer is an independent source of meaning and motive to the people participating in it. A hollowed-out institution derives its meaning from outside its own realm. Like an ancient tree with dry rot, it often looks the same as any other old tree, but it is empty on the inside—rotted out. In spite of hollowing out, the American family will continue, but its meaning will not. "Family" used to mean a largely self-sufficient procreating group. But families are no longer self-sufficient, and a significant number no longer procreate. The production of goods and services has been almost completely removed from the home to the factory, office, school, hospital, restaurant, or other outside establishment. The traditionally low birthrate of upper-class families has spread to the middle class, and the childless marriage is no longer an oddity. So the family no longer has the same degree of self-sufficiency as it did in an earlier, more pluralist age. Nor does it automatically procreate. Furthermore, the family used to mean caring for and teaching others. But both the teaching and caring functions have been moved out of the family as well. The school, hospital, nursing home, and welfare office perform most of those functions now. The family now means much less to most of us than it once did. Other values, from other spheres of life, have gained significance.

Puritanical Beginnings and Revolutionary Changes

Although the American family has been shaped by many traditions and socioeconomic forces, its origins are in seventeenth- and eighteenth-century Puritan New England. The Puritans had fled what they considered to be a decadent and immoral society in England. They came to the New World to establish a New Jerusalem. Each Puritan family was headed by the father, who was responsible for the proper behavior and moral upbringing of all family members. The father followed his patriarchal calling sternly, as if his soul depended upon it. There were very few unattached individuals in Puritan society, for both moral and economic reasons. Unattached individuals, particularly young men, were considered ripe ground for the devil's work. Moreover, unattached individuals found it almost impossible to survive in the wilderness, for the family was the basic production unit in the Puritan agricultural economy. Little society-wide division of labor was practiced. The Puritan family farm was largely self-sufficient, producing most of what it needed itself. Family members often included unmarried relatives and servants. The model Puritan family was the large, extended family, dominated by the father.

Women were extremely important to the survival of the Puritan family. The women grew much of the food and did all of the food preserving and preparing. They also made from scratch most of the family's clothes. They spun the thread, wove the cloth, made the patterns, cut out the cloth, and sewed it together. In spite of their disproportionately large contribution to the family's well-being in the wilderness, women were subjected to the authority of men. Because of the high mortality rate among women, men frequently remarried. John Winthrop, for example, married four times.[1]

In this sealed-off, patriarchal society, the famous witch trials were to be expected. Nevertheless, as more non-Puritan immigrants came to New England, and as the wilderness gradually opened up to the Europeans, the Puritan's grip was loosened. It became easier and easier for dissidents simply to leave the Puritan communities and move elsewhere. A far more contemporary-looking individualism began to emerge. The Puritan experiment left a lasting mark on American values, however. Among other values, an anxious fear of failure, a strong drive to work, and a stern, even callous, devotion to success in one's calling are still with us, albeit in the increasingly distorted form of corporate careerism. Furthermore, the Puritan disdain for waste, ostentation, and sham have played a major role in the shaping of the U.S. character, at least up to now. So too, unfortunately, has puritanical patriarchy. And the Puritan distrust of centralized, clerical power structures has had a profound effect on religious life. These values undoubtedly were maintained by the challenges and opportunities of the American frontier. For while the frontier did loosen the grip of the Puritan family and community on the individual, it also was a place where an ambitious individual could get ahead, with little need to resort to sham and ostentation. Two centuries of frontier expansion forged the ideal American into the man on the make and altered his family accordingly. The frontier, with its scattered form of land settlement and the constant lure of greener pastures farther west, narrowed down the extended Puritan family, as servants and young sons and daughters found it possible to strike out on their own. It also made the exercise of centralized authority of any kind very difficult. Communal self-help and self-reliance became almost essential in the expanding Jeffersonian democracy. The American Revolution had resulted in the expulsion and expropriation of the aristocratic loyalists, and although their elitism reemerged with the Federalists, the Jeffersonians and then the Jacksonians moderated the inevitable postrevolutionary reaction. By the Civil War, the extended family of the Puritans had evolved into a slimmed-down but still self-reliant model—the pioneer family, led by the man on the make and largely supported by the unrecognized and unpaid work of the man's wife.

With the defeat of the Southern planter aristocracy and the passing of the Homestead Act, the field was open to the pioneer family. The Plains Indians were killed or subdued, and Jim Crow put the former slaves back in their place. The white, patriarchal, pioneer family became the standard model. However, it soon began changing once again, this time under the twin influences of commercialization and industrialization. The commercialization of agriculture dramatically reduced the economic self-sufficiency of the family farm. It soon became totally dependent on the fluctuating market prices of the agricultural commodities in which it specialized. Not only did the self-sufficiency of the family farm begin declining, but the number of family farms soon began declining as well. By the 1920s, the United States was predominantly an urban, nonfarm society, and those families still on the farm—particularly the black sharecroppers of the Deep South—were hard pressed to survive there. The short-term condition of family farms has fluctuated widely with the market prices of what they produce, but the long-term prospects have steadily deteriorated. The farm family is now insignificant as a source of meaning and value in American life. (Less than 3 percent of Americans now live on the family farm.) It has been replaced by the urban family, which itself is tied to the economic position of its breadwinners.

The Industrial Revolution urbanized the American family and took the father out of the family's inner circle. The father became an outside earner of income instead of an internal producer of crops. His work took him outside of the family, into an urban setting of factories and offices. This is not to say that the Industrial Revolution eliminated the father's role in the home. In America, the role was reduced and changed, but not eliminated. In Europe, the effect of the Industrial Revolution on the family was more complex. Not only did the father's work move outside the family circle, but the opportunity to create a family circle in the first place was significantly enlarged. That opportunity had been enlarged in America, even before the Industrial Revolution, by the opportunities of the frontier. But in Europe, before the Industrial Revolution swept the remnants of feudalism away,

marriage was, in brief, a kind of privilege, a prerogative, a gift bestowed by the community. One had to wait until there was a house or a cottage available, or until permission was granted to build a house or cottage on the commons. A place had to be vacant.... The European marriage pattern, in effect if not in intent, imposed a means test for marriage.[2]

So in spite of all the exploitation that early factory work entailed, the opportunity of factory work did allow more men and women to strike out on their own and start families in the growing urban centers. Organized worker resistance to the lengthening of the workday eventually resulted in legal restrictions on hours and conditions. In industrializing Europe a kind of bargain eventually was reached, though not by any conscious design. It traded eight hours of the day for a subsistence wage and a chance to form a family outside of the old limitations of the feudal village economy.

But it was a harsh bargain, particularly in America, where the marriage option already had been opened up earlier by the frontier and where government regulation of working hours and conditions was very long in coming. (It finally arrived in 1938, the year of the Fair Labor Standards Act.) Most of the native-born refused the bargain offered by industrialization, if there was any way they could stay on the family farm. And they still refuse it. Hence, the massive waves then and now of immigrants seeking work in the United States and the chance to form their own families, even if those families involve absentee fathers and, increasingly, absentee mothers as well.[3] The immigrants, through great ingenuity and struggle, formed ethnic enclaves of factory families. The U.S. steel industry and many other industries owe their existence to those ethnic communities. The factory family that made up the ethnic communities was far more resilient than the melting pot theorists thought. In Polish communities, for example, the parish and the "society" provided lasting self-help institutions, and the union, usually after a long struggle for recognition, provided a degree of economic bargaining power for a while.[4] Furthermore, the ethnic women did more than their fair share to provide for the family's welfare. Many of them worked in the factories and then worked just as hard in their homes, where they prepared the food, made the clothes, tended the sick, and taught the ignorant while their husbands gathered for drinks and talk at the corner tavern.

Only with the contemporary trend toward deindustrialization have the ethnic communities and the factory families that composed them finally been seriously threatened. Yet even in the heyday of the ethnic community, this stronger variant of the American family was only a shadow of the Puritan-pioneer ideal. The factory family was far from self-reliant, yet it struggled to be self-supporting. The father struggled to be head of the family, even though he was absent most of the day. The mother tried to be nurturing, in spite of the fact that an ever larger part of the food preparation, education, and caring were done outside of her family circle. Even the ethnic family, in its little enclave, suffered from a hollowing out. The traditional family lost its meaning as it lost its function. With the children in school, with medical experts, social workers, and with even the courts usurping the family functions, the ethnic family did not die out, but it was transformed. Most important to the evolution of corporate hegemony, even the ethnic family began to lose its power to give independent value and meaning to life. Not that the meanings and values it gave were those of the Enlightenment, for they were not. More often than not, racism, sexism, and superstition were among the values imparted by the ethnic family in the ethnic neighborhood. The point is, however, that at one time the ethnic family was able to impart values and meanings that were independent of corporate values and meanings. But now it cannot. None of its weakening was due to coordinated action or social purpose. It was merely due to a convergence of trends and changes—the blind drift of history.

Family "Breakdown"

The Industrial Revolution, driven by the dynamic nature of capitalism, had a profound impact on the traditional extended family of Europe and eventually on the Puritan-pioneer family of the United States. On the one hand, the Industrial Revolution had an antifamily effect. It stripped the extended family of its extended membership. Spinster aunts, uncles, less-favored children, and domestic servants were able to strike out on their own in the burgeoning factory towns. On the other hand, the Industrial Revolution also had a pro-family effect. It gave the opportunity to form families to the previously excluded members of the extended family. The opportunity was not a golden one. Leaving the extended family to found a family of one's own in the factory towns involved long hours of wage labor, terrible working conditions, periodic unemployment, a slum environment, and a truncated family. Yet family life is life itself, and most of those presented with such an opportunity, slim though it was, did try to form their own families. But the Industrial Revolution and the continuous technological change that induced it, coupled with the capitalist drive for more profit and capital, led to a massive increase in the scale, scope, and complexity of enterprise. Corporate rather than individual enterprise became the rule, and with corporate enterprise came corporate bureaucracy and corporate career. Career is proving to be a far more corrosive factor in its effect on the American family than all the other changes combined.

To repeat, the family is not dying out, nor will it die out in the future. True, the divorce rate is about five times as high as it was at the turn of this century, and the rate of illegitimate births has increased. Furthermore, the rate of first marriages continues to decline (from 87.5 in 1960 to 64.9 in 1981, per thousand single women aged 14 and over). Nevertheless, while the divorce rate per thousand married women rose by 146 percent from 1960 to 1981, the remarriage rate per thousand divorced women rose by 144 percent over the same period. So the family, albeit in changing form, is just about holding its own, at least for the population as a whole. This is not the case for poor black people, however, where the effect of poverty on marriage and family formation has been catastrophic. For them, the 1980s have been a watershed period. During the 1980s, the proportion of black people who are married has fallen below half, presumably for the first time since slavery.[5]

With the tragic exception of poor black families, marriage and the family are surviving in the United States, but in changing forms. From the extended family of Puritan New England and feudal Europe, to the slimmed-down pioneer family and the ethnic factory family, the trend has been toward a smaller, nuclear family composed of mother, father, and one or two, occasionally three or four children. Furthermore, with the rising divorce and remarriage rates, the trend is also toward a sequential or modular nuclear family. The family is becoming sequential in that it involves a sequence of mothers and/or fathers, rather than just one. The family is becoming modular in that its different units can readily be removed and replaced. The father or the mother can be unplugged and a replacement mother or father plugged in, so to speak. The same with the children, though they generally are interchangeable parts only when changed with one of the spouses. (Modular children fall into three classifications: his, hers, and ours.)

Just like the Industrial Revolution allowed more people to found their own families by breaking away from the traditional extended family, the sexual revolution is allowing more people to found their own kinds of families by breaking away from the traditional heterosexual family. Some gay couples, on the leading edge of the sexual revolution, are establishing their own kind of family group and are successfully raising their own children. Furthermore, a few women, not necessarily gay, are banding together in creative new ways to raise their own children. The rising numbers and successes of the nontraditional families are one of the brightest spots on the cultural horizon. For these developments in nontraditional family life offer a potentially independent source of meaning and value, perhaps a source that eventually will challenge the dominant corporate way of life.

These changes do not mean the end of the family. Instead, they represent the adaptations of a resilient institution to changing conditions. The most important change is the increased value placed on career success. For most of us, that career success means success in a corporate career. It no longer means being a successful pioneer, factory worker, or independent entrepreneur. The effects of corporate careerism are still slight in the higher circles of the upper class, in family businesses, and in a few insulated areas of ethnic family life. In those three social spaces, quite traditional family life can still be found. But in middle-class circles the corporate career is changing the family in three major ways. (1) Pursuing a corporate career requires frequent geographical relocation, particularly in the early stages of a successful career when the careerist gets promotions to more important districts, branches, or subsidiaries located in distant cities. Then when the careerist gets his or her really big break by moving to the corporate office, geographical moves become less frequent. (2) The middle-class careerist, unprotected by the kind of maximum-hour legislation that protects the working class, gets overused by the corporation. The workday thus extends far beyond eight hours, and the workweek stretches into Saturday and Sunday, absenting the careerist from the family proper for longer and longer periods and forcing an attenuation of his or her family role. Before the 1970s, this affected primarily the father. (3) During the 1970s and into the 1980s, the speedup spread from overuse of the father to the children and the mother. Hard times and increasing pressure to keep up with the rising standard of middle-class living drew more and more mothers into the work force. The rising levels of unemployment and middle-class strain put greater pressure on middle-class children to become careerists themselves at earlier ages.

The effects of corporate careerism on lower-class and working-class families have been more indirect than those on the middle-class family. In the lowest circles, the rising standard of living of the corporate careerist has had a discouraging and alienating effect. The realities of permanent unemployment, dependence, and a chronic lack of income simply do not square with the high standards of life bombarding the poor through every medium of communication. They cannot live up to those standards, particularly the men, who are supposed to be able to make and spend big money. So, in the lowest circles, the family is disintegrating under the pressure. The disintegration is manifested by the flight of impoverished males from the family itself. In the working-class families who manage to stay above the poverty level, the pressure from the rising standard of living, set by corporate careerists, has forced most mothers into the work force to help make ends meet. A rising tension, foreboding the fate of the impoverished family, can be discerned between the spouses of working-class families as inadequate income and loss of male self-esteem begin to take their toll. The family really does break down when it becomes chronically impoverished. This is why marriage and family have disintegrated among poor black people—because they are chronically deprived and discouraged, not because they are black.

The traditional family, though increasingly in serial form, remains strongly entrenched in the higher circles of the upper class. These families are largely free from the economic pressures that burden families below them. This allows upper-class families to look down on the restructuring of the families below them with a self-righteous scorn and an exaggerated sense of effrontery.

The reason marriage and family have been strongly affected (not destroyed, not yet) by corporate careerism among the middle class is made clear in the following statement of a higher-level executive describing his corporation: "Successes here are guys that eat and sleep the company. If a man's first interest is his wife and family, more power to him—but we don't want him."[6] To a factory worker, a job is a job. If protected by a union or by legislation, the worker usually can go home when the eight-hour shift is over. Not so for the white-collar worker on the make who is protected by nothing at all. To the ambitious corporate trainee—that is, to the corporate eunuch desired by corporate recruiters—a job is an all-absorbing career. The kind of choice forced upon budding young corporadoes, the kind of absolute commitment demanded of them, used to be demanded only of soldiers or initiates in Catholic orders. The corporation demands their life, not just their time for eight hours of the workday. This is particularly true for women trying to move up into the highest corporate circles. More likely than not, they will have to give up children and family to rise to the very top. Overcoming sex discrimination will take their unrestricted commitment. It will take a blank check—written on their lives, not on their bank accounts.

Career Choices: Yours or Ours?

While the extent to which a factory worker's family is absorbed by his job is very limited, the extent to which a corporate careerist's family is absorbed into career is much greater. Thomas J. Watson of IBM described the corporate career relation as seen from the corporate side: "We always refer to our people as the 'I.B.M. Family' and we mean the wives and children as well as the men."[7] Until the 1970s, corporate careerists were almost all men. Their wives had to work for the corporation too, but without pay. They played the role of supportive homemaker. And the wives could see, from their perspective in the home, what effect their husband's career was having on the family and on the husband. It was consuming the man, and tying the family to the corporate career. While it was making the husband an absentee family member, it was drawing the family in to perform an unpaid supportive role and forcing the family to adopt the husband's corporate social circle as a kind of substitute community. At least some kind of community was needed, particularly by families undergoing frequent relocations. (Wags claim that IBM really stands for "I've Been Moved.") The fate of corporate careerist fathers is obvious:

Except as providers they are quite expendable, for it appears that what fatherless families mainly suffer from is low income or poverty, deprivation due to lack of income, not lack of his presence. Fathers who are good providers are nice to have around. They may even be fun and useful around the house. Conceivably they might occasionally play ball with you or read to you or take you to the circus.[8]

Until very recently, and with the exception of William H. Whyte, Jr., investigators of the corporate world assumed that normal men easily integrated their roles of husband-father and corporate executive. Of course, employed women, on the other hand, were assumed to have difficulty integrating their roles of wife-mother and outside worker. Eyes finally began to open, however, with the rise of women's lib. With women's lib, not only were the traditional assumptions about women reexamined, so too were those about men. While it remained clear that women did, in fact, have difficulty integrating their family and work roles, it also became clear that men had similar difficulties too, and had encountered them all along.[9] It is impossible to say whether it was the rise of women's lib as an ideology or the rise in women's participation in the work force that changed our understanding of family and career. But in the 1970s, profound changes took place both in family practice and in family theory. In the 1950s, theory and practice focused on the two-person career. In the 1980s, theory and practice focus on the two-career family. That is, in the 1950s, the successful managerial family involved one career—the man's—but two adults worked at that one career, the man and his supporting wife. She raised his kids. She took care of his aged parents when they were still around and arranged to bury them when they died. She kept things at home on an even keel for him. She mediated between his lack of understanding and the children's need for it. She made excuses for him and his absences, both of body and spirit. She was his hostess and goodwill ambassador. She supplied the community spirit and participation that he lacked and could not give. She kept his house and made the purchases necessary to maintain his good repute. She seduced him if he was too tired to get it up himself. Or, at least, she was supposed to do all these things, if he was to be a success in his career. When the career choice was made, the wife automatically sacrificed her career to his. So in the 1950s, theirs was a two-person career, but the career was his. In just two decades, all that has changed. She has a career too. Now, in the 1980s, they are a two-career family, or trying to be. And that makes for much harder career choices.

The Wife's Breakdown

The two-person pattern still survives at the very highest levels of corporate management, where the economic pressures are eased by bloated salaries, fringe benefits, and expense accounts. But the two-person career is rapidly dying out at the middle and lower levels, as women's lib—or necessity—put most middle-class women into the career competition along with their husbands. In the process, middle-class women have been freed from automatically playing second fiddle to their husband's career. They have been freed from being the subordinate, supportive housewife, and that is a gain. "In truth, being a housewife makes women sick."[10] Nevertheless, many 1950s-model supporting wives and second fiddles used to report that their marriages were very happy ones. Jessie Bernard explained why:

We do not clip wings or bind feet, but we do make girls sick. For to be happy in a relationship which imposes so many impediments on her, as traditional marriage does, a woman must be slightly ill mentally. Women accustomed to expressing themselves freely could not be happy in such a relationship; it would be too confining and too punitive. We therefore "deform" the minds of girls, as traditional Chinese used to deform their feet, in order to shape them for happiness in marriage.[11]

The very same could be said about the 1950s-model middle-class man being "deformed" in order to make him happy in his conflicting roles of corporate careerist and family man. In fact, it *was* said, by William H. Whyte, Jr., in his famous article for *Fortune*, "The Corporation and the Wife." He argued, "it would almost appear that she and the corporation are ganging up on the husband."[12] The model wife of the 1950s wanted success just as badly as the husband, and the way for her to get it was to push him to achieve it. Apparently, many men obliged. But now, in the 1980s, because the middle-class strain has become so intense, she is going out to help get it herself. Some call this women's liberation. In one sense, it is. Women are being liberated from the social pressure to perform one single role—that of supporting wife. Yet in another sense, it is not women's liberation at all. Instead, it is the speeding up of wives. Now they too must work for the corporation in order to keep their family's joint income rising as fast as the emulation-determined standard of living for middle-class families on the make. Middle-class wives have been liberated from the social pressure to perform one single role, only to find themselves performing two roles. Unless she is married to an unusually sensitive and supportive man, or unless she is not married at all, she now must be the supportive wife and mother while also being a careerist in her own right.

The two-career, middle-class family is a logical outcome of the continued struggle over the speedup. The working class responded to being sped up by organizing their resistance. Union-negotiated and/or state-enforced maximum-hour constraints were imposed to protect workers from exploitation. Restrictions were placed on child and woman labor to protect them from exploitation as well. These working-class protections were long-delayed in America. Nevertheless, they were largely in place by the end of the Great Depression, and the protections withstood the reactionary era following the Second World War. Traditionally middle-class occupations, however, were largely unprotected. This lack of protection became extremely significant when the period of postwar expansion fizzled out in the 1970s. With the working class protected, and with their kinds of jobs rapidly disappearing anyway, the squeeze had nowhere else to go but onto the unprotected and burgeoning middle class. Middle-class men, primarily in managerial jobs, were already working far beyond the eight-hour day and the five-day week. So as the standard of living for middle-class families rose higher than the income of middle-class men could support, their wives were sucked into the work force to help them keep up. Now it takes twice as much work from the middle-class family (two careerists when one used to suffice) to earn enough to make its middle-class ends meet. This is not to say that the real earnings of managers have been declining, for they have not. However, the required income of a middle-class family has risen much faster than the real income earned by just one middle-class worker. The required income is that amount of income a family needs to keep up with the competition, and the competition is composed of other middle-class families, all trying to improve their status at the expense of their neighbors. Their competition for status through consumption has driven the required level of consumption to ever-higher levels. The net result, not planned by anyone, has been the speedup of the middle-class wife. There are no villains in this speedup, for no one planned it. However, the lack of villains does not make the speedup any less real or binding. Nor does it ease the plight of those being squeezed.

It does, however, reduce the wife-mother role in middle-class families. To the extent that wives follow their husbands into corporate careerism, they too are absented from the family for the larger part of the day. Since they are simply *not there* much of the time, they cannot fulfill all of the old role demands. A few supermoms are the exceptions that prove the rule. Furthermore, to make the new two-career family a going concern, substantial adaptations are being made. Some corporate employers have opened up well-staffed and well-equipped day care centers to ease the burden on career wives. Career women and working women are pushing hard for decent day care and preschool institutions for their children. Some career husbands have eagerly pitched in to help their career wives with child care and housework. Most of the adaptations have been made by the career and working wives themselves, and by their children.[13] Television, the new babysitter, has helped. So too have fast-food restaurants, microwave ovens, no-wax floors, and prepared foods. The kids can learn to help out, even if their dad resists. Furthermore, the obsession with cleanliness of the 1950s model housewife can be dispensed with, unless it is necessary to impress and entertain one of the bosses at home. (There are two bosses to impress now—his and hers.) The resiliency and adaptability of career wives and their children is quite remarkable. But they are only human, and not even the so-called quality time spent with the family can completely compensate for the sheer magnitude of time spent on the career.

In spite of their resiliency and adaptability, an unavoidable narrowing down and hollowing out of the mother-wife role is taking place among two-career families. The same had occurred earlier in the father-husband role when the middle-class men were drawn into their corporate careers. The irony of the situation cannot be ignored. The middle-class women are still following the lead of their men, even in these liberated times. The speedup has lengthened the workday and workweek for managerial workers, forcing them, whether male or female, to narrow down their noncareer functions. With only so much time to spare, some things that fathers would like to do, as fathers, simply cannot be done. And now the wife can no longer cover for him. She has a career of her own and is discovering the limits of the twenty-four-hour day and the seven-day week. Some things that mothers would like to do, as mothers, can no longer be done. And so the meaning and value, essential to human life, that she used to draw from her wife-mother role are drawn increasingly from her career, just like her husband before her. As the career role gains in motive and meaning, mother and wife roles lose. That is, the mother-wife role is hollowed out. Both husband and wife now derive more meaning and motive from their careers than from their families. For them, the value of family life has been hollowed out. So it is now easy for them to relate to the family as interchangeable parts. Husbands and wives can easily be unplugged from one family and plugged into another one. The children are a bit of a problem, but they are resilient and adaptable too. Besides, careerism is seeping down to lower and lower age levels, and the children of the two-career middle-class family are finding meaning and value in their career preparations in the career-priming machine called school. They too are becoming less dependent upon their families for meaning and value. So far as they are concerned, the family is being hollowed out as well. That is, it means much less than it used to mean, and it is valued much less than it used to be. This hollowing out has occurred to a much lower degree in the working-class family, and very little in the upper-class one. Among the impoverished, however, the family has virtually disintegrated, particularly for the urban poor. Latino families, even impoverished ones, may represent partial exceptions to the main drift.

This congeries of social trends, institutional adaptations, and economic pressures has put us in a most curious position. The main drift has hollowed out the family. For centuries now, egalitarians have criticized the family as a bastion of reactionary values and constricting socialization processes. Many have called for its abolition. We should be cheering. For although the family has not been abolished, it has been hollowed out. It no longer confines and deforms women to the same extent that it used to do. Within its tender embrace, they are no longer forced to perform only a single role. They have broken free from it, only to be caught up in another kind of intimate embrace. The children have broken free from it as well. Now they spend most of their time at school, or at something that resembles a school. Why then are we not celebrating? The reason should be obvious: the family's place—to a large extent—has been absorbed by the corporate career, so that it no longer is an independent source of meaning and value. We no longer learn racism, sexism, and superstition while sitting on our mother's knee. Now we learn careerism, a more rational but still more dangerous variety of character deformation.

Moral Majority to the Rescue

The degeneration of the impoverished family is well known, but with a few exceptions, the hollowing out of the middle-class family has gone largely unexamined by social critics and egalitarians.[14] However, others have noticed the declining value and meaning of the middle-class family, particularly of the wife-mother role within it, and they have reacted savagely. Since no real villain is responsible for the decline, the reaction against it has had to focus on scapegoats or side-issues. The reaction has organized to form the Moral Majority, which rose to prominence under the leadership of the Reverend Jerry Falwell. At first it seemed that supporters of the Moral Majority were mostly poorly educated, highly religious, Protestant, white, female southerners. Subsequent research, however, has shown support to be more diffuse and middle-class. Most supporters of the Moral Majority and reactors against the declining significance of the mother-wife-family trinity are highly religious and female, but they are not as southern and poor as was originally thought.[15] What seems to bind the group's supporters is not so much their regional location or education, but their attitude toward the wife-mother role within the family. In short, they are responding to a perceived threat to the value and meaning they place on their own role as wife-mother. The reactors and Moral Majority supporters are vehemently opposed to abortion, for example. Although opposition to abortion also has moral-religious origins, the anti-abortionists perceive abortion to be more of a lifestyle-status threat than a moral-religious threat. Abortion, though not perceived as such by many of those who are vehemently opposed to it, is actually a side issue in the transformation of the American family. Resistance to abortion is really a symbolic reaction, a defensive reaction, to the hollowing out of the American family and of the women's role within it. As such, it completely misses the mark.

The Moral Majority's supporters also vehemently oppose women's lib. But women's lib is more a scapegoat than the real cause of the transformation of the mother-wife-family trinity. Even if the Moral Majority could succeed in completely repressing women's lib as a movement, the hollowing out of the American family and the women's role within it would continue unabated because the growing influence of career would continue unabated. Furthermore, the Moral Majority and other reactors are strongly opposed to what they call secular humanism in the schools. So they push for more parental control over the curriculum in public schools, as well as for prayer in public schools. Or they push for public financing, through vouchers and tax credits, of the private schools their children attend. They also react strongly against sex education, busing, and Darwin's theory of evolution. Of course, they are reacting to their own loss of status, their loss of influence over their children, and to the rising influence of the school (that is, the rising influence of the career-priming machine we call the school). Perhaps they should react to the narrowing of their own parental and familial realm of influence, but banning liberal textbooks, banning Darwin, banning black children, banning sex education, imposing prayer, and purging teachers with religious convictions different from their own will do little to infuse more meaning into the family and the parent-child relation. Nor will public funding of private schools rectify things. Nor will further institutionalizing paranoid attitudes toward homosexuals improve matters. Those are not the things that have hollowed out the family and the parent-child relation in the first place.

In spite of their confusion, their scapegoating, and their diversion onto side issues, the Moral Majority and their like are really onto something. The family and the parents, as independent sources of meaning and value, have declined dramatically. But the decline has come about for reasons other than those addressed by the Moral Majority. Social critics and egalitarians should join them in their cry to save the family, for their cry signifies real anguish. But the family should be saved from what really threatens it, not from the scapegoats and side issues of the Moral Majority. It should be saved not so that it can propogate physical abuse, intolerance, sexism, racism, and superstition, but so that it can better serve an independent, nurturing role within a truly enlightened and egalitarian pluralism.[16] Saving the family along these lines would not involve any of the side issues and scapegoats of the Moral Majority. Instead, it would have to begin with a fundamental transformation of the corporate world and the careers we pursue within it.

Furthermore, saving the family does not mean saving the traditional structure of the family. The family function is essential. The particular structure of the family is not. That is, human beings must be reproduced and nurtured, but any number of different kinds of social structures can do those jobs. The family can be a kibbutz. Healthy, happy children can be raised in the kibbutz. The family can be matriarchal. Women can raise children without being dominated by men. The traditional, patriarchal family can be replaced with a different structure that performs the same function. The function could even be performed better.

The Effects of Class

Class can dampen or magnify the effects of corporate career on the family. The upper-class family is largely unaffected by corporate career. The upper-class family does not have to make it; it already has it made. The lower-class family, living below the poverty level, also is largely unaffected by corporate career. The lower-class family has no chance to make it, so the family does not have to try. The working-class family is somewhat protected by traditions of solidarity, by union contract, and by the forty-hour workweek. But the middle-class family is strongly affected by corporate career. The middle-class family tries hard to make it, and corporate career is the way to do so. Farm families, though they too may be middle-class, are not affected by corporate career to the same extent as urban middle-class families, unless they are pushed off the farm.

The upper-class family's wealth serves as a strong focal point for its members. Being controlled by the older members of the family, the wealth serves to maintain the grandparents' power to subjugate the grandchildren, lest they be disinherited. Furthermore, the wealth also insulates the middle generation from the corrosive pressures of corporate career by either allowing them not to work at all, or giving them a head start over their non-wealthy competitors. Their head start usually does not involve something as direct as a top job at a family-controlled corporation. Although that does occur, for sons the head start usually takes the form of an Ivy League degree and powerful family connections. The head start for daughters is still almost exclusively in the form of a good marriage, but it sometimes takes the form of a career head start. The head start provided to the second generation of upper-class families ties it into the family very effectively. The third generation in an upper-class family—that is, the grandchildren—are tied into the family in two different ways. First, they are subjugated to the inheritance. Second, they are raised up by the inheritance, so to speak, because they are the major instruments of their benefactors' dreams for continuing the family name and the family power.[17] So all three generations of an upper-class family—grandparents, parents, and grandchildren—are tied together by wealth into an ongoing family, albeit they are tied together in different ways.

The working-class family is not tied together by wealth, but as long as the principal breadwinner does not suffer a period of sustained unemployment, which drives the family into poverty and disintegration, it remains tied together as an ongoing family far more so than the middle-class family. Many working-class occupations are covered by maximum-hour legislation, and sometimes also by union contract. These are major accomplishments that serve to protect the husband–father role from being truncated by excessive work. It also, to a lesser degree, protects the wife–mother role, because working-class wives and mothers generally receive even less help from their husbands than middle-class ones do. The protection of the working-class family should not be overdrawn, however. Its workers are not protected at all in a second job, and only limited protection against mandatory overtime is provided through some union contracts. The middle-class family, though, is totally unprotected. Both husband–father and wife–mother are "free" to devote as much time and effort as they wish to their career. This means that they are unprotected from its corrosive impact on their family roles, and that their family roles are being hollowed out.

Although pressure to succeed in a career is exerted on the children of some working-class families, the pressure is more widespread among the children of middle-class families. So working-class children, when compared to middle-class ones, are relatively free from the educational manifestation of the speedup. Their "freedom" is reinforced, in a negative way, in schools serving predominantly working-class children. Children are not prepared for successful careers in such schools. Instead, they are prepared to be the traditional hewers of wood and drawers of water. In schools serving middle-class students, far more emphasis is placed on career success—the need to work hard and get ahead. More is demanded of the students, and the children frequently attend preprimary schools at an early age to give them a head start on the long career ladder. Those that finally emerge with M.B.A. in hand have learned to compete successfully and put their careers first. After all, that is what their middle-class career parents wanted them to learn, or was it? (According to Russell E. Palmer, dean of the Wharton School, about 50,000 M.B.A. degrees were handed out every year in the mid–1980s by some 650 business schools.)

Career is the central focus of the middle-class family on the make. And career is a centrifugal force to the family, not a centripetal one. That is, career pulls the family apart rather than pushes it together. The young, the children, are strongly affected by the centrifugal force of career. Particularly in two-career families, the children are an incredible drain on resources that could be devoted to career advancement. As infants, they require constant care. So one of the family's careerists, usually the mother, must redirect time away from her career to change them when wet, clean them when dirty, feed them when hungry, and nurse them when sick. It is easy to see why housebreaking them and getting them their shots are the first order of business. Once domesticated and weaned, both of which are done as quickly as possible, they can be placed in the proper preprimary school. From then on, the career begins to pull them farther away from the family. After all, there is little of meaning or of value to hold them there in the first place. The final break comes soon after graduation from college, but numerous little breaks began almost in infancy. For even in infancy, children of career families are more like dependents than family members. As infants, their dependence draws upon too much parental time, time more lucratively spent on career matters. As preschoolers, their private school tuition or nursery school bill is a drain on the family's ability to finance a vacation home and a Mercedes, neither of which is purchased for its use value to the family but for its display value to the career. The cost of educating (career priming) the children rises continuously until they finally get the M.B.A. The money is spent to get the children good jobs, not to enlighten them—to make them self-supporting, so their drain on the family budget can be stopped, and so they can be placed in positions that reflect favorably on the parent's good standing. Almost from the beginning, their relations to their parents are the monetary relations of a dependent rather than the personal relations of a family member. Cash is the real nexus. In the 1980s this cash connection seems to have stretched out past college. Middle-class parents, particularly upper-middle-class ones, are having a harder time weaning their children from the parental purse. At one time, for middle-class youth, the cash connection ended after college. The children then become completely self-supporting. But the later models of budding careerists hang on to the parental purse much longer than the earlier models, drawing on it for such extras as Rolex watches, BMWs, and Caribbean cruises. However, once the cash is gone for good, so are they.

The real puzzle is why careerists have children in the first place. All indications are that careerists do understand where babies come from. The U.S. birthrate did fall through the 1960s and most of the 1970s, with a slight uptick in the late 1970s and early 1980s. In 1982, the birthrate per 1,000 women aged 18 to 44 who were not in the work force was nearly three times the birthrate for those in the work force (125 versus 45). So women who work do seem to have far fewer births than those who do not. Furthermore, the birthrate per 1,000 women seems to fall, the higher the woman's family income. In 1982, women with family incomes under $5,000 had a birthrate of 99 while women with family incomes of $25,000 or more had a rate of only 56. The birthrate also falls with rising education, except for very highly educated women. So, careerists do have children, but they appear to have far fewer than other women.[18] Furthermore, after careful investigation, Jessie Bernard stated, "The general conclusion warranted from the research is that childless marriages tend to be happier than those with children, and that small families tend to be happier than large ones."[19] With the time pressures of career and the conspicuous-consumption pressures to maintain reputable appearances, there are just not enough family resources left over to be a happy family.

If such pressures could be measured, they would be found to rise exponentially with the number of careers pulling at the family. That is, the two-career family would be found to be under more than twice the pressure of the one-career family. And you can easily guess which members of the family will bear the additional pressures (probably not the husband). In the one-career family, the 1950s model, the husband was the careerist, but his career was a two-person career. His wife was the second person. She played second fiddle, but her efforts on his behalf were very real nonetheless. In the two-career family, the wife competes against many men who are backed up by their wives. Furthermore, while competing against all those two-person careermen, she is also pressured at home, as a wife, to back up her man in his own career. If she has children, she is pressured as a mother to nurture the children. And as a wife, she is pressured to cover for the aloofness of her career husband toward the children, even though she has her own trouble staying emotionally involved with them. If she does not have children, many of the internal pressures on her are reduced. Emotionally, she does not have to cover for her husband's aloofness nor struggle against her own. Physically, her cleaning, cooking, laundering, and other chores are reduced considerably. She will not have to drive kids around nor stay home with them when they are sick. But with relief from these internal pressures comes increased external pressures, sometimes subtle and sometimes not. As she gets older, the farther she gets from prime child-bearing age, the more her friends and parents ask her about her childless state. If she has had an abortion, she starts having second thoughts or, at worst, profound guilt. Perhaps her career success, if it comes, compensates her, or perhaps not. If she has remained single to pursue her career, these kinds of pressures are multiplied several fold. Furthermore, not so subtle remarks about dikes and frigid women can cut her to the bone.

On his part, unless he is a completely insensitive clod, the husband of a careerist takes pride in his wife's success but also feels some degree of inadequacy for not being successful enough himself to keep her at home. Furthermore, at the very highest level of corporate power and status, the two-career family is still rare. C.E.O.s of Fortune 500 corporations generally have 1950s model wives who play second fiddle for them. This invidious example does not go unnoticed among the lower ranks of aspiring young male C.E.O.s, leaving them with nagging feelings of insecurity and insufficiency. When big promotions come, if they do, direct conflict is the result. Their nagging feelings about this and that quickly become minor in comparison, because unless the careerist has already acquired a position at the corporate office, promotion usually involves a move to another city, and moving would disrupt the wife's career. His promotion at XYZ would take him to the branch office in Minneapolis, but her position is at the ABC St. Louis office. Something must give: her career, his, or the marriage. Usually her career gives, but increasing numbers of career couples find a middle ground in the commuter marriage. He moves to Minneapolis, she stays in St. Louis, and they meet when they can in Chicago for a quickie at the O'Hare Hilton. This is marriage in its most stripped-down, hollowed-out form. But taking careerism to its logical conclusion, this is the future for the two-career "family." Weeks of constant work, interrupted with a conjugal visit—sounds more like a prison sentence than a marriage. Nonetheless, humans and their families are remarkably resilient. Even under incredible pressure, many families pull together in times of hardship to support ill children, parents, or grandparents. After all, home is still the place where they have to take you back.

CONCLUSION AND FURTHER REFLECTION

The Assumption of Separate Spheres

With a few exceptions, the connections between work and family life have not been carefully explored.[20] In large part, this neglect is due to an implicit assumption: work life and family life are two separate spheres that do not really overlap. In this separate-spheres assumption, the worker— usually understood to be the man of the house—leaves his family life behind him while on the job. When he returns home at five o'clock, he leaves his work at the factory or office to pick up his family life where it left off in the morning. This compartmentalized life, assumed as the norm, may apply to some workers from the ethnic, factory family. But it does not apply to middle-class careerists. For them, the family compartment has been invaded by the work compartment. Careerists carry their work home with them. What little time they spend at home in the first place is contaminated by their career. This invasion of the family compartment, still generally assumed not to occur, is what I have called hollowing out. Literally speaking, it has resulted in the hollowing out of the so-called family compartment of modern American life, emptying it of meaning and value and filling the corporate career with what the family has lost. Ask a middle-class corporate manager who they are and they respond with descriptions of the work they do and the career goals they hold. They will tell you that they are the district marketing manager for 3M. They probably will not tell you, in a casual conversation at least, that they are the father of Johnny and the husband of Marsha. That is, they will describe themselves in terms of their careers rather than in terms of their families. This is only slightly less true of female corporadoes than of male ones. The females will also describe their husbands' career prospects and hopes; maybe she will go so far as to describe her aspirations for her children's careers as well. In sum, we derive meaning and value for our lives from our corporate careers, not from our families. We are corporadoes, not family members.

Hollowed Spheres

Our families have been hollowed out by a common thread running through American culture, and by a series of historical accidents or convergences. The hollowing out is not by conscious design, nor by class conspiracy. In fact, class conflict has played only a modifying role—class conflict has protected the working class to some extent, and thereby has focused the pressure on the unprotected middle class.

The common thread running through American culture and contributing to the hollowing out of the American family reaches from the Puritan family of seventeenth-century New England all the way to the two-career family of twentieth-century corporate America. That thread is a certain coldness or aloofness toward others, even loved ones. It is the callousness of the "called." Puritans had to harden their hearts against the temptations of this world and resist even gentle feelings toward kith and kin. The Puritan god was a jealous god. He must be served, *his* will be done. The Puritan god gave the Puritans a calling. To pursue that calling, to assuage their fear of being among the damned, to be true to their god, they could not give themselves completely to others, not even to their wives and children, lest they give offense to their jealous god.[21] This callousness of the called was also due to the fear of failing in the calling, a fear not at all unlike the fear of the contemporary careerist. The Puritan and the careerist are tied together by a common thread. For the Puritan, it was his calling; for the careerist, his career.

In addition to this common thread, five convergences or accidents of history have reinforced the hollowing out of the American family. First was the long period of open opportunity on the moving frontier combined with the raw egalitarian heritage of the American Revolution and the anti-loyalist kind of populism it sustained. These molded the American into the man on the make, the man perpetually on the move who was more than willing to sacrifice other values and other meanings to his quest. Second was the final closing of the frontier, which was followed by the opening up of career jobs in growing corporate organizations. The man on the make moved off the farm and out of the frontier into the city and onto the corporate career ladder. His slimmed-down family moved with him. Third, as a result of the Great Depression, came at least a modicum of protection for the working-class family in the form of union contracts and maximum-hour legislation. But this left the middle-class family unprotected. Here is where the callousness of the called and the man on the make heritage were strongest in the first place. The postwar boom that followed the Second World War provided a temporary respite from the coming speedup, but the hard economic times came soon enough. Fourth, in the 1970s and 1980s, the squeeze was focused principally on those least protected from it. The middle class was sped up. (The poor were defunded.) Fifth came the rise of the rational management of conglomerates, with its profit center speedup à la Harold Geneen–style management. As the hard times of the 1970s sucked the middle-class wife into the corporate career, the middle-class family ceased altogether being an independent source of value and meaning. The corporation and the corporate career have filled the vacuum. Corporate career values and meanings now dominate. Family values and meanings are subordinate. This unplanned cultural development is of profound significance to the evolution of corporate totalitarianism in America. A major source of institutional resistance to corporate domination is being lost.

In the next chapter we turn to the other institutions that could offer continued resistance. We will find that although institutions other than the family could resist the corporation, by and large they do not. They too are hollowing out. This is leaving their social space clear for expanding corporate influence. Education is being hollowed out. Education now means career preparation, more than it means enlightenment. Education is now valued in cash, in how much more a college graduate earns than a high school graduate, and an M.B.A. than a B.A. Similar fates are befalling the church, the community, and the state. They too are losing their former meaning and value. That is, they too are being hollowed out.

5

The Hollowing Out of Noncorporate Institutions

Yea, much bitter dying must there be in your life, ye creators!
—Friedrich Nietzsche

HOLLOWING OUT

The Decline of Personal Bonds

The first personal bonds are forged in the family and then, later, in the school. But those bonds are becoming decreasingly significant in our personal lives. Family and school bonds contribute less and less to human solidarity and to the common meanings and values that are our cultural heritage. The family and the school are being hollowed out, drained of independent meaning and value. The school means a place where the career is started; and the more it is valued as such, the less it can be anything else. Not only does the school stop being a potential source of enlightenment, but it also stops being a place to make friends. Lacking family support, students can get so very lonely and depressed that they become suicidal. Unfortunately for them, the family is coming to mean little more than a place where you go after school or work to do homework or to eat and sleep.

For some, school and family are not yet that empty. These people make dear friends in school and keep them, as well as have rewarding ties to their families and old friends. Nevertheless, the main drift is clearly in a different direction, particularly for middle-class careerists. For them, for the corporadoes, the network of career allies has replaced the old gang of school friends. The favorite teacher or priest, the older confidant we could always count on, has been replaced with a career mentor. For the corporadoes, personal bonds have been turned to account.

Geographic mobility has played a very large role in the transformation of personal bonds. The more frequently a corporate careerist is transferred to a new community, the harder it is for her to maintain meaningful contact with her old friends and mentors outside of her corporate sphere of life. Striking up new friendships and finding new confidants, outside of the corporate sphere, also become harder, even pointless, since another transfer promises to nip any new friendship or confidence in the bud. As contacts with her noncorporate friends become less frequent, the personal bonds become more tenuous. Her personal relations decline while her instrumental relations increase in significance. Finally, the corporado finds herself with no friends and no confidants, only with a network and a mentor. An extraordinary contrast exists between the geographically mobile corporate careerist, who has ambitiously taken advantage of any transfer that came along, so long as it advanced the career climb, and the geographically rooted blue-collar worker, who has clung tenaciously to neighborhood roots even when it meant unemployment. On the surface, a kind of trade-off has been chosen: one has obtained lucrative employment at the expense of personal bonds, while the other has maintained personal bonds at the expense of lucrative employment. But at a deeper level, the path each followed has determined not only the lifestyle, but also the subsequent values, meanings, and beliefs of each.

Old Ends Become New Means

In addition to the family and school, common meanings and values are also forged through participation in the union, church, community, state, and mass media. But these institutions all pale in comparison to the corporation, for they all are being hollowed out. They contribute less and less to individual human character because they are losing their independent meaning and value. Each of these institutions is becoming a means rather than an end. Career success in the corporate world is becoming the premier end, and the other institutions are becoming the means for achieving it. As means, the school, family, union, church, community, state, and mass media have become meaningful and valuable only to the extent that they serve the greater end. The independent significance of each has declined. In a sense, these institutions are waning from gemeinschaft to gesellschaft—

from giving support based on strong personal commitment as a matter of principle, to providing support based on weak personal commitment as a matter of expedience. At the same time, the corporation and the corporate career pursued within it are waxing toward the opposite direction, from gesellschaft to gemeinschaft—from commitment as a matter of expedience, to commitment as a matter of principle.[1]

The subordinate position of the school was described earlier. It has become a means to noneducational ends. The school is more a means for furthering corporate career than it is an independent institution for pursuing personal enlightenment and social awareness. Students are less and less committed, as a matter of principle, to those ideals. Instead, school is an institution for pursuing personal advancement and a status-bestowing degree. Students go to school more out of expedience than commitment. Their teachers have had little luck in changing their lack of commitment to the educational principle. What the students are really interested in, and their teachers know it, is getting their degree as painlessly as possible. They do not value education in and for itself. They pursue an education because getting ahead requires it. Education—the school—has been hollowed out for them. School is merely a means to an end. And the end is of the corporate world, not of the educational world. So the school has become a means to corporate ends, and those who seek to reform the school do so with an eye to making it more useful to the corporation. Educational reform now means promoting "computer literacy," not citizen competence.

The computer literacy campaign demonstrates the point. Computer literacy is a real boon—but to the corporation, not the school. The drive for computer literacy aids the corporate world in two ways. First, it requires school districts, colleges, and universities to spend billions on computer hardware, software, and assorted paraphernalia—all produced in the corporate sector. Second, it produces the technically competent and personally indifferent employees needed by the corporate sector. Corporate employees need technical competence in computer operation, particularly in the middle-management levels. But corporate employees also need to be indifferent to the pervasive intrusion of the computer into their work and their life. They must be taught to accept a computer-paced worklife. Students of the 1960s objected to being computerized, to being reduced to holes on an IBM card. The 1960s generation attacked university computer centers as they sprang up in campuses across the country. That animosity toward computerization had to be overcome, and has been overcome in the new generation of college students. The 1980s generation happily buys their own little computers.

The subordinate position of the family has also been explained—it too has been hollowed out, but not to the same extent as the school. The family still means something to its members and they still value it. Nevertheless, for middle-class careerists, meaningful family participation is becoming increasingly difficult. Corporate careerists are being drawn out of their family roles. The family is losing its meaning and value to them. Like the school, it too is becoming more a means than an end. That is, the outward appearance at least, of a happy family life is becoming more a means of furthering career prospects than it is an end in itself.

Serendipity

The same hollowing out, the same loss of meaning and value, has occurred to a greater or lesser extent in the other, major noncorporate institutions. But the hollowing out process for each of them has been slightly different from that of the school and of the family. That all major noncorporate institutions are losing their value and meaning at roughly the same time owes much to the increased meaning and value of the corporation. By force of attraction, it is sucking the meaning and value out of other institutions.

But the corporation's rise to dominance is also another one of those remarkable accidents of history. Presented with a social vacuum left by the declining significance of family, friendship, school, church, and union, the corporation is expanding rapidly to fill the available social space with the meanings, values, and beliefs of corporate career. Our lives must mean something. If family, friendship, school, church, and union do not give meaning to our lives, then we will find that meaning elsewhere—the corporado finds it in their corporate career. Our lives must be worth something, must be of value. If the corporate institution is the only source of value, if participation in the corporate world is valued above participation in other institutional spheres, then our lives will be valued in corporate terms. Furthermore, we must believe in something. If our family, friends, school, church, and union give us little of social relevance to believe in, then we will turn to our corporation. We will do so, not because we are coerced, and not because of a conspiracy of corporate leaders, but simply because we have nowhere else to turn. And as we turn to the corporation for meaning, value, and belief, the result is corporate culture. More to the point, the result is corporate hegemony.

As the birth of pluralism was largely accidental, so too is its death. My thesis is a premature postmortem, an autopsy by way of forecast—for the victim is not dead, not just yet. Noncorporate institutions still show signs of life. Their remaining vitality, however, is easily diverted into blind alleys and scapegoats. This is the real significance of serendipity. We want to find enemies. We want to find someone to blame, someone to fight. But our plight is due largely to happenstance, not to conspiracy, so our rage has no place to go. We invent phantoms and attack them, while serendipitous social and historical forces driving us onward remain unchecked.

THE UNION

Union Functions

The modern-day union is generally understood to serve as a counter-vailing power against the power of the large corporation. Through collective bargaining, the union can offset the power of large corporate employers to push down wages and working conditions. So the origins and functions of the modern-day union can be traced to the power of large corporations.[2] This view has some truth to it, but only a little. Strong unions also have sprung up in industries where the large corporation exercised little power over wages and conditions. In the construction industry, strong building trades unions did not spring up to function merely as countervailing powers. Furthermore, unions failed to take hold for many years in industries where their countervailing power was needed desperately—the steel and auto industries are notable examples. In those industries it took far more than the need for countervailing power to bring in the union. It took the formation of the Congress of Industrial Organizations (CIO), the devotion of leftist organizers, the sit-down strike, the Wagner Act, and the unusual political and economic conditions of the 1930s to establish unions in steel and autos. So there is much more to modern-day unions, at least in their organizing phase, than the provision of countervailing power through collective bargaining.

Workers organized unions not only to bargain collectively, but also to create and share meanings and values as equal human beings. Neither skilled tradespeople nor unskilled industrial workers could look to their bosses for the meaning and value of their lives. Their bosses saw them merely as means to an end. To the bosses, the workers were of little value or meaning as humans. But to other workers, even the unskilled factory hand was of some value. She meant something more than another hand. Workers were alienated from their bosses and their work, but not really from each other. Unlike the middle class, banding together seemed quite natural to many in the working class. So while the middle and upper classes could take heart from the American dream of success and compete savagely among themselves for the main chance, the working classes could take heart from one another and try to band together accordingly. Even so, outside of the trades, organizing unions was a very difficult task in the conservative and individualistic environment of the United States. The closest thing to a genuine labor movement in this country was the Knights of Labor, which reached its heyday in the 1880s and then quickly declined. Industrial workers were organized in the 1930s and 1940s, but even in those years unions remained essentially weak in the United States. Their principle successes have come only on bread-and-butter issues. They have never been very effective at

Table 3
Union Membership in the United States, 1930–80

Year	Total (in millions)	Percent of Nonagricultural Employment
1930	3.6	11.6
1940	8.9	26.9
1950	15.0	31.5
1960	18.1	31.4
1970	20.7	27.4
1980	22.8	25.2

Source: U.S. Bureau of Labor Statistics, *Statistical Abstract of the United States* (Washington, D.C.: Government Printing Office, various years).

giving value and meaning to the rank and file. Nor has a labor party of any significance ever existed in the United States. As shown in Table 3, the postwar years have seen union power, weak as it was to begin with, erode even further.

Union Decline

Although the total number of union members has continued to rise through the past three decades, the percentage of employed persons in labor unions has gradually declined. What little dynamism the labor movement had at the beginning of the postwar period clearly had fizzled out by the 1980s. Several factors have contributed to that fizzling out. First, in historical terms, came a purge of labor's best, most militant organizers. The purge began immediately after the Second World War with power struggles in the CIO. Walter Reuther of the United Auto Workers and Joe Curran of the National Maritime Union gained control over their unions from more leftist and militant factions, and the presidential candidacy of Henry Wallace caused a severe split between renegade CIO unions, which supported him, and the CIO executive board, which did not. Soon after, unions that refused to expel their leftist leaders were themselves expelled from the CIO. Then the Taft-Hartley Act and the Communist Control Act completed the purge of many of the labor movement's best organizers. Section 9(h) of the 1947 Taft-Hartley Act required union officials to sign an affidavit that they were not members of the Communist party. Noncompliance cost the union its certification by the National Labor Relations Board. The Communist Control Act of 1954 took away virtually all standing in law of any union found

Table 4
**Employment in States with Right-to-Work Laws and Total Employment,
1950–83 (in Millions)**

	Right-to-Work	Total
1950	15.3	60.2
1983	30.5	100.2
Increase	15.2	40.0
Percentage Increase	99	66

Note: Excludes Alaska and Hawaii.

Sources: Bureau of the Census and Bureau of Labor Statistics, *Statistical Abstract of the United States* (Washington, D.C.: Government Printing Office, various years).

to be "Communist infiltrated." Both the Communist Control Act and Taft-Hartley Section 9(h) fed the predatory drive of opportunistic labor leaders. They could attack other unions and take over control by smearing the unions' leadership as Reds.[3] The spirit of class solidarity and community spirit left most unions, leaving them mere bargaining units, incapable of infusing independent meaning and value into working-class life.

The Taft-Hartley Act further weakened unions by allowing individual states to adopt so-called right-to-work laws, which allow workers to receive the benefits unions have won without paying any of the costs of maintaining the union. A total of nineteen states adopted such laws, which make it difficult to maintain union membership. As Table 4 indicates, employment has grown much faster in right-to-work states than in the nation as a whole.

The faster growth of employment in right-to-work states than in the country as a whole has contributed to the decline in union membership, but so too has the feminization of work. Outside of a few more progressive unions, unions have never done well in organizing drives among women workers. As more and more women have entered the work force, the proportion of workers belonging to unions has declined. According to the Bureau of Labor Statistics, women were only 30 percent of the civilian labor force in 1950, but 43 percent in 1983. Union membership has also declined because of the changing occupational structure. White-collar workers, outside of public school teachers and some government workers, seldom join unions. As white-collar occupations have gradually replaced blue-collar ones, union membership has declined. This replacement has been occuring for many decades and has totally transformed the civilian work force in the United States, as shown in Table 5.

With the majority of experienced civilian workers now in white-collar

Table 5
White-Collar Workers as a Proportion of the Total Experienced Civilian Labor Force, 1900–1980

Year	Number	Percent
1900	5.1	18
1910	8.0	21
1920	10.5	25
1930	14.3	29
1940	16.1	31
1950	21.3	36
1960	27.0	40
1970	37.9	47
1980	53.5	51

Note: White-collar includes managerial, professional, technical, sales, and administrative support workers.

Source: Bureau of the Census, *Statistical Abstract of the United States* (Washington, D.C.: Government Printing Office, various years), and *Historical Statistics of the United States: Colonial Times to 1970* (Washington, D.C.: Government Printing Office, 1975).

occupations, and with unions still having difficulty breaking into the white-collar ranks, it is little wonder that only a minority of U.S. workers are union members. Nevertheless, from the standpoint of pure self-interest, the sustained decline in union membership is quite puzzling. The empirical and historical evidence is quite clear that unions do raise the incomes of their members by anywhere from 10 to 30 percent. Furthermore, unions increase the fringe benefits received by their members, reduce capricious differentials in wages, increase job security for senior workers, and provide members with a say in how their work is done.[4] In short, unions do provide members with solid economic benefits. However, unions do not provide meaning and value to their members' lives. That is the real rub. Unions do not serve as sources of meaning and value that are independent from the corrosive values and meanings of corporate career. They provide a shrinking minority of workers with economic protection from corporate exploitation, but they provide no one with cultural protection from corporate totalitarianism. This could change, but it is unlikely. In fact, the leadership of most unions in the 1980s has adopted a cooperative attitude toward management in a desperate effort to keep the plants open.

THE CHURCH

The Varieties of American Faith

Unlike the unions, the churches in the United States do serve as sources of meaning and value to their members' lives, but those meanings and values have been vastly different in different periods and for different people. All churches, regardless of denomination, provide the same thing. Whether Protestant, Catholic, or Jewish, all religions provide faith. Members of different religious denominations emphasize their denominational differences. Nevertheless, such differences are of little significance. What is significant is the nature of the faith itself rather than its denominational manifestation. Faith comes in two forms: as a social gospel or as a doctrine of individual salvation. A social gospel is a set of beliefs about the meaning and value of human beings in society. A doctrine of individual salvation is a set of precepts for becoming one of God's chosen people. The balance of emphasis placed on the two forms—social gospel versus individual salvation—is extremely important to the nature of the faith, far more so than mere denomination. The emphasis placed on one or the other form has varied widely between churches and over time within the same church. When individual salvation is emphasized to the exclusion of social gospel, the faithful have lost their faith and their interest in each other and have replaced them with faith and interest in their own personal God. The reverse is also true. When social gospel prevails over individual salvation, the believers have lost their faith and their interest in their own personal God and have replaced them with faith and interest in each other. Under the influence of a gospel of individual salvation, the faithful lose their concern for the plight of others and focus their attention on their own individual plight. The gospel of individual salvation represents a faith in retreat. It offers little of positive value or meaning to human beings trying to make their way in the social world of human relations. Instead, it encourages a retreat into spiritual privatism. On the other hand, under the influence of a social gospel, the faithful lose their concern for their own private plight and focus their attention on the plight of others. The social gospel, then, represents a faith on the march. It offers a source of positive meaning and value to human beings trying to bring their faith to life in the social world of human relations. In the United States in recent times, we generally have had more faith in our own personal gods than in each other.[5] That is to say, our faith has been of the individual salvation variety rather than of the social gospel variety. Our rising faith in our personal gods and declining faith in each other have reduced the ethical commitment to society and the social good and have increased the commitment to personal holiness and personal salvation.

If human beings were of the species homo economicus (economic man), then the poor would follow their own economic interest by supporting churches that emphasize the social gospel. Such is not the case. Instead, the poor, particularly in the United States, frequently support churches emphasizing the doctrine of individual salvation. When the poor turn to religion, as many of them do, they generally "turn not to a faith in revolution, but to a more radical revolt against faith in their fellow man."[6] Revivals among the U.S. poor generally lead to socially and economically regressive social movements, usually dominated by authoritarian leaders and often racked with a frightened conformism, racism, and jingoism.

The Social Gospel Movement

Such has not always been the case in the United States, however. When corporate career began drawing many into a new sphere of life, a social gospel movement of real strength arose. Although it really was not a poor people's movement, during the two decades before and after the turn of the twentieth century, a social gospel movement among U.S. churches did attract many followers. Catholics, Jews, and Protestants were all strongly affected by the movement. Its message of faith in each other was simple. Since we are all brothers and sisters, we should be cooperating instead of competing. Furthermore, the social gospel placed great faith in the Golden Rule, which was to be implemented through political, social, and economic legislation. Antitrust action, slum clearance, woman suffrage, labor legislation, profit sharing, and many other specific reforms were all backed by the social gospelers. Yet the fate of one of the most outspoken social gospelers is quite instructive. George D. Herron, a Congregational minister from Indiana and later the vocal occupant of a Chair of Applied Christianity at Iowa College, went one step too far. In 1899 he stated, "I think the people are ready for a great socialistic movement that shall be political in its aspects and yet wholly religious in its spirit."[7] The college trustees dismissed him; his former students had difficulty obtaining pastorates, and he eventually moved to Italy. Other leading social gospelers were Washington Gladden, a Congregational minister who refused to accept a gift to his church from John D. Rockefeller; Richard T. Ely, an academician who helped found the American Economic Association; and Professor Walter Rauschenbusch, a theologian whose writings strongly influenced the young Martin Luther King, Jr.

These men were all Protestants, but American rabbis were active social gospelers as well. Strong statements on social justice were made by leaders from all three branches of American Judaism. American Catholics also became active in 1919 with the drafting of the "Pastoral Letter of the American Hierarchy." This letter, belatedly but firmly, brought American Catholic clergy in line with Pope Leo XIII's 1891 encyclical *Rerum Novarum*. The Catholics, though latecomers, have been far more persistent than the

Protestants. They have continued to stress equality, social justice, economic regulation, and cooperation. Pope Pious XI rounded out the social principles of Leo XIII. Then John Paul II, though very conservative in many ways, has carried the tradition into the 1980s with his encyclical *Laborem Exercens*. The Catholic hierarchy has continued to speak out because it is hard for angered college trustees or church laypersons to fire Catholic popes and bishops—not so with Protestant professors and preachers. Even though the social gospel movement died out in the 1920s, the latest American Catholic statement on social justice is firmly in the tradition of the old social gospel movement. In their first draft of a 1984 "Pastoral Letter on Catholic Social Teaching and the U.S. Economy," the American bishops came out strongly in favor of income redistribution, economic democracy, and welfare reform. The second draft of the letter, written in 1985, was watered down in response to conservative lay reaction to the first draft. Nevertheless, even the second draft is still strongly in the social gospel tradition of religious faith. However, the linking up of progressive Catholics with other progressive religious elements still is largely barred by the Catholic church's positions on birth control, abortion, divorce, and women's lib.

Although the original social gospel movement around the turn of the twentieth century was not a black movement, the black clergy took up the spiritual call for social justice once again in the 1950s and 1960s with the civil rights movement. Dr. Martin Luther King, Jr., paid for it with his life, as did many others. Outside of the Catholic hierarchy, the social gospel movement had died out in American churches, but the black clergy's faith and blood revived it, only to have it fade again in the 1970s.

In the 1980s members of the clergy like the Reverend D. Douglas Roth from Clairton, Pennsylvania, continue to preach the social gospel. Reverend Roth and about thirty other ministers in the Pittsburgh area banded together to preach and protest against corporate disinvestment in the Monongahela River valley steel industry. The original members of his congregation petitioned Roth's Lutheran synod leadership to dismiss him. They finally prevailed, but had to have him arrested to remove him from his church.[8] Obviously, it is not the social gospel that dominates spiritual life in America. Rather, it is the doctrine of individual salvation.

On most social issues and during most social crises, the silence from the pulpit is deafening. For example, during the turmoil of the Martin Luther King, Jr., assassination in 1968, a team of researchers studied the sermons given by Protestant clergy in California. The researchers found that the good clergy "had not devoted a single sermon mainly to racial problems during this year of death, turmoil, and tragedy."[9] The silence of the evangelical pulpit on the broad social issues of equality and peace is notorious. It is broken only by truculent references to the sanctity of white middle-class values and to the Christian's duty to fight godless communism and (Moslem) terrorism. The truth is, most Protestant churches are neither strong enough nor independent enough to speak out for equality and peace in a world of inequality and war. At the parish level, clergy are least independent because of their need for lay support. At higher levels in church organizations, however, a degree of autonomy is achieved because, at those levels, professionalism manifests itself. That is, church officials above the parish level are oriented more toward the values of other church officials than toward the values of the laity. This gives them a degree of autonomy from the social conservatism of the laity. Centrally controlled church funds and centrally directed church activities can then become vehicles for social activism, unless it is internally opposed by the church hierarchy. An excellent example of the social activism possible under the proper conditions is the World Council of Churches and its occasional deviation into social gospel.

In addition, the social gospel can manifest itself even at the level where the clergy meets the laity. An example of this is the social activism of many clergy in campus ministries. When the lay group dealt with is young and liberal or activist, the church organs dealing with them often stress the social gospel rather than individual salvation, even in Protestant circles.[10] In the campus ministries is a potential for preaching the social gospel. The potential may develop into a social movement if the campus and world struggle over disinvestment from South Africa intensifies. Another social gospel potential exists in the sanctuary movement, in which a network of congregations and religious individuals have created the twentieth-century equivalent of the old underground railroad for helping refugees from the U.S.-sponsored war on Central American peasants and Indians. Related to the sanctuary movement is the "witness for peace" movement, in which over two thousand U.S. Christians and Jews have already toured the war-torn areas of Central America in solidarity with the war's victims. These religious movements might just infect the U.S. religious with a virulent strain of the social gospel—liberation theology.

Despite the efforts of the campus ministry and sanctuary movement, Dugger's theorem states that the closer the clergy to the laity, the weaker the emphasis on the social gospel, all other things being equal (Dugger was trained as an economist). The theorem has a corollary: the greater the dependence on the support of the laity, the greater is the emphasis on individual salvation. The theorem explains the continued emphasis Catholic clergy place on the social gospel. Its corollary explains the continued emphasis the Protestant evangelicals place on individual salvation. The Catholic clergy are supported by centuries of clerical tradition and very substantial clerical wealth. The Protestant evangelicals have no such tradition and little permanent wealth. The one can take an independent stand; the other cannot. The one must adopt the ethics of competitive capitalism; the other can resist.

So in Latin America, while the evangelicals are busy shoring up the repressive status quo by preaching individual salvation, many of the Catholic clergy are busy undermining it by preaching their Third World version of the social gospel—liberation theology. Although the current pope (John Paul II) is taking a dimmer and dimmer view of his revolutionary priests, they are continuing their work, even in Nicaragua. In fact, liberation theologies have sprung up in many beleaguered Third World countries. The Philippines, Jamaica, and South Africa have all spawned liberation theologies. These Third World versions of the social gospel, Cornel West argues, "result from the inability of capitalist civilization to provide contexts and communities wherein meaning and value can be found to sustain people through the traumas of life."[11] West sees a strong point in favor of the Third World, where the corporation is still an intruder. In the Third World, the church may develop into a powerful source of opposition to corporate capitalism and its corrosive values of individual career. The church in America did so when corporate capitalism was in the process of transforming America. That resistance turned out to be futile, through perhaps it will not in the Third World. Now in the United States, where the corporation has become an entrenched institution, it, not the church, provides meaning and value. For here, individual career success is such a powerful value in the material sphere of life that it forces its complement (individual salvation) into a dominant role in the spiritual sphere of life for the middle class.

So far, the social gospel has not taken root in the contemporary middle class. This is not to say that religious faith has not taken root there—far from it. The U.S. middle class can only be described as extraordinarily devout. But its faith is of the harmless variety, harmless to the corporate status quo, that is. The middle-class corporado's faith is in his own personal God and in his own individual salvation, not in a God of all people and not in the salvation of humanity. The middle class' God offers personal solace at day's end to the harried careerist, and meets the careerist's special need for individual salvation and psychic security in a savagely competitive world. So the middle class can be as devout as any pantheon of saints, but its faith will never serve as a source of meaning and value independent of the corporate world. This kind of faith does not enable the middle class to transcend that world, merely to accomodate to it. In fact, the middle-class world of corporate career seems to be corrosive of any socially meaningful faith. In a fascinating recent book, Michael Harrington has argued that entering the corporate world of work actually reduces the degree of faith of the entrants.[12] So a liberation theology is not likely to develop among the American middle class.

Although a few of the rich may feel a special need for individual salvation, the spiritual sphere of life generally means little to the upper class in the United States. Its financial relation to the church is important—to the church, but not to it. For the rich are not of the church, but above it. They are a special variety of "domestic heathen." The very rich "are outside the pale of organized religion; they are not objects of charity, but all other mortals are such objects to them. They are the 'angels' or patrons of religious bodies, but usually feel superior to the bodies they patronize."[13] Of course, this is probably why some of them financially patronize the churches, out of motives of conspicuous piety rather than spiritual commitment. Be that as it may, the upper class in America presents little opportunity for a revival of the social gospel. Rich Americans are not likely to develop a liberation theology.

The chance of such a development among the American poor is only slightly less likely than among the rich. The very poor, the destitute, are outside the church. With the exception of many southern blacks, the very poor, like the very rich, are "domestic heathens." They are objects of pity and charity rather than members of a spiritual community, and many of them know it. They are not of the spiritual life, but object lessons for it. So the very poor in America show little sign of developing an autonomous religious source of value and meaning. That is, they cannot be expected to develop a new social gospel.

Perhaps the black poor are another matter. A revival of black spiritual consciousness along the lines of what occurred in the 1960s is a possibility. A middle-class black revival, sans the poor, would inevitably drift into traditional middle-class channels—concern for individual salvation and faith in God would outweigh concern for social improvement and faith in humanity. But a lower-class black revival might move into a different channel. It might result in a call for social reform through political action. That is, it might result in a revival of the social gospel that provides meanings and values that are more humane and more fit for free adults than the meanings and values of corporate careerists. Martin Luther King, Jr., in the last book he wrote before his murder, was very critical of the inhumane, intolerant values of American culture. To him, it smacked far more of hegemony than of pluralism, and he believed that the black civil rights movement was America's best chance of transcending itself. If the movement leadership—largely middle-class—never forgot that "the salvation of the Negro middle class is ultimately dependent upon the salvation of the Negro masses," then King believed that the challenge of transforming the United States could be met. He stated:

Let us, therefore, not think of our movement as one that seeks to integrate the Negro into all the existing values of American society. Let us be those creative dissenters who will call our beloved nation to a higher destiny, to a new plateau of compassion, to a more noble expression of humaneness.[14]

Just like black musicians gave us an authentic American music, the black churchmen of the civil rights movement could have developed an authentic liberation theology, a revived social gospel in the United States. But soon after the Reverend King wrote those words, he was shot dead.

COMMUNITY

The Main Drift

With a few possible exceptions, there is little in the way of a social gospel in the United States to serve as an alternative source of values and meanings. Furthermore, with the exception of a few ethnic enclaves and isolated rural margins, there is little in the way of self-contained community either. We have separate business districts, bedroom districts, tenderloin districts, industrial "parks," shopping malls, and college towns, but few whole or self-contained communities. We have geographic clusters that differ from each other, each with their own charm. But that does not make them real communities. Real communities are organic social systems, not just geographic clusterings of similar activities. Community is created by the quality of human relations between the members of the community. It is based on gemeinschaft, on close and continuous interpersonal relations. Geographic clustering of similar activities creates the very shallow and discontinuous interpersonal relations of gesellschaft. In a community, relations are based on personal emotional commitment; in a geographic clustering, relations are based on impersonal functional expedience. In a community, interpersonal relations include all of the different roles each person plays. That is, people relate to each other in many different ways—as worker, churchgoer, schoolmate, and neighbor. In a geographical clustering, interpersonal relations include only one of the different roles each person plays. That is, people relate to each other strictly as coworkers or strictly as neighbors, but not as both. The close and continuous interpersonal relations of the community create and enforce shared values and meanings. The shallow and discontinuous interpersonal relations of geographic clustering do not create shared meanings and values. When we work, shop, eat, sleep, worship, study, and play all in the same place with the same people, we participate in community and come to acquire a set of community values and meanings. But when we work in one place with one set of people, shop in another place with another set of people, eat in a third place with a third set, sleep in a fourth, worship in a fifth, and play in a sixth, then we do not participate in community, nor do we acquire community values and meanings. Most of us, particularly most middle-class corporadoes, follow the second pattern of working, shopping, eating, sleeping, worshipping, studying, and playing in different places with different sets of people. So most of us do not acquire community values and meanings because we do not organize our various activities along communal lines.

Pointing out this lack of community in American Life is in no way an endorsement of the "Chicago School" view of sociologists who studied the anonymity and social disintegration of the American city of the 1930s. They were strongly anti-urban in their approach to the city, being largely from small towns themselves, and based their conclusions on studies of Chicago during a period of economic depression and social disintegration.[15] The growth of cities and the decline of rural towns are not the real problem addressed here. Rather, the real problem is the lack of effective institutional resistance to the growing influence of the values and meanings of corporate capitalism.

Even if we were to eat, sleep, work, etc., all in the same place with the same people, most of us would not do it for very long. Our jobs, our careers, require us to move too often. We seldom have time to send down roots in any one place with any one group of community members before we move somewhere else. According to the Census Bureau, only about half of the U.S. population lived in the same house in 1980 as it did in 1975 (53.6 percent, to be exact). In 1982 alone, 38 million people moved to new addresses. For most of us, this constant churning makes real community impossible. Even for those of us who do stay in one place and pattern our activities along communal lines, the frequent moving of other would-be community members makes real community difficult.

Our lack of community, combined with our lack of any meaningful social gospel, leaves us with no social center to the meanings and values of our lives. A faith in individual salvation is an inadequate substitute for the vacuum we feel, for try to accommodate to our individual isolation as we may, human beings are social animals. We need some kind of social center to our lives. It need not be the stifling closeness of Sinclair Lewis's *Main Street,* but we seem to need something nonetheless. This yearning, left unsatisfied, seems to lead to a kind of reactionary nostalgia. Robert A. Nisbet, conservative pundit, celebrates this yearning: "the root ideas and values of early nineteenth-century conservatism have found their way straight to our own generation and have become the materials of a fresh and infinitely diversified veneration for community." Furthermore, in contemporary America, he claims that "belonging, not escape, is the imperative moral value."[16] Except for the minority living in ethnic enclaves or isolated rural communities, our search for a social center to our lives cannot be satisfied by belonging to a community.

The minority, still living in real communities, provide a rather poor model for the rest of us. White ethnic communities do provide social meaning and value to the people living in them, but those values and meanings simply cannot serve as a social center for the vast majority. The values and meanings of white ethnic communities are not cosmopolitan enough to be fulfilling to the larger population, composed as it is of a very diverse racial, spiritual, and ethnic mixture. Nor can the social values and meanings of isolated rural communities serve the more diverse whole as anything more than the stuff of nostalgia. Life on the move can never mean the same as life in a small country town, and the drive for career success is incompatible with the values of the quiet life. So the majority turns elsewhere. Even when we retire and can live wherever we want, most of us do not try to become members of small rural communities or ethnic communities. Quite obviously, we would not fit in. Instead, if we can afford it, we move to enclaves of retirees in Florida or Arizona.

A Note on Friendship

Social meanings and values are not found in the church, and most of us cannot find them in the community. Our families are seriously weakened, and if we would be successful in our careers, we dare not turn to our friends for social meaning and value. Friends present real problems that are inherent to career. A careerist needs allies for networking and sponsors for mentoring, not friends. Friends get in the way because some of them inevitably fall behind us or rise above us. If they fall behind, continued association with them can threaten our own rise in status. And if they rise above, they remind us of our own shortcomings. The ones that fall behind tease us and say we have the big head. The ones that rise above give us pointers, unsolicited, and say we should think big, like them. And so, one by one, we allow our friends to fall away from us. We replace them with allies in our network, and we become protégés to powerful mentors. But allies and mentors are not friends. They are tools. We use them; and they use us. And we are lonely. So if we can find their addresses, once a year we send our old friends expensive cards with beautiful scenes of holiday fellowship reproduced on the front and maudlin messages of cheer and goodwill printed on the inside, and we hope that they will send us the same cards. We call them Christmas cards and send them out through the mail in bunches in December. Some of them, more each year, come back to us marked "no forwarding address." And we turn elsewhere to fill the vacuum inside us.

THE STATE

The Paradox of Patriotism

In the 1980s many Americans, particularly young, middle-class males, seem to be turning to the state as a source of social value and meaning. In the light of recent history, their patriotism is paradoxical: President Kennedy committed troops to defend the tyrannical regime of Ngo Dinh Diem in South Vietnam and then turned on Diem, allowing him to be ousted by his generals. President Kennedy allowed United States-backed Cuban expatriates to invade Cuba at the Bay of Pigs. Kennedy did both in the defense of freedom, so he said. President Johnson was elected as the peace candidate, while planning massive escalation of the Vietnam War. Then Richard Nixon was elected as the peace candidate. He escalated the war even further, waging his own secret air war against the people of Indochina, but won reelection anyway, only to resign in disgrace in the Watergate scandal. President Ford pardoned Nixon. Carter and then Reagan became president, each following their own prophetic mission to save America. Both were false prophets. In spite of more than twenty years of presidential scandals, lies, and disgraces, recent years are witness to a profound resurgence of patriotism, particularly among the more gullible and truculent of the young.

To the new patriots, war is a spectator sport, a kind of game played by others for one's own enjoyment. It comes with its own sportcasters and instant replays. The sportcasters are the likes of Dan Blather, Walter Chronic, Eric Severe, and Tom Brokejaw. The instant replays are even repeated on the ten o'clock news for the convenience of those who missed them at six o'clock. In a different time, the nightly carnage in our living rooms was a source of anguish. But not this time, at least not for the new patriots. And yet, in a sense, not even the worst of the new patriots should be judged too harshly. Perhaps Hunter S. Thompson is right. Maybe the young new patriots have nothing better going for them:

With AIDS and acid rain, there is not much left in the way of life and love and possibilities for these shortchanged children of the '80s. In addition to a huge and terminally crippling national debt, and a shocking realization that your country has slipped to the status of a second-rate power, and that five American dollars will barely buy a cup of coffee in Tokyo, these poor buggers are being flogged every day of their lives with the knowledge that sex is death and rain kills fish and any politician they see on TV is a liar and a fool.[17]

Be that as it may, the Reagan administration has boosted the new patriotism by finding the policy mix that minimizes domestic resistance to foreign military adventures. To maintain popular support of military adventures, we use other people to do our fighting for us, and we borrow the money to pay for it. Our war against Nicaragua is being fought by the former henchmen of the Somoza regime. In El Salvador, we have enthusiastic, indigenous death squads do the retail killing on the ground and well-trained local pilots do the wholesale killing from the air. Moslem religious fanatics serve our purpose in Afghanistan, and a whole array of Cambodian renegades have reopened our Indochina front for us. The Reagan administration relearned, from its own experience in Lebanon, not to use American troops in dirty fights. The meaning of war gets too close to home when the bodies come back to the States in flag-draped boxes. So Americans are used only in quick, clean operations like Grenada or in night air raids on Libyan civilians. War is best when others do the real fighting or when the victims cannot fight back. The Reagan administration, while pledging to keep the armed services strong, had enough sense not to reinstate the draft. War is also best when we do not have to pay for it right away. Even though somebody always pays in the end, wars financed by budget deficits instead of taxes create far less domestic resistance. So the Reagan administration, while pledging to balance the federal budget, by constitutional amendment if necessary, knew not to raise taxes. The resulting war-spending deficits were simply blamed on the wasteful spending of liberals in Congress.

We have learned our lesson from Vietnam, and this is what we have learned: the Johnson administration, in particular, made two mistakes in the war. First, Johnson raised taxes to help pay for the war. That is lesson number one. DO NOT PAY FOR WAR WITH TAXES. Second, Johnson committed a large number of American troops to the actual fighting. That is lesson number two. DO NOT SEND AMERICANS TO FIGHT.

The Corporate Use of Patriotism

If Americans are kept home and taxes are kept down, the post-Vietnam generation's patriotism can be turned to account very easily and for an extended period of time. This generation's support is as good as money in the bank for major Pentagon contractors. How much money the public's support of the Pentagon is worth overwhelms the imagination. Americans are willing to give the Pentagon big bucks. Seymour Melman, an excellent student of Pentagon capitalism, estimates: "Without considering the full social cost to the American community, the combined Pentagon budgets of 1946–1988 represent a mass of resources equivalent to the cost of replacing just about all (94 percent) of everything manmade in the United States (excluding the land)."[18] President Reagan raised the ante rapidly. In his first term of office alone, he spent $780 billion on national defense, excluding veterans benefits and services.[19] The military spending plans for his second term were even more grandiose—$540 billion in the first two years alone. He ran up a total deficit of $600 billion in his first term of office. In his second term, the deficits continued. Massive sums now have to be paid to banks, insurance companies, foreign lenders, and other financial intermediaries for lending the Pentagon money. In Reagan's first term alone, net interest paid on the mounting national debt totalled $356 billion, a massive transfer of income to the upper income groups that surpasses even the grandest redistribution schemes of President Johnson's War on Poverty.[20]

So long as public support can be maintained, the new war spending is incredibly beneficial to big defense contractors and big bankers. Corporations now benefit twice from it: once when the bidding corporations are awarded the lucrative contracts, and then again when financial corporations lend the Pentagon the money to pay the contracts. It is a nice racket, as long as public support for it can be maintained. That support rests on the patriotism of the post-Vietnam generation. Its ultimate purpose is corporate profit from war spending. And now that the war makers have learned not to pay for war with taxes, not only the nonfinancial but also the financial sector of our corporate economy can share in the profits. How nice—the pie has another slice.

The problem is, no one really trusts the pie maker. The state, of course, is baking the pie for the corporations to share. It is being baked in the name of patriotism, but these new patriots have no faith in the baker. American patriotism in the 1980s is a different kind of patriotism. The post-Vietnam generation feels no reverence for the state as a system of government. State officials and even war veterans are looked upon with suspicion, hostility, and disdain. In fact, the national government and those who serve it are new kinds of scapegoats. Although the national governing system has continued to run rather well, we blame it for almost all our problems.[21] Its welfare programs are blamed for poverty, its regulatory programs for inefficiency and pollution, and its taxes for tax cheating. The solution, public action through responsible government, is now widely viewed as the problem. Both Jimmy Carter and Ronald Reagan ran aggressive presidential campaigns against the very government they wanted to head. In this topsy-turvy world, the new patriotism is not a support for the works of government, but a reverence for the new symbols of government. The new patriots worship power, status, and wealth. They do not support the rule of law, active citizenship, or economic equality.

The current resurgence of American patriotism cannot be taken either as a sign of democracy on the mend or as support for democratic reform and progressive revitalization. It must be understood for what it is—a profoundly regressive and authoritarian retreat into dreams of power, status, and wealth. The new patriots are not asking their government to revitalize their democracy. They are not asking their government for progressive reform of their economy. Instead, they are asking their government to right perceived wrongs done them; to get them the respect they think they deserve. They are asking their government to give them theirs, at the expense of whoever. Their demands will never amount to any resistance to the continued enlargement of corporate power. Instead, their demands have been easily turned to corporate account. And that is the point. The state as an institution is not resisting corporate dominance of U.S. society.

The New One-Party State

The United States has developed its own version of the one-party state. Two major parties actually exist here, but they are little more than separate branches of one big party. The one big party remains unnamed, but its two branches call themselves Democrats and Republicans. The corporate giants understand the nature of the political game being played, so they give campaign contributions to both branches of the one big party. Since the two branches are really of the same party, neither branch really minds that its campaign supporters are also supporting the so-called opposition. So the Democrats and Republicans both take money from the same corporate Political Action Committees. The result is a system of grossly overfunded plebiscites. Voters can vote for one of the candidates of the one big party and against the other candidate of the one big party. The one big party always wins and the voters always lose. Some voters have caught on and stopped voting. The one big party does not offer voters any real choices. Instead, the voters can vote for a reactionary and against a conservative; or they can vote for a conservative and against a reactionary. Voters are never presented with real choices between capitalism and socialism. Instead, they can choose between conservative capitalism and reactionary capitalism. The conservatives are grouped in the Democratic branch of the one big party, while the reactionaries are grouped in the Republican branch. Only once in recent memory were voters presented with somewhat more substantial fare.

In the early 1970s, a few liberals sneaked into the Democratic branch of the one big party. The sneak attack on the one big party was led by George McGovern in 1972. He offered voters something of an alternative. He offered them liberal capitalism and peace instead of reactionary or conservative capitalism and war. The modest choice drove conservatives out of the Democratic branch of the one big party in droves. The offending liberals frightened the reactionary wing of the party so much that the wing's leadership adopted a series of "dirty tricks" against the interloping liberals. One of the tricks was an illegal breaking and entering adventure in the Watergate complex. The adventure indicates the length to which the one big party will go to keep out dissenters, critics, peaceniks, and other un-American groups. The liberals were soon soundly defeated. Now former liberals try to hide their questionable past, calling themselves "neoconservatives" and doing their utmost to show their devotion to the principles of the one big party. The principles are "Where's Mine?" and "Me Too!" Needless to say, these principles do little to inspire respect for the state as a vehicle of social justice.

This peculiar one-party state severely restricts the range of political representation in the United States. Reactionary and conservative views are solidly represented in the separate wings of the one big party. But liberal views are only sporadically represented; while socialist and communist views are almost never represented. So the political game in the United States is not played with a full deck, so to speak. What with the liberals barely able to reach the voting public and the full-bodied critics never really reaching the voting public at all, the political game is fixed in favor of the giant, capitalist corporation.

THE MEDIA

Print Media

The era of yellow journalism, of whipping up war fever to sell newspapers, is gone. The print media, particularly the *New York Times* and the *Washington Post,* showed their independence during the latter part of the Vietnam War by publishing stories on the Pentagon Papers and the Watergate coverup. For a brief time, liberals were able to get their views discussed in some of the big dailies. That was the high point of mainstream American journalism in recent years. It was a time when investigative reporters were willing to put their jobs on the line to get their stories published. Mainstream journalists can point to their past performance with justifiable pride. They won many battles against internal and external censorship. But in the end, they lost the war. They did not lose to the media censors. They lost to the media managers.

The media censor tries to squelch the radical article, the uncomfortable fact. He is against journalists. To him, journalism is propaganda and the investigative reporter a subversive. He thinks in terms of ideology and propaganda. He keeps a file of friends and enemies in his head. Is the article friendly? The censor peddles lies and represses truth, and he brings forth much righteous indignation. Journalists resist him. As a result, he is far less effective than imagined. Even censorship in the Soviet Union is less effective than the censors imagine. Somehow, many truths still filter through the net. But the media manager does nothing of that sort. The media manager has the best interests of the journalist in mind. He is for journalists. The media manager wants the newspaper to be a success. To him, journalism is a business. He thinks in terms of advertising revenues and circulation figures. He keeps a running file of such figures in his head. What will the article do for the numbers? The media manager peddles bonuses and promotes circulation. To him, the investigative reporter is an expense to be minimized, not a subversive to be repressed. The media manager is not against investigative reporters. He just cannot fit them into his cost-benefit ratios. He can measure their cost, but not their benefit. The benefit of investigative reporting is in terms of journalistic integrity, but journalistic integrity does not fit into the media manager's numbers, only the reporter's salary and contingent legal fees to defend the paper fit into the numbers. Salary plus legal fees are costs, measurable ones at that, while the benefits are abstract at best.

Since the media manager meets much less righteous indignation than the censor, resistance to him is less focused, less emotionally charged, and in the long run, far less effective. The media manager does not fire reporters for writing critical articles. Instead, he downsizes the reporting staff for the health of the paper, not for reasons of propaganda. Investigative reporters are fired anyway, but they are not repressed. They are not locked up. They are not threatened. They remain free to investigate and write whatever they please. But their articles seldom are written while on the payroll of the major dailies, and seldom appear in them, not because of censorship but because of costs and benefits. The major dailies have their own reporters to write the stories they need. So the investigative reporting can still be done, but usually at the reporter's own expense. Furthermore, the investigative articles can still be published, but not in the big dailies that reach millions of readers. Instead, they appear in much smaller circulation vehicles such as *The Nation, Mother Jones, In These Times, The Village Voice,* and *The Texas Observer.* The big dailies are big businesses. Their managers prefer circulation builders like Ann Landers over muckrakers like Jack Newfield. Nevertheless, both the circulation builders and the muckrakers are perfectly free to write whatever they want. Getting it published for the millions to read is another matter.

And so the news in the big U.S. dailies is not politically censored. It is commercially censored. It is trivialized and homogenized, and if it builds circulation, it is also syndicated.[22]

Broadcast Media

The same applies, even more so, to the broadcast media. Popular radio is into sex, drugs, and rock and roll—none of which are necessarily radicalizing or liberating (Timothy Leary to the contrary notwithstanding).[23] Sex, drugs, and rock and roll have commercial entertainment value, which is why radio specializes in them. Some radio stations object to rock and roll, with its emphasis on sex and illegal drugs. In its place they play country and western music about sex and legal drugs (mainly alcohol) and throw in some evangelical preachers to broaden their appeal. A few radio stations run talk shows about sex and drugs, and cut the music entirely. In sum, radio fare is pitched to the lowest common denominator of lobotomized teenagers of all ages. The trivial and banal is where the advertising audience is.

All this fun has aroused the fears of self-appointed censors. The Parents Musical Resource Center has sprung up to monitor rock lyrics. Led by such musically gifted personages as Susan Baker, the wife of President Reagan's Treasury Secretary, and Tipper Gore, the wife of Senator Albert Gore, Jr., the Center has joined hands with the National Parent-Teacher Association to insist on rating and labeling records. The American Civil Liberties Union has sprung to the defense of the freedom of music. But the conflict will never rise much above the level of low farce. It is much to do about nothing. Even if the juvenile obsession with sex and drugs is driven back under covers, little will change in America. If the radio is cleaned up, fewer people will listen to the radio.

A somewhat more serious conflict has emerged over television. The content of TV entertainment is just as trivial and banal as radio. Television merely downplays drugs and sublimates sex. However, the major television networks, CBS in particular, have pretensions of broadcasting the news. These pretensions rose to threatening levels during the Vietnam War and the Watergate scandal. The TV cameras brought the killing in Vietnam and the lying about Watergate right into our living rooms. TV coverage of the Watergate hearings made a heroine out of a black woman from Texas—Barbara Jordan. And what was worse, she deserved it. She was really heroic. The TV coverage of Vietnam showed us fighting a determined enemy who was not about to give up, while our leaders kept telling us that we were close to winning the war. The TV coverage of Vietnam and Watergate had committed a cardinal sin. It violated social norms. According to social norms, black women from the South do not have voices like Barbara Jordan's or give us lessons about the Constitution on national television. Furthermore, according to social norms, Americans easily win wars against little Asians, particularly little Asians who run around in black pajamas. The violation of those norms made TV journalism appear biased. Of course, it was not. In fact, it was often courageously and painfully objective. "But if the norm of society is corrupted, then objective journalism is corrupted too, for it must not challenge the norm, it must accept the norm."[24] For a brief interlude, TV journalism did not accept the norms. In the Vietnam-Watergate era, TV journalistists and news broadcasters ran stories that were truly countercultural. Now, in the post-Vietnam era, they are paying dearly for it.

The TV newspeople have been put back in their place. It is unlikely that they will step out again. CBS, Inc., learned an especially expensive lesson. Not only was it dragged into a costly libel case brought against it by General William C. Westmoreland, who headed our Vietnam war effort, it also had to fight an even more expensive takeover battle against Senator Jesse Helms, media mogul Ted Turner, and the Fairness in Media group. The takeover attempt, like the libel suit, was unsuccessful, but they both put CBS on notice. Had the takeover been successful, the Fairness in Media group and its allies would have eliminated what they considered liberal bias in CBS's news. Something new was injected into the television news equation. Media managers have known all along how much network news staffs cost in terms of direct salaries and expenses. And, all along, the media managers have had difficulty fitting the news staffs' benefits neatly into a cost-benefit calculation. But now two more costs have been added to weigh in against the unmeasurable benefits—the corporate cost of defending against the takeover bids of right-wingers and the legal cost of defending against libel suits, often encouraged by same.

Freedom of the Press

Freedom of the press is still intact. But the willingness to exercise it has been shaken. Formal freedom is still possessed by broadcast and print media alike, but for very similar reasons, both are reluctant to exercise it. The reasons for the reluctance have nothing to do with censorship. They have everything to do with management. Investigative reporting and broadcast news that violate social norms—the norms of corporate culture—are not illegal. They are expensive. And since all mass-market radio, television, and print outlets are big businesses now, they all curtail their news. But they do so by cutting expenses, not by cutting critical stories. Nevertheless, the result is the same. Their business school–trained managers do not intend to act as censors, merely as good managers. So as print and broadcast media both evolved into big businesses, managerial criteria came to replace journalistic criteria. And it is the application of managerial criteria to the production of the news that stifles critical and investigative reporting.

An excellent example of this managerial revolution in the media is the evolution of the *New York Times* from an aggressive newspaper in the late 1960s and early 1970s into a media conglomerate in the 1980s. The old *Times* newspaper ran stories in 1966–67 about the indiscriminate bombing of North Vietnam. The old *Times* also published the Pentagon Papers, and did its part in publishing the Watergate scandals. The stories changed the course of the war, and perhaps the course of history as well. But the new *Times* of the 1980s has gone soft. The stories it should be running about indiscriminate bombing in El Salvador and civilian slaughter in Nicaragua are either not run at all or are so wishy-washy as to lose all impact. America is at war by proxy in El Salvador, Nicaragua, Afghanistan, and Cambodia, but a reader of the new *Times* has to dig very hard and read between a lot of lines before they can find out. The new *Times* has gone soft because it is no longer just a newspaper run by journalistics or by people who love journalism, but it is now a media conglomerate run by managers who love the bottom line. By the end of the 1970s the *Times* conglomerate had pushed its annual sales up to $650 million and its annual profits up to $35 million. It owned three magazines and three book publishing companies, nine newspapers in Florida and North Carolina, radio and television stations in New York, Memphis, and Fort Smith, Arkansas, major interests in three Canadian pulp plants, and major interest in a pulp plant in Maine. In addition, it also owned several information systems and information sytstems companies. The conglomeration of the *Times* is not an exception. Other media outlets have expanded even further into the world of corporate finance and conglomeration than the *Times*.

Now only small, nonbusiness-oriented media outlets consistently take chances on critical stories and investigative journalism because only they are free of professionally trained managers with their business career objectives and their cost-benefit ratios focused on the bottom line instead of on the good story. But the audience that these independents reach is so small that their impact on evolving U.S. culture is minimal. They are incapable of stopping the main drift. At best, they only slow it down.

NATURE HATES A VACUUM

Liberalism Has Lost More than Its Nerve

What America is experiencing is not just a failure of its liberal-plural nerve. The liberals and the pluralists have lost that, sure enough, but they have lost much more. They have lost their foundation. They have lost the very institutional structure that created and supported them. That structure was an economy composed of small-scale firms and a society composed of independent institutions. The small-scale producers, most of whom were farmers, were the economic foundation of liberalism; while the independent institutions were the societal foundation of pluralism. The economy of liberalism has long since passed into the hands of large-scale, conglomerated corporations and their career-obsessed managerial cadres. And the society of pluralism has evolved into a hegemonic system composed of a set of hollowed-out institutions dependent upon one dominant institution. The spawning grounds of liberalism in the political sphere and of pluralism in the cultural sphere have gone sterile. Since pluralism-liberalism represents the central values and meanings in American life, the American center is not holding. Nor can the liberal-plural faith be revived, for the wellsprings of that faith have gone dry. As a result of its collapsing center, America is drifting to the right, the far right. Far more than just a swing in the political pendulum is involved in this move. The pendulum may swing back toward the center in the 1990s, but each time it swings back, it stops sooner and sooner. The pendulum will continue swinging, but over the long haul the center will continue shifting to the right.

The move to the right is not planned by a conspiracy, but it is led by a dominant institution. The dominant institution is the conglomerate corporation. Our other, formerly independent instititions have been hollowed out and offer little resistance to the main drift. The hollowed-out institutions are the school, family, union, church, community, state, and press (both print and broadcast). Let us review the emptiness and consequent transformation of these dependent institutions, one by one.

Filling the Vacuums

Education used to mean enlightenment, and the school used to be valued for the knowledge and wisdom it imparted. Of course, to Americans, school also meant social mobility. But now, that is its primary meaning. School is not meaningful, nor is it valuable as an educational institution, in and for itself. School is valued as the start of a career, preferably a head start over the other careerists. School is valued to the extent that it leads to a lucrative career, usually a corporate one. School does not really suffer from dry rot. At least for those on the make, it is not meaningless and valueless, but a valuable and meaningful career center. Even the teachers can look forward to having career ladders built into their profession that will make it possible for some of them to rise above the status and pay of their friends and colleagues by becoming "master teachers."

The meaning and value received from family relations are roughly proportional to the time and effort put into them. First the middle-class father and then the middle-class mother have put less and less time and effort into family relations, not because they do not care, but because the force of circumstances has taken them out of the family for longer and longer times. The circumstances responsible for absentee parents are intimately connected to the pull of corporate career. The degree of absentee parenting is directly proportional to the degree of career commitment, so the rising career commitment of men and women has caused a rise in parental absence. Parents who are not there cannot derive much meaning and value from their family roles. Nor can they impart much meaning and value into their families. So the family, too, is being hollowed out. It means far less to family members than it once did. It has not been able to resist the corrosive effect of corporate employment and career obsession. Rather than resisting, the family has adapted in a curious fashion: the Puritan calling has become the corporado's career. While the Puritans hardened their hearts against all that would detract from God's call to them, the corporadoes have hardened their hearts against all that would detract from the pursuit of their career. Some resistance to the hollowing out of the family has surfaced. But so far it is largely regressive in nature. Groups such as the Moral Majority and the Eagle Forum have taken up the call against eroding family values, but they have focused their attention on side issues and scapegoats. Abortion and women's lib take the brunt of their reactionary ire. So their resistance has amounted to nothing of any value.

The union also has been unable to resist the growing influence of the corporation. Purged of its radical heart by anticommunism, the modern equivalent of the witch-hunt, and lacking a labor party to support it politically, the American labor movement is little more than business unionism. The business union means little to its member beyond its ability to push up wages and protect working conditions against corporate assault. It does not impart class solidarity to its members so it does not serve as a bulwark against the rise of corporate hegemony. It is even becoming less and less capable of reacting against corporate assaults on wages and conditions.

The church in America has adapted well to corporate hegemony. Faith, as purveyed by the pulpit, does not mean faith in the believer's fellow men and women. It does not mean faith in social progress through social action. It does not mean postive faith in a universal God. It means faith in each believer's personal God and faith in each believer's individual salvation. This faith in the doctrine of individual salvation is perfectly adapted to fulfilling the corporado's need for psychic security in a savagely competitive world. American faith is more a faith in individual salvation than a faith in the social gospel. Exceptions exist among some of the clerical staff of the established denominations and among some of the black clergy. Examples of a vital social gospel also come to us from Third World religious movements. Nonetheless, a social gospel strong enough to resist corporate hegemony has not yet sprung up in American religious circles. So far, those who have prophecied against or judged our corporate world have been cast out of the temple themselves. Douglas Roth was merely defrocked. Martin Luther King, Jr., was murdered.

The community in America has never been as strong as the community in Europe. Outside of the early Puritan communities, America has never really been a nation of communities. The land settlement pattern did not result in the formation of peasant village communities. Instead, it resulted in isolated farm families with scattered trading towns commercially preying upon them. The Industrial Revolution brought a wave of immigrants to work in the factories. The immigrants did form communities, and many of their ethnic communities survived. But they are not in the mainstream of American life, and the deindustrialization of the 1980s is destroying what remains of the ethnic community in America. Career values have largely replaced community values, and careers are made in the corporate world, not in the neighborhood world. The man and woman on the make do not make themselves in the neighborhood. So the community serves only poorly as an independent source of meaning and value. It only weakly resists the spread of corporate hegemony.

The ability of the state and the free press to resist seem weakened as well. The state, meaning the federal government in America, is a source of independent meaning and value. It is a source of patriotism. But the new patriotism of the post-Vietnam generation has been easily turned to corporate account. Under the Reagan administration a new formula for patriotism has been found. Other people fight our wars and other people pay for them. The corporate world benefits in two ways: first, by supplying weapons through lucrative Pentagon contracts; and second, by financing the weapons through underwriting the federal deficit. We now have a military-industrial-financial complex, and it grows fat sucking the juices of patriotic fervor. The lessons of Vietnam have been learned, after all, but far too well. The free press is still free, but the media that reaches the millions has gone soft under the leadership of the media managers. The alternative press is as lively and as ignored as ever.

So the formerly independent institutions of American pluralism are falling under the sway of corporate hegemony. Under the current dispensation, the opposing institutions seem enervated and virtually incapable of resistance.

6

Power Processes

Our true condition is that in relation to a complicated economic and social organization which we have not learned to control, most of us are factually servants, allowed the ordinary grades of upper, middle, and lower, insistent on the marks of these grades or resentful of them, but, keeping our bickering within its terms.

—Raymond Williams

FORMS OF RETREAT

We are moving into corporate hegemony because of serendipity, because of the blind drift of retreat, if you will. The corporate elite is not conspiring to take us there, even though a corporate elite exists and is very powerful.[1] Class conflict is not taking us there either, even though classes with conflicting interests clearly exist in the United States. These forces are important and have been crucial at one time or another in the course of events. But right now, and right here, the blind drift of retreat is taking us there. We like to think that we are in control, and we try mightily to determine our own fate, but at this particular juncture, a force beyond our control is moving us into corporate hegemony. That force takes on a different concrete form in each major institution. It takes the form of privatization in the state, reaction in the church, vocation in the school, truncation in the family, commercialization in the media, and trivialization in the culture itself. Each of these is the concrete form of retreat for that particular institutional sphere. Make no mistake about it—all U.S. institutions, save one, are in retreat.

State Privatization

Reeling from defeat in Vietnam, the disgrace of Watergate, and continued disdain for its welfare functions, the government is having its functions stripped from it in a broad movement called privatization. The first major federal government step in that direction was taken nearly fifty years ago when President Franklin D. Roosevelt decided to rely almost exclusively on private contractors to supply the weapons and material for the Second World War. Every war conducted by the federal government has had its share of private sector profiteers, but war contracting has become extraordinarily profitable now, what with the insatiable military appetite for very expensive, high-tech gadgetry. The use of private contractors rather than national armories is the largest single case of privatization. With the rise of private defense contractors, the government was stripped of its most important inherent function—the making of war, or the searching for peace.[2] Various corporate defense contractors, most of whom are giant conglomerates, now conspire with each other for lucrative contracts as they struggle against Congress and the taxpaying population for ever larger defense appropriations, which are justified by ever larger doses of public paranoia. Although war is the largest public function to be privatized, other functions are being stripped from the government as well. Privatization at the state level has taken an interesting turn. State prisons are on the verge of being turned into new corporate profit centers, as more states experiment with contracting out their prison populations to private corporations. After all, the free population has been tapped by corporations in every conceivable fashion. Why should the prison population be free from the corporation when the rest of us are not? Who *is* free, anyway?

Religious Reaction

While the government is privatizing, religion is sinking into reaction. Without a viable social gospel to give it the life and the fighting spirit it needs, religion in the United States is sinking into a deeply reactionary position. The popular churches are not acting as guiding forces of moral enlightenment. Instead, most churches are caught up in knee-jerk reactions to the fears of their parishioners. The deterioration of the family, the rise of spouse and child abuse, the strains of caring for elderly parents, the moral dilemma of abortion, the stress of divorce, and the pressures of unemployment and inadequate income are all very real forces tearing at the lives of congregations everywhere. Yet little moral guidance on these modern problems comes from the pulpit. Even worse, each time a fundamentalist makes a fool of himself over the issue of human evolution, religion loses more of its credibility for intelligent people. On the burning issue of feminism and equality, the popular churches are not staking out the high ground of moral principle. Instead, the religious are being pushed by their own fears into taking the lowground. Who could have guessed a few years ago that religious zealots would begin bombing hospitals and clinics? Each time someone detonates another antiabortion bomb, the church as a moral force dies a thousand deaths. This is not to deny the morality and nobility of thousands of committed churchmen and churchwomen in America. Their sacrifices are real and herioc. But, at least into the foreseeable future, the religious in the United States will probably remain in retreat.

Vocational Education

While religion in the United States is dying as a moral force, the school has been dead for years (except in the minds of paranoid fundamentalists who live in dread of secular humanism). The church has fallen victim to reaction; the school, to vocation. Unless our families teach us so—a very unlikely possibility in our careerist age—none of us learn that, "On the strength of . . . a strong will to achievement in some field, one can be an efficient or important, but never a good (kind) human being."[3] Furthermore, schools do not teach the value of artistic or intellectual pursuits. They are not supposed to do so. Such values are excess baggage to careerists. Instead, schools teach valued skills. They teach the skills valued by potential employers, not the skills valued by citizens, artists, or intellectuals. Schools also teach a kind of maudlin, degraded patriotism in the more truculent of times. But beyond that sort of thing, and with the exception of the truly gifted and committed teacher laboring on against all odds, the rest is a wasteland of vocationalism. The school has become merely an extension of the corporate personnel office. As such, it might as well be privatized along with other former government functions. Simple vocational skills fit for hirelings probably can be taught more efficiently by profit-seeking corporations than by the government anyway. Following the logic of corporate hegemony, the government should be stripped of the educational function by some kind of voucher system that contracts out to profit-maximizing, corporate Fagins, the training of promising young corporadoes. These for-profit institutions surely would not tolerate any inefficient youthful high jinks, frivolity, or free inquiry. The educational voucher has the further advantage of granting a subsidy to the upper-class parents of the "better" children who, on their way to leading roles in the corporate world, need to spend a few pleasantly expensive years in prep schools and Ivy League colleges. The voucher and the privatization of schooling represent democratic education in retreat.

Family Truncation

Along with the government, church, and school, the family is in retreat as well. The impoverished family has been ground down by poverty, so it no longer counts for much as a positive, independent cultural force. The middle-class family is counting for less and less, because it is being truncated, pruned way back. First, the middle-class father was removed by the attractions and compulsions (different sides of the same coin) of corporate career. Now the mother is being removed as well. Furthermore, the children are having their roles changed from that of family member to careerist. While the rich family has been largely exempt from truncation, and the working-class family has been protected to some extent by a limitation on the length of its workday, the middle-class family has borne the brunt of the corporate speedup, at least since the Second World War. Typically now, in the 1980s, both father and mother pour the substance of their life into their corporate careers rather than into their family roles. And so, typically, their middle-class families are truncated by their sacrifices, by their willing participation in their own exploitation by corporate capitalism. Marx theorized that the working class would be immiserated by the evolution of capitalism. However, in a curious twist, it is the middle class that has been immiserated, and in very novel ways. Rather than getting poorer in an absolute sense, the middle class has gotten poorer in its family relations and in the growing difference between its rising aspirations and its stagnating real income.

Media Commercialization

While all this was going on, the mass media, print and broadcast, lost its critical voice. Where once it roared bravely, now it squeeks meekly. In the 1980s commercialism has driven out journalism. But before it was able to do so, the journalists showed the mass media at its best. During the Vietnam War and the Watergate coverup, some U.S. journalists criticized their corrupt and imperialist government on the front page. Some broadcasters did the same on the evening news. War scenes and corruption were brought into the living room of every American home. They were electrifying. Unfortunately, they soon stopped. They were not censored. But the resulting libel suits were expensive, even though the media often won. The new media managers are timid. Critical journalism just cannot be justified to the corporate office in terms of its contribution to the bottom line. Besides, critical journalism is too hard to capitalize. To oversimplify a bit, what has happened is that the old individual publisher or broadcaster with his personal ax to grind has been replaced by a corporate behemoth with its bottom line to watch. More often than not, the axes the old individual publishers ground were profoundly reactionary. William Randolph Hearst and Col. Robert Rutherford McCormick were not progressives. But they were journalists. In spite of their faults, the values they espoused were sometimes as journalistic as they were commercial. That is not true of the new media manager. The new media manager is a purely commercial phenomenon.[4]

The Trivialization of Culture

The upshot of all of this retreating—of privatization, reaction, vocation, truncation, and commercialization—is the trivialization of all sources of culture in the United States, save one. The beliefs, values, and meanings of government, church, school, family, and media are in danger of becoming trivial. They are in danger of becoming inconsequential, when compared to the beliefs, values, and meanings of corporate life. When a former source of culture becomes trivial, it does not necessarily disappear into the woodwork. Often it continues to generate controversies and raise new issues. But the controversies lack a real cutting edge. Like our elections, they do not move people to take action. For example, creationism is an issue raised by the evangelicals in America. But, as a modern issue, it is as trivial as the question of whether the Earth is flat. Creationism is an extreme example of a trivial controversy raised by an institution pushed to the margin of American culture. The point is that as an institution is pushed to the margin of a culture, the controversies it raises and the issues it poses no longer challenge individuals in the mainstream of the culture to take positions and defend their beliefs and values. As more and more institutions retreat to the margins of the culture, individuals who participate in that culture are confronted with fewer real controversies; they are challenged by fewer real issues. So they have fewer and fewer opportunities to mold their own values and beliefs out of the controversies and issues they are forced to deal with. The only things they are forced to deal with are trivial. Trivial issues and trivial controversies are insufficient for us to mold our own character into that of a truly independent human adult.

To put some steel in us, we need real challenges. Unfortunately for us, our increasingly hegemonic culture does not provide the challenges once provided by a more pluralist culture. The greatest gift of pluralism is being lost, as most of our institutions retreat to the margins of our culture, leaving the mainstream to be dominated by a single institution—the corporation.

Dominating the center, as it does, the corporation is becoming the fountainhead of mainstream belief, meaning, and value. In addition to the widespread retreat of opposing institutions, four social processes have further solidified corporate power; emulation, contamination, subordination, and mystification have all contributed to corporate hegemony. All four of them are power processes that have expanded the cultural impact, the power, of the corporation. Emulation is seeking social standing through imitation. Emulation is imitation with envy. Contamination is replacing the motives of one role or institution with those from another role or institution. Contamination injects inappropriate motives into institutionalized roles. Subordination is raising one motive or meaning above another. Subordination subjects one institution or set of meanings to another institution or set of meanings. And mystification is confusing one set of meanings and symbols with another. Mystification makes corporate hegemony into free enterprise. The ways each of these processes works and the ways they affect our culture warrant careful explanation.

EMULATION

The Rationalization Myth

Max Weber, one of the most influential sociologists of the twentieth century and a very close student of organizations, argued that humans were rapidly rationalizing their world through a thorough application of the modern principles of organization to both the private and the public sectors. The modern organization, Weber argued, was based on bureaucracy—on the impersonal and rational application, by trained specialists, of formal rules to the achievement of specified goals. Modern organization, bureaucracy, was to apply to both the public agency and the private corporation. These modern organizations would replace the old-fashioned distinctions of honor and status, which used to result in inequality, strife, and inefficiency, with the formal bureaucratic distinctions based on measured performance and efficiency. The bureaucratic principle would promote rationality in all large-scale organizations. Rationally organized human activities would be the wellsprings of progress, banishing the outmoded, honorific behaviors that used to interfere with coordinated human action in pursuit of goals, or so Weber and most mainstream social scientists thought at the beginning of the twentieth century.[5] But in analyzing the impact of the organizational revolution, Weber underestimated the importance of emulation, particularly in corporate capitalism. Contrary to Weber's position, the organizational revolution did not reduce envy and spite. The bureaucratic organizational revolution actually increased envy and spite, particularly in the United States.

A bureaucratic organization unavoidably puts people into a finely graded system of ranks. Each rank fits into the well-known pyramid of authority or organizational chart shown in all the business management textbooks. Higher ranks supervise the lower ranks, making sure that the goals of the organization are achieved. This ranking of supervisional authority may help get the job done, but it also greatly aggravates the envy and spite of a business-oriented people, fresh from the individualism of the frontier. So the bureaucratic organization of business corporations greatly intensified emulation in America. Grouping individualistic careerists close together and putting them in ranks, particularly when they are out to make a buck for themselves in a business career, makes them more personally competitive and more acutely aware of gradations in status. The constant personal contact between rivals that occurs in corporate hierarchies has intensified emulation in an already envious people; and this has not made us more rational.

The Importance of Emulation

Emulation is of fundamental significance to pluralism because it eats away the separating walls so important to the theory and practice of pluralism. A pluralistic society is supposed to be composed of separate, independent institutions. Within each institutional sphere, participating individuals partake of and contribute to the values, beliefs, and meanings of that sphere. As long as the institutions are roughly coequal, the beliefs, meanings, and values of each can more or less coexist. But with the rise to preeminence of one institution, the individuals participating in all the different institutional spheres begin to take on the values, beliefs, and meanings of the one preeminent institution. Emulation facilitates this interpenetration because it allows a corporate leader to usurp leadership roles in other institutional spheres without the participants in those other spheres objecting. Although they lack expertise in other areas of life, successful corporate leaders can use the aura of status that surrounds them as leaders in the corporate sphere of life to support them in other leadership roles. Because high-level businessmen are emulated by those in all walks of life, clergy, educators, government officials, and family members accept the status claims of a corporate leader, even in noncorporate affairs. The acceptance of status claims is not reciprocated, however. This last point is extremely important. Emulation is a strictly one-way relation. For example, while a high-level educator would feel very hesitant about telling a high-level businessman to mind his own business, particularly if the businessman is a contributor to the endowment; a high-level businessman would feel far less status anxiety in doing so to a high-level educator, even though the educator supplies the businessman with needed employees.

Another way to look at the corrosive effect of emulation is to note that corporate leaders can give advice to anyone they choose. And, of course, they do so freely—witness the predominance of businessmen on presidential advisory commissions, university governing boards, church boards, and the various philanthropic boards. Furthermore, although businessmen give advice to everybody else, they accept advice only from other businessmen. The token representation of clergy and educators on the boards of directors of large corporations is merely the exception that proves the rule. Nonreciprocity in emulation allows the corporate institutional sphere to penetrate the other institutional spheres while remaining inviolate itself.

Those who think that American society is still pluralist go to great lengths to separate wealth, power, and status *in theory,* as if doing so would keep us safe *in fact* from the emerging corporate hegemony.[6] But emulation ties all three together. That is, emulation makes the power of the wealthy legitimate and the wealth of the powerful respectable by inducing the ambitious among us to admire them both. So emulation protects the use of corporate power by cloaking it with the status of legitimacy, thus turning raw corporate power into accepted authority. Emulation also protects the accumulation of corporate wealth by admiring it, thus turning the spoils of power into the fruits of enterprise. Emulation is the strongest integrating force working on our culture. Unfortunately, the first major social scientist to explain the integrative effect of emulation on American culture, Thorstein Veblen, did so in a writing style so droll that after reading him, it is hard to take emulation seriously. His *Theory of the Leisure Class,* published first in 1899, is a literary classic and is still widely read as the definitive statement on emulation in American culture.[7] "Conspicuous consumption" and other phrases from it have become standard parts of the language. But rather than just something to snicker at, emulation gives the lie to the pluralist picture of America.

Not only does emulation allow the corporation to break through the walls of other institutional orders without reprisal, and to integrate all three forms of social standing—wealth, power, and status—into an impressive whole, but it allows the corporation to recruit and coopt into its lower ranks a steady stream of highly ambitious and highly talented young blood from whichever institutional spheres of life or social strata it desires. The young man or woman on the make admires and envies the successful corporate executive, not the politician, the clergy, or the teacher, and certainly not the housewife. However, many young Americans admire rock groups and athletes more than they do corporate executives. Here lies another glimmer of hope, of sorts.

Nevertheless, emulation penetrates so deeply into our culture that it poisons the simple things in life. Not even Thoreau and his *Walden* would be exempt from the effects of emulation. Were he alive, his gardening technique would be sold in serial form to women's magazines, his little cabin would be duplicated all over upstate New York and New Hampshire, and he would be besieged by new commercial offers night and day. His picture would be on the covers of *Time* and *Newsweek* simultaneously, making him a celebrity for fifteen minutes. The simple, contemplative life has become virtually impossible for any self-respecting American. The hippies were the last ones to try it seriously and look what happened to them: their clothes were turned into high fashion, their hair became a smash Broadway musical, their slang became high English, their neuroses became the stuff of avant-garde psychology, their recreational drugs became the cutting edge of consciousness, and their symbols of rebellion became cultural icons. After the hippies, even status-seeking Muscovites wear blue jeans. So hungry is this world of hirelings for new things to emulate and so boring is this world of corporate conformists, that any simple act of creative living will be immediately snapped up and commercialized, and all of the fun will be completely emulated out of it forever. The best example of the emulative dry rot is in physical fitness. The simple, creative act of being more physically comfortable with oneself by cutting out cigarettes and drugs and by getting some fresh air and exercise has turned into a fitness mania. Smokers, in addition to drug users, now face legal sanctions and social ostracism. And while participation in health clubs, spas, and diets is becoming mandatory for everyone, joggers and bikers have taken over our sidewalks. World-class athletes gobble steroids like candy, to get just a little more out of their already overdeveloped bodies.

Emulation has even touched our debauchery. You cannot just roll one of your own, light up, pass it around, and get stoned. Before you do, you must finish an elaborate, emulative ceremony. First you have to discuss the genetic origins of your grass, describing how and where it was grown: indoors or out, artificial or natural light, and what kind of soil, trying all along to impress everyone with the quality of you cannabis and with the stylishly advanced nature of your personal knowledge of drugs. Next you must state whether it came from a male or a female plant, and compare it, invidiously, to the local, national, and international varieties available at the time. Only then will people consider having a hit with you. But after all that, the thrill is gone. For those who prefer legal drugs, getting drunk on cheap wine is now out of the question, even for the lower classes. For all but the destitute, wine drinking has become a highly competitive sport, complete with specialized magazines, newspaper columnists, wine-tasting classes, and snobbery raised to the nth degree. With wine in permanent decline, beer swilling is being ruined by imported brands, and hard liquor is running against the grain of the physical fitness craze. No wonder people are drying out and going straight. The fun is gone from drinking and drugs. They are both too competitive.

So, of course, now the detox centers and rehab programs are being redesigned for the emulative. What with the wife of one former president opening up her own substance abuse center for rich and famous alcohol and drug abusers (Betty Ford), and the wife of another former president visiting substance abuse centers to sell them and herself on national television (Nancy Reagan), the repentant abusers are all paying $400 a day to dry out in the proper style. Pity the old-time ex-junkie who has turned straight and just wants to help others do the same. He has no one to help. They are all tastefully straightening themselves out at high-brow drug centers, rubbing elbows with the elite, getting on national television with Nancy Reagan, and crowding out the honest, simple abuser who just wants to quit. Drinking and drug use will never be the same again. Because of emulation, even recreational drug use has become a competitive pastime for middle-class climbers, and visits to expensively stylish detox centers have become symbols of arrival. The spreading drug phenomenon in America shows the strength of emulation and the relative weakness of advertising in the shaping of American culture. For it is emulation, not advertising, that has led to the widespread use of illegal drugs.

The spreading drug phenomenon also shows something about the U.S. labor movement. Labor leaders are not joining hands with their membership in the name of national sanity and class solidarity to overthrow their drug-crazed masters. Instead, in the name of progress, the most aggressive trade unions are pushing for insurance coverage of detoxing at substance abuse centers in their collective bargaining contracts. The labor leadership is eager for their membership to share in all the good things in life. So, of course, is the membership. It does not want to transform the way of life, but to have more of it for itself. Labor is striving mightily not to be left behind in the mad emulative scramble. Emulation is the American way. Emulation, not sanity, and certainly not class solidarity, shapes the folkways of the U.S.A.

Emulation's Impact on the Institutional Order

Emulation does more than just poison the folkways. It also distorts the entire institutional order by forging it into hegemony rather than plurality. Emulation makes the corporate leader's prestige count in noncorporate institutions, insuring corporate domination of the noncorporate world. Businessmen have long tried to buy their way into positions of respect and power outside of their own narrow fields of activity. Nevertheless, like gangsters, they have found it difficult to *buy* status in the eyes of those outside the business. However, with the rising prestige of corporate leadership roles, the position of the businessmen occupying those roles has changed fundamentally vis-à-vis those outside the business world. Now corporate leadership roles can be used to transform their occupants' high standing in the corporate world into equally high standing in the noncorporate world. The emulative transference of role status can do what money alone cannot—give a businessman the same status and power outside his business world as he has attained inside it.

In the educational sphere, the emulative transference of role status allows corporate leaders to assume leadership roles in the schools. For example, when educational leaders at the national or state level desire a new direction in education, they often turn to corporate leadership to provide it. In 1985 when the state of Texas tried to develop new directions in education, it turned for leadership to H. Ross Perot, founder and former CEO of the old Electronic Data Systems Corporation (EDS was acquired by General Motors, along with Hughes Aircraft, in a major diversification move in 1985). So too, apparently, has the United States Post Office turned to Perot.[8] Corporate leaders always dominate the governing boards of universities and colleges, even state ones, giving a decidedly corporate flavor to university fiscal affairs. Corporate domination goes beyond the fiscal office into the curriculum itself. Business schools are the most notorious, being little more than vocational training centers for corporate-bound youth. Of course, most colleges and universities, when accused of shortchanging the educational needs of their students by selling out to corporate vocational interests, point with indignation to their liberal arts traditions and programs. The trouble is that most students avoid the liberal arts, enrolling primarily in the business school.

Even in the pure liberal arts college with no business school at all, corporate vocationalism is advancing rapidly in the form of runaway enrollment in the college's economics department. In such instances, the economics department capitalizes on its new-found emulative popularity by offering mostly vocational courses of a decidedly business school nature, like accounting, marketing, management, and finance. When a true economics course is offered, like micro, macro, or development, its content is often distorted. The content of many economics courses has been influenced, more or less for two decades now, by the Joint Council on Economic Education. The Joint Council is a corporate dominated group that funds workshops, seminars, and curriculum guides for economics teachers all over the country.[9] The substance of its workshops, seminars, and curriculum guides is free enterprise, pollyanna economics. It is boringly upbeat, optimistic, American, and pro-business. The course content is dished out as if it were the result of rigorous scientific investigation. While dishing it out, many instructors surround themselves with a false aura of scientific objectivity, referring to the laws of supply and demand as if they were the equivalent of the laws of physics. And, though many are poor mathematicians, they speak a language of mathematical rigor.

Some teachers of economics have resisted this corruption of the discipline with great courage and imagination. Theirs has been a valiant but losing battle. When forced to do battle with the objectivity of science, the rigor of mathematics, and the prestige of the corporate executive, the simple honesty of the schoolmarm and intellectual integrity of the college prof are outclassed. In the educational sphere of institutions, the struggle is being lost to corporate emulation.

In the religious sphere of institutions, many American churches have long been dominated by the business animus, if not by the businessman himself. Among the smaller churches, most of which are constantly on the verge of financial collapse, church leaders must be more businessmen than churchmen. Survival requires financial, not spiritual ability. Here the effects of emulation are the strongest. The television and radio churches are organized on a business basis from the very beginning. They buy airtime to deliver a spiritual service over the public airways, and they solicit a monetary payment for it in return. If what they pay for the airtime and their solicitation and related expense is less than what they receive from those they solicit, they earn a profit. If they prosper, they soon diversify into additional products and services. Oral Roberts, for example, has so far invested in a hospital, a university, and a retirement real estate community. Now he can birth them in his hospital, book them in his university, and bunk them in his retirement village, all the time while he continues to save them on his television show. His is a vertically integrated ministry with a diversified portfolio run by an inspired businessman (himself).

Churchmen on the make long have emulated successful businessmen, distorting the church as they did so, giving it that Elmer Gantry flavor so unique to American spiritual life. But interestingly enough, unlike the role transference in education, high-status corporate leaders have seldom tried to transform their high business status into equally high status in the religious field. Instead of corporate leaders turning their status to account in the church by becoming leading churchmen, leading churchmen have increased their own status by becoming leading businessmen while remaining churchmen, at least in name. So the distortion of religious life in America has been done by the churchmen themselves, with little direct transference into the religious field by corporate executives. Not all churchmen and churchwomen have participated in this degradation of their roles. Many have bravely resisted, but to little avail.

In the governmental sphere of institutions, the impact of emulation has been obvious. While the status of corporate managers has been raised by emulation, the status of government officials has been reduced. So when the government needs decisive action or new direction, corporate leaders, not government ones, are tapped to provide it. When the government wants to save money, for example, the president of the United States does not call on the leaders of government agencies to determine what is to be done. Instead, he asks corporate executives to form a commission and draft a report for use in attacking the very government it was aimed to help. (The Grace Commission and its catalogue of suggestions to dismantle or cut back the welfare state is the most prominent example from the 1980s.) Privatization is another example of the mindless denigration of government combined with the mindless emulation of the corporation: when government at the national, state, or local level needs to step up its efficiency, the government level involved does not improve its own operations. That would be too obvious. Instead, it just sells the operations. That is, it resorts to privatization—to selling off the right to perform public functions to private corporations. This, in our mindless age, allegedly raises the efficiency of the auctioned-off functions. Because of emulation, we think anything done by a private corporation is done more efficiently than if it were done by a government entity.

In an earlier mindless age, the French king, before the 1789 Revolution, was also in the habit of privatizing many of his functions by selling them in the form of rights to private investors. After all, it was the prerevolutionary French economists, the Physiocrats, and not Adam Smith, who first invented laissez-faire. In an early French experiment that blended privatization with monetary quackery, the king even sold the government's right to coin money to a private speculator, John Law, who promptly ruined the currency.[10] This historical episode, unknown by most contemporary economists, foreshadowed the outcome of the more recent American experiment of a like nature, which also mixed monetary quackery (monetarism) with privatization (supply-side economics). Privatization in France certainly raised the short-term revenues of the Crown, giving it temporary help in reducing its growing deficits. The practice seemed to reach a peak right before the French Revolution, during which the king lost his head. The relations between privatization, monetary quackery, deficits, laissez-faire economists, regicide, and revolution are all quite complex and problematic. And far be it from me to suggest that history can repeat itself, particularly if we are ignorant of it. Nevertheless, emulation has blinded us to the folly of making government work better by dismantling it and auctioning off the pieces.

In the family institutional sphere, emulation has distorted the women's liberation movement, just like it earlier distorted the men's labor movement. It has blinded both to the importance of family. It has attracted both men and women on the make, drawing them away from the narrow confines of family-imposed tradtions with the promises of a corporate career. For women, the forward attraction of corporate career has proved stronger than the backward drag of sex stereotyping. So for women, corporate career has been a mixed blessing. On the positive side, the possibility of a corporate career has provided many middle-class women with an alternative role to play as they free themselves from the stultifying sex stereotypes imposed upon them by the traditional patriarchal family. But on the negative side, which far outweighs the positive side, the emulative attraction of corporate career has turned the women's liberation movement, like the labor movement before it, toward the traditional careerist goal of more for me. In search of more for me, the energies and imaginations of women are turned to corporate account rather than family account. Women are trying to teach men how to work with them on an equal footing in managerial roles when they could be teaching men how to grow with them in familial roles. Men, and now women too, are inventing new products for corporate marketing when they might be inventing new roles for living together. Talented men and women are designing new personnel programs for huge corporations when they might be designing new types of families. We will never have enough creative ways of living together as loving human beings, but we have enough manipulative personnel programs. Men, and now women too, are designing better ways of making things when they might have been designing better ways of raising people. We have enough things, if only they were shared more equally, but we can never have enough loving people. Emulation in the form of corporate careerism has meant major opportunities lost in the art of living together in exchange for minor opportunities in the scramble to get promoted before your rival. It removed men and then women from the home, weakening not just the patriarchal home, but the caring and nurturing home too, the one that men and women should be trying to construct together.

To sum up, emulation has touched every major American institution in a way that has always raised the status of the corporation and its roles above the status of alternative institutions and their roles. The result has been a strengthening of corporate hegemony.

CONTAMINATION

In addition to emulation, corporate totalitarianism is made more powerful by contamination. The spread of motives originating in one institutional sphere to another institutional sphere is contamination. The two processes, emulation and contamination, are closely related because emulation promotes contamination. When people from different institutional spheres emulate the leaders of one particular institutional sphere, they adopt the motives of the emulated leaders, whether or not those motives are appropriate in walks of life different from the one being emulated. If everyone emulated corporate executives, then the motives of corporate executives would seep into the church, the school, the state, and the family. Then, even if corporate motives would be very destructive when pursued by, say, clergy and educators, corporative motives would still contaminate the church and the school. This is precisely what has happened, but beyond just the church and the school. Corporate motives have contaminated all walks of life: church, school, government, family.

Contamination of the School

Educational institutions—the school, for short—labor under a double burden. Not only is the school in the United States contaminated by the corporation, but it is also contaminated by an agency of the state. It is also contaminated by the military. The military motive is an aggressive patriotism. My country, right or wrong, is the military's motto. It is also, to greater or lesser degree, the school's motto. But it is usually very subtle. So in classes on civics or current events, for example, if students study the international intelligence community at all, they do so in terms that prejudge the issues. They read about how U.S. intelligence specialists are needed to deal with communist spies. They do not read that Soviet intelligence specialists are needed to deal with capitalist spies, unless they are reading a Soviet textbook in the U.S.S.R. To the extent that military contamination has been effective, free inquiry—the educational motive—takes a backseat to patriotism—the military motive. That extent varies from school to school. Generally speaking, schools with a more authoritarian atmosphere and more traditional curriculum, discipline, and grades, are more contaminated with a truculent patriotism than are the less authoritarian and less traditional.[11]

Patriotism in small doses is not fatal to free inquiry in schools. After all, it often plays an important role in maintaining support for adequate state funding. The same is true of vocationalism—the corporate motive in education. It too helps maintain financial support for schools. But keeping the doses of patriotism and vocationalism small enough to do little harm is difficult. Schools react to them as if they were addictive drugs, with a built-in tendency toward ever larger doses. This is strikingly true of vocationalism during periods of high unemployment, because students and their parents, particularly the ones who count—the middle-class ones—see good schools as career-priming machines. When middle-class parents fear that their children will be unemployed and, therefore, remain at home for a good part of their lives, the parents cannot get enough vocational education in the schools. The same is not true of the growing under class. Rising unemployment seems to mobilize the middle class to seek more vocational training; but it seems to demobilize the underclass, leading to massive dropping out from school. Rising unemployment has little effect on the upper class, as its members are not directly dependent on income from work.

The U.S. school is deeply contaminated with vocationalism, with the desire to get a good job and a good start on a corporate career. At the very least, vocationalism leads to the premature tracking of high school students into either the pre-college track or into the non-college track. This marks the non-college track student for lower-paying occupations. At the very worst, vocationalism crowds everything else out of the school, leaving the school little more than the crude Rube Goldberg career primer described in Chapter 3. Then the school ceases to exist as a school and becomes an extension of the corporate personnel office. As such, it comes to serve a private purpose at public expense. As such, it functions as a subsystem within the larger system of corporate hegemony. It has turned the school from pursuing inquiry to pursuing career.

Contamination of the Church

Contamination may have pushed corporate motives deepest into the school, but it has touched the church as well. Religion is big business in the United States; exactly how big is impossible to tell. Contributions to the top forty U.S. churches totaled over $10.9 billion in 1982, with the giant Southern Baptist Conference accounting for $3.1 billion itself.[12] No trustworthy estimate of total U.S. church wealth or income exists, though total wealth must be in the hundreds of billions of dollars and total income must be in the tens of billions.[13] Since church income and wealth are largely untaxed, none of the municipalities, states, or federal agencies makes a cataloguing of church assets. And unlike other nonprofit organizations, to qualify for their federal nonprofit status, religious organizations rarely have to report or account for their financial practices to the IRS.

The degree of church contamination by corporate motives is not measured by the extent of church wealth, however. Instead, contamination, or the lack thereof, is indicated by the goals pursued by churchmen. The evangelists are the most contaminated because they are the least financially secure of churchmen. Unfortunately, they also typify U.S. churchmen. Their roots go back to the traveling salesman and the medicine show. Like their forebears, they must diligently pursue the almighty dollar in order to stay on the air or on the road. If they are the old-fashioned, camp-meeting, traveling revivalists, they must pay their traveling expenses from what they can collect at each revival meeting. Theirs can be a hard life, lived close to the vest. No mercy is shown potential contributors, when mercy is a luxury, and the bus needs a new engine. The lowest of the traveling evangelists have to work the dwindling stock of rural fears and superstitions for all they are worth. In fact, the pure traveling evangelist is a vanishing breed, put out of business by new communications technology. Billy Graham and his associated crusaders probably represent the best and the last of the traveling breed. Even though he likes his expensive suits and his coiffured hair, Billy Graham probably is less contaminated with pursuit of the almighty dollar than those traveling evangelists who are less well-financed and less well-connected. He is less contaminated because he can financially afford to cut himself some spiritual slack. Graham has also managed to be a cross-over artist. He has crossed over into broadcast evangelism, a more lucrative field.

There he competes with the true masters of the new communications technology, the spiritual impresarios of broadcast mass media, God's electronic entrepreneurs. In the 1980s, the king of the broadcast evangelists is Pat Robertson of the 700 Club and the Christian Broadcasting Network. The crown prince—or maybe the court jester—is Jerry Falwell of the Moral Majority and the Old-Time Gospel Hour. The triumphs and tragedies of broadcast evangelism are played on a much larger stage than those of the traveling evangelists. So the business expenses are much greater. Air time is costly. Production budgets soar. Putting together a religious program with the accompanying plea for contributions represents a major capital investment for the businessman–evangelist. When he is starting out in the business, he must be a real risk taker, a true entrepreneur, because at first he cannot be certain of the returns of his investment in the production and broadcast of a show. He must trust God and the new communications technology. The new communications technology has transformed evangelism into a sophisticated, high-stakes, high-tech business that is run by people with full-blown business motives.

These high-tech preachers want the same thing that corporate executives want, and they are willing to do the same things to get what they want. They want wealth, power, and status. And they are willing to invest their supporters' money and to risk their own status in their business venture of delivering religion to people in their homes via radio and television. The broadcast evangelist, the most powerful spiritual force in the United States, and the most uniquely American religious leader, differs very little from the typical corporate owner and corporate executive in motives. He is thoroughly contaminated. So the broadcast evangelist offers no independent source of resistance to corporate values. He offers no independent, critical reappraisal of the corporate world. He offers no alternative spiritual meaning to life. He does not preach the social gospel and he will not be found among the ranks of the liberation theologists. At his worst, he offers scapegoats and superstitions, sidetracking the religious from partaking of far more substantial spiritual fare and making a mockery of the faith he proclaims, and doing it right in the living rooms of the multitudes. At his best, he offers individual solace to his viewers. But anyway you look at him, he is the high-tech future of religion in corporate capitalism.[14]

Contamination of the Family

The school and church show deep contamination with corporate motives, and so does the family—the middle-class one, that is. In the school it takes the form of vocationalism; in the church it takes the form of high-tech evangelism; and in the middle-class family it takes the form of careerism, both vicarious and actual. Vicarious careerism is the malignant form, which manifests itself in the parents who try to achieve through their children the career success that eluded them in their own lives. Actual careerism largely takes the form of benign neglect. Parents actually obsessed with their own careers simply do not have enough time for their children or spouses. So children and spouses are ignored rather than infected. But in either case, the careerist family member has adopted a motive inappropriate to the family sphere of life, allowing the corporation to contaminate the family with foreign motives of wealth, power, and status. And yet, except for the most career-oriented families, the family values of love, sharing, and responsibility can prove to be remarkably resilient, providing some with a desperately needed harbor in a corporate sea.

In the case of vicarious careerism, parents who either never had the chance to pursue a career or were less successful than they wished to be, infect their children with a strong drive to succeed where they failed. The parents can then relive their own lives through their children, or so they try. The results are often monstrous, particularly for the child. Pushed and prodded by their parents during their childhood and all through school and university, they become grim overachievers who fill every waking hour of their lives with work or study. And their very grimness and single-mindedness usually precludes the career success they burn for. So they burn out. Hyde Park, around the University of Chicago, is full of these victims of vicarious careerism. Around Hyde Park, they form a lumpen professoriate, dropouts from the graduate school who have no place to go. Vicarious careerism is best known in the form of the mother who pushes her daughter into a stage career, sometimes to the mutual destruction of mother and daughter. But stage careers being rare and corporate careers plentiful, this little tragedy is played out more frequently in the corporate world than anywhere else.

In the case of actual as opposed to vicarious careerism, parents have little time left over from their work, usually for the corporation. When only the father was a corporado, the mother usually tried to cover for him and do her share as well. But now with the mother a corporado too, ambitious, middle-class parents have little contact with their children at all. This is a more healthy arrangement for the children than vicarious careerism. In fact, it may be one of the few bright spots in the corporate contamination of American institutions. If they are left to their own devices by both parents for long enough, and if they are not devoured by street life or authoritarian educators, the latchkey children of the 1980s might be the rebels of the 1990s.

Contamination of the State

Contamination of the state by the corporation is obvious in the lobbying, deregulating, campaign financing, bribing, bid rigging, contract jobbing, and influence peddling that goes on daily at all levels—federal, state, and local. This form of state contamination is corruption, and it is so common in the United States that we have come to accept a certain amount of it as unavoidable.[15] State contamination also takes the form of privatization. Privatization is not just a case of reversing an earlier socialization of the means of production. It is not just selling back a previously nationalized railroad to a private speculator after refurbishing the railroad at public expense. That sort of thing is bad enough, but privatization involves far more than that. It involves the amputation of essential governmental functions. Privatization is a potlatch spectacle whereby pieces of the state are ceremonially auctioned off to the highest bidder. So through a thousand weeping wounds of corruption and privatization, the state is infected by a thousand sucking mouths, in a thousand revolting spectacles, repeated daily all over the land, in full view of the children.

Contamination also occurs in a subtle way. Plato established the ideal for the state in his *Republic*. It was justice, and it was our ideal for the state for two thousand years. But efficiency has become more important than justice. Efficiency is a question of money, of revenues minus costs. Efficiency is a corporate concept, a question of net gain or loss. Justice, however, is of sterner stuff. Justice is a concern for truth and beauty. Justice is the age-old question of virtue itself. Justice holds the polity together, giving it enduring life and vitality. This is not to say the polity should be inefficient. Gross inefficiency would grind it to a halt. Nevertheless, while men will water the just state with their lifeblood; they will only pay their taxes to the efficient state, and that begrudgingly. Efficiency can be ugly, false, mindless, and cruel. Justice cannot. The Nazis efficiently murdered millions of Jews by gassing them. That could never have happened in a just state, but it did happen in an efficient state. Factories need to be efficient. States need to be just. But the contamination of the state with the motive of the corporation has blinded most of us to the simple difference between the two.

In sum, all of our basic institutions have been contaminated by the corporation. Schools perform career training functions or patriotic indoctrination, not education. Churchmen, particularly the uniquely American ones—the evangelists—pursue the almighty dollar as avidly and with the same high-tech fervor as the corporadoes. Families, particularly those of middle-class careerists, reflect the motives of corporate career. And the state is corrupted, privatized, and made more efficient. None of our basic institutions seem to have motives strong enough to resist their own contamination with motives from corporate life.

SUBORDINATION

Subordination links the weakened institutions of church, school, state, and family to the strengthened corporation. It subjects them to a new kind of feudalism. As pluralism is dying out and hegemony reviving, all other institutions are being subordinated to the corporation. Subordination turns their ends into corporate means in a hierarchical ordering of institutional means and ends. The ends of noncorporate institutions get reduced down to the level of mere corporate means. At the same time, corporate ends get raised above all others. Corporate power, wealth, and status become cultural imperatives. As they do, the purposes of noncorporate institutions lose their independent meaning. The church, state, school, and family are demeaned as independent cultural entities. The other institutions come to mean something, if they mean anything, in terms of the corporation. If it's possible, their meaning is reconstructed in reference to the corporation. They either become corporate satelites or they fly off into the void. This is the meaning of innovation for the leader of an outlying institution—the innovator re-shapes his institution so that it will fit into the new corporate dispensation. To save his institution and himself from becoming irrelevant, he must make it and himself relevant to the new corporate world. He must make himself and his institution useful to the corporation.

Subordination of the School

The U.S. school has never meant much as a purely educational institution. Idle curiosity and free inquiry have been more or less tolerated, but schools in the United States have always meant something else, something far more important to the main drift of the culture than free inquiry. For the early Puritans and other Protestants, schools meant places to learn to read the bible. Schools also meant places to train ministers. Most Ivy League colleges were founded for that explicit purpose. To latter-day educators, Horace Mann and others, school meant a place to train citizens and to Americanize immigrants. To military leaders, both early and late, school has always meant a place to inculcate patriotism and respect for authority. To corporate leaders, school is a place to train new workers and managers. Only to a few cranky educators—John Dewey being the most notable—has school meant free inquiry.[16] So the schoolteacher has had to serve many masters. Today she serves a corporate one, and behind him, a military one. She might also have to serve a religious leader if the fundamentalist Protestant and conservative Catholic fear of secular humanism in the schools becomes widespread.

The corporate subordination of the school has been easy, since the school was never strongly independent in the first place. The burdens of vocational training rest easy on most educators' shoulders. The major difficulties en-countered in subordinating the schools have had to do with which level of corporate work a particular school or curriculum track should serve and with how to choose the particular students and teachers needed to fit into those tracks or schools. Emulation and the accompanying obsession with status has made it hard to get some students and their parents to accept the lower, noncollege curriculum track or school. I.Q. scores and college en-trance exams come in handy. They enable educators to avoid making the crucial decision themselves. All the educator has to do is determine the needed cutoff point in the distribution of I.Q. and entrance exam scores. Students can then be informed of their fate by formal letter and science can be used to back up the decision. Of course, science has nothing to do with it. The results are determined by socioeconomic class. The upper class scores high and goes to college. The lower class scores low and does not. A few middle-class students, particularly black ones or brown ones, make for hard choices, but no system of discrimination is perfect.

Some teachers and some schools, particularly at the college and university levels, resist assignment to the lower level of training as well. Most schools serve a student body and a corporate training niche determined by long tradition. But new schools are occasionally founded and some schools become upstarts under the persistent goading of ambitious leaders. At the school level, this leads to much rivalry and duplication of effort. The new schools and the upstart schools are constantly jostling each other and the established schools for better position. Programs are duplicated and vast sums are spent on advertising and public relations, much of it in the form of college sports. The established schools are drawn into the rivalry to protect their positions. The physical result of educational competition is massive waste due to duplication and puffery; the intellectual result is severe distortion of the educational tenor of the United States into the hysterical boosterism encountered at football games between rival small-town teams.

Rivalry between teachers, particularly at the college and university levels, makes academic life more petty than corporate life. It also results in a mountain of worthless "research." The more articles published in refereed journals, the more likely that a job in a higher-level university will be snagged by the research careerist, the academic equivalent of the corporate careerist. So thousands of articles are written and hundreds of editors are cajoled into publishing them, not so much because the writers have something important to say, but because they need more publications on their résumés. Students are ignored and other duties shirked in order to crank out another status-raising article that will be published in a refereed journal that nobody reads, not even the referees.

Research careerists are just as busy as corporate careerists, and they both do extensive damage to themselves and to those around them in their lust for career success. Being preoccupied with all their busywork, and being ambitious, they are easily subordinated. They take the easy way with their teaching by accepting the frightened vocationalism of their students. Teaching twenty-year-olds what they think they need for a job is easy and financially rewarding. Academics on the make take the easy way with their research as well. Getting funds for research of interest to the corporate world or to a particularly powerful subset of the corporate world, the military-industrial complex, is easy. So ambitious young academics, rather than do their own research, do corporate or military research, and are highly rewarded for it. Of course, in the process, teaching free inquiry and doing free inquiry get pushed off the academic agenda because academe has been subordinated. Having been turned to corporate account, education itself counts for little. Education is only valued for what it brings in the corporate world.

Subordination of the Family

Self-appointed advocates for the family abound in America. Everyone from the president down to the poorest tenant of the Chicago Housing

Authority notes the decline of the traditional family. They are descriptively correct. The traditional family is declining on a broad front. For the disadvantaged, poor black tenant of the Chicago Housing Authority, the traditional family is dead. Poverty and unemployment killed it. Even Ronald Reagan's family was severely wounded. The pull of separate careers is even felt by presidents. Reagan's own Hollywood divorce left two badly divided sets of children and loyalties. Christmas Eve at the Reagan White House was not a family affair. Nor is it in the apartments of the Chicago Housing Authority. So the decline is felt from the very top to the very bottom of American society. Debt and falling prices plague the family farm, as they have done on and off for a century or more. And although the biggest pressures are now exerted on the middle class, the lower-class family having already collapsed, no level is completely exempt.

Who dares attack the American family? What villain is to blame? A hue and cry can be heard all across the land. The culprit must be found and run to Earth. Politicians blame the welfare system and threaten to force poor (black) families to stand on their own two feet by taking away the only financial support they have. But not to worry, for according to the sadistically self-righteous, hardship strengthens the spirit. It teaches the less righteous the importance of getting out of the welfare-dependency trap set for them by devious welfare bureaucrats and ignorant liberals. The poor family, if freed from government interference, will pull itself up by its own bootstraps.[17] (Of course, it has no boots to begin with.)

The preachers, particularly those of the Moral Majority, have also found the culprits. They have run to ground the villains who would destroy the American family, who would subvert motherhood. The villains are secular humanism and evolutionary theory in the schools, and they must be ripped out, root and branch. It will take the great courage and moral strength of men like Jerry Falwell to do so, but replacement with prayer and the Christian belief in creationism will reestablish family strengths and values in American society. The villains are also the women's liberation movement with its support for abortion and the gay rights movement with its support for sodomy. These subversive movements also must be destroyed, root and branch. Or so supporters of the Moral Majority sincerely believe.

Their desire to defend their children and families from a perceived threat is to be commended. Their willingness to stand up for their values, in face of what they perceive to be widespread ridicule and contempt, is also to be commended. Although they create scapegoats, they have courage and purpose. But they will not save the family as they know it. They are failing to address the real problem of the family. The real problem is that the family has been subordinated to the economy, to the capitalist corporation. The subordination is not complete, for the family is a resilient institution. Nonetheless, the family now serves corporate ends as a career central. The family is more the social space where careers are coordinated than it is an independent sphere of life. The young people get the financing and guiding needed to start their careers from the family. Active careerists seek solace and encouragement from the family. Corporate leaders conjure up images of the family to encourage greater work effort and loyalty. So the family still exists for the great middle class, but it exists as something of use and meaning to the corporate world. It is used by the young as a bank and by the old as an insurance policy. More and more, the U.S. family is coming to resemble a combination financial intermediary and union business agent more than it resembles an ancient human institution. It could be replaced by a highly efficient combination of artificial insemination, in vitro incubation, and cleverly programmed personal computer. Such a replacement certainly is needed because it could exercise tight surveillance over the children, eliminating from the family sphere of life even the remotest possibility of insubordination.

Insubordination in the family sphere is at least a possibility because, left to their own devices, the young may take counsel together and attempt another youthful rebellion against the roles adults want them to play.[18] Of course, if the youth band together just to share recreational drugs, beat each other up, and engage in other juvenile amusements, no system-threatening rebellion will take place. Nevertheless, the system is less secure because subordinating the family to the corporation has removed the parents from the family circle. And this parental absence leaves a gap in the social conditioning process, not completely filled by early careerism in school. This gap is even wider now than it was in the 1960s because most mothers were still at home during the first outbreak of youthful resistance. They could at least attempt to rein in their children. Now, most mothers are at work. The potential for insubordination is correspondingly greater. A glimmer of hope exists.

Subordination of the Church

The burning ambition of the most prominent churchmen in America, the electronic evangelists, has made them eager to serve the powers that be. Since those powers are corporate, the evangelists have subordinated their preaching to the needs of corporate hegemony. Their self-righteous wrath is always directed at safe targets. With great courage, they attack Arab terrorists, homosexuals, and radical feminists. They never attack corporate price-fixers, corporate lobbyists, or corporate polluters. With much noise and self-congratulation, they point out the evils of communism, atheism, and secular humanism. They never mention capitalism, imperialism, sexism, racism, or careerism. They never attack the powerful. In short, they direct the fears and frustrations of their followers into safe channels.

The corporation's rise to power has wrought profound changes in U.S. culture, changing family, church, and state. The changes have been mainly for the worse, when viewed from the pluralist ideal. And U.S. churchmen have helped defuse the popular response to those changes. Rather than our spiritual leaders turning against the most materialistic of all human institutions, the corporation, they have turned against its critics. In a curious twist, spiritual spokesmen in the United States do not criticize the materialistic corporation. Instead, they criticize its intellectual and spiritual opponents, thereby undercutting their own spiritual positions. This puts thoughtful believers on the defensive, blunting their dissent from the rampant materialism of corporate careerism. Worse still, when the self-appointed protectors of our spiritual values attack the scientific theory of evolution, they make spirituality itself, not just themselves, a laughing stock. To a large extent, this is what happened to the social gospel and the Populist Progressive movement accompanying it in the early part of this century. It committed suicide at the Scopes Monkey Trial when Clarence Darrow, the indefatigable defender of labor and free inquiry, was forced to destroy William Jennings Bryan, at one time a rousing populist orator and presidential candidate, who had turned fundamentalist bully and buffoon.

Then as now, the spiritual leaders of the United States managed to silence the culture's spiritualistic critics rather than soften the culture's materialistic excesses. Notable exceptions like the Reverend Martin Luther King, Jr., struggled mightily against the general drift. But the exceptions were drowned out by louder voices. According to the electronic evangelists, "Americans" (white Christian Anglos who were born in the U.S.A.) are God's chosen people and "America" his chosen nation. We were chosen to build a city on a hill that would provide a shining example to all the other peoples and nations of the world. The electronic evangelists strike a deeply resounding chord in the national character. The spiritual myth of the city on the hill goes back three and a half centuries to a famous speech given by Puritan leader John Winthrop to his pilgrim followers. So from the very beginning of the great experiment, the city-on-a-hill image has profoundly shaped how we see ourselves and others. It is the image that gives a stiff spiritual backbone to U.S. arrogance toward "non-Americans" and a sadistic self-righteousness to the peculiar American intolerance of dissenters.[19]

During the long frontier period it served as the spiritual justification of manifest destiny and Indian genocide because it encouraged the white Christian Anglos' belief that their God had given this continent to them. Now it justifies corporate domination at home and massive intervention abroad. Corporate careerism and corporate multinationalism are both sanctified national institutions.

Subordination of the State

The ends of the state also are being turned into corporate means. The state (meaning the governing apparatus at all levels: federal, state, and local) is not only being privatized and corrupted, it is also being subordinated. The most striking example of this subordination has occurred in the making of war. War is a major end of the state. To defend itself from the attacks of other nation-states or to mount attacks against them is an important state function. And this function, this end, has become a corporate means. War, or more precisely preparation for war, is used to finance corporate research and development, to finance corporate training, and to finance corporate sales. The financial drain of corporate defense contractors on the public coffers has become infamous. It approaches the level of unilateral disarmament through holding the taxpayers up for corporate ransom. That is, corporate defense contractors charge such high prices for such oversophisticated and unreliable weaponry, that the state is nearly being stripped of its financial and technical ability to wage war against a determined opponent. Weapons are purchased that kill the wrong men (air-to-air missiles); that rely on foreign production lines (all weapons using semiconductors); that frequently break down (the aborted helicopter rescue of American hostages in Iran); that require supersophisticated servicing (the F–15 fighter plane); and that are easily jammed (the AWACS plane). Communications systems are purchased that do not deliver urgent messages. (The *Liberty* was sunk by Israeli planes in 1967 because it failed to receive orders to leave the area in time to do so, and the *Pueblo* was seized by North Korea in 1968 because it failed to receive a warning message.) Communications systems that deliver incorrect messages are also purchased. (NORAD, deep beneath the Colorado rockies, frequently gets false warnings of nuclear attacks.) Space capsules are purchased that burn up the astronauts sitting in them on the launch pad. Space shuttles are purchased that blow up the astronauts riding them. Star wars systems are purchased when we do not even know if they will work. Civilian airliners are shot down by mistake. And the cost of all this oversophisticated, high-tech junk that corporations sell to the government just keeps going up.[20] The government has been turned into a deep-pocketed financier of corporate boondoggles. The government's war function has been subordinated to the corporation's finance function.

In most economies, the government owns or regulates public utilities to protect consumers. But protecting the public interest in public utilities is another government function being subordinated to the corporation in the United States. Government ownership of utilities is rare in the United States, and many of the government agencies charged with regulating the utility corporations have been captured by the corporations they were supposed to be regulating. Since a regulatory agency is said to be captured when it comes to serve the interests of the public utility corporations more than the interests of the consumers, capture serves as a prime example of subordinating the government to the needs of the corporation. Be it the Interstate Commerce Commission, the Civil Aeronautics Board, or the Federal Reserve Board, agencies that regulate specific industries often come to serve the interests of those industries. The ICC was originally intended to protect farmers and smaller shippers from exorbitant freight charges. But the ICC ended up protecting high rail and truck freight rates against competition from unregulated carriers. The Federal Reserve Board, intended to regulate the banks, has ended up protecting the bankers' high interest rates and tight money against the outcry of the bankrupted farmers and small businessmen. The CAB, intended to regulate the airlines, ended up protecting them against competitive fares. The ICC, CAB, and the Fed were all captured.

Under President Carter's administration, many of the abuses of the federal regulatory agencies were removed through deregulation, particularly of the CAB and the ICC. However, the Federal Reserve Board still serves the interests of bankers by protecting their high interest rates and tight money, and numerous federal and state regulatory agencies are still working hard to serve their own corporate clients as well. Deregulation missed them. Furthermore, as deregulation continued into the Reagan presidency, more good regulation than bad was eliminated. In retrospect, it is hard to tell which is worse—deregulation or capture. With capture, the regulatory agency allows the industry being regulated to raise its prices and keep them up by stopping potential competitors from coming in and driving prices back down. But with deregulation, the ruinous competition of new companies threatens industry safety and product quality, and the severe price-cutting drives revenues below the industry breakeven point. What with the capture of many regulatory agencies and the deregulation of many others, the government is failing to protect consumers' interests on a very broad front.[21] The government, at the federal, state, and local levels, has been subordinated to corporate interests. And so too has the school, the family, and the church. They all serve as means to corporate ends.

So why do so few of us cry out against this cumulating corporate hegemony? The main reason is that we are confused. We are mystified by the state of our own lives and by the state of our culture.

MYSTIFICATION

Symbolic Values and Scapegoating

Mystification is the subordination of symbols. Mystification is the usurpation of one institution's valued symbols by another institution. Taken to its sociohistorical conclusion, mystification is the hegemony of symbols, achieved when one institution usurps the positive symbols of all the other institutions and displays them for its own uses. This gathering together of symbolic value into one fasces concentrates symbolic authority in one institution and covers that institution with a protective shield of valued symbols. That powerfully bundled institution in the United States is the corporation. The corporation has usurped the symbols of value of other institutions, wrapped itself tightly in those symbols, and now emerges as the most powerful institution in the culture. The symbolic values of family, church, and state have been usurped and gathered together by the corporation, stripping the other institutions of their symbols of value while clothing itself with theirs. The family, church, and state now stand naked and embarrassed for all to see, while the corporation stands fully dressed. Magnificent in its new clothes, the corporation is admired by all, and their admiration is turned to account by the usurper. To indicate how far the symbolic drift has taken us, remember that at one time patriotism was the best refuge of a scoundrel. Wrapped in the flag, you could get away with anything. But now, free enterprise is the best refuge. Now, wrapped in the free enterprise system, you can get away with anything.

Mystification involves not only the elevation of an institution, but also the denigration of another institution. While the elevated institution becomes associated with all the positive symbols of the culture, the denigrated institution becomes associated with all the negative symbols. And while the elevated institution gets credited with every success, the denigrated institution gets blamed for every failure. The elevated institution acquires the aura of invincibility, while the denigrated institution acquires an aura of defeat. Then when the elevated institution suffers even a slight setback, scapegoating is born because it provides an easy excuse. Under the influence of scapegoating, most people will believe that the invincible institution only failed because of the diabolical plotting of the denigrated institution. Given enough setbacks or failures suffered by a highly valued institution, scapegoating will tip the cultural scales so far in favor of the one institution and against the other that the culture will slide off, imperceptibly at first, into hegemony.

In the case of the United States, the abuse of government could plunge to gutter level and the celebration of the corporation rise to surreal heights, given enough failures of the corporation to provide full employment, a safe environment, and a stable price level. More corporate failure could lead to more scapegoating of the government and to more elevating of the corporation, until the corporation appears to be the source of all good and true things—things that would be within our grasp, if only the government could be pushed out of our way. Aided by scapegoating, we could come to believe that government bureaucrats are intentionally thwarting us with their rules and regulations. We could come to believe that these rules and regulations are enforced by a growing army of government regulators. We could come to believe that the government is growing out of control because of the desire of government bureaucrats to build ever larger empires for their own benefit. We could come to believe that gay liberationists, radical feminists, environmental extremists, and welfare activists dominate the government. We could come to believe all of this, and possibly much more, in spite of clear evidence to the contrary.

Furthermore, we could come to believe that "free enterprise" will save us from job stagnation, price inflation, rising pollution, and international imbalances. To be more specific, we could come to believe that freeing giant corporations from government regulations will stop inflation. We could come to believe that freeing giant corporations from collective bargaining will stop the loss of jobs. We could come to believe that cutting the funding for the Occupational Safety and Health Administration and the Environmental Protection Agency will reduce pollution. And we could come to believe that deregulating international trade will balance our international economic relations. Then, when none of this saves us, we could come to believe in it even more. In short, we may be seeing the birth of our new "religion." Supply-side economists are already trying to rally a march of the faithful.[22]

Will the Drift Be Reinforced or Resisted?

The scales, tipping steeply in favor of the corporation, could be brought back to balance if other institutions could weigh in against the main drift. Unfortunately, most institutions do not resist it. The state and the school have been the worst in this regard. The state has allowed itself to be scapegoated for the harm done by corporate power. The state has also soiled itself by allowing its international standing to be used to protect U.S. multinational corporations from the actions of foreign peoples and governments, some just and some not so just. The school has given up its free inquiry by allowing its grades and degrees to serve as screening devices in the corporate career game, and by allowing its lingering reputation for free inquiry to be used to protect the corporate propoganda gushing forth from its economists and other social scientists. That leaves us with the church and the family as possible centers of institutional resistance.

The family offers little hope of effective resistance. The family has been sucked deeper and deeper into the corporate circle. Both spouses now typically pursue corporate careers and place great importance on corporate symbols of success. Their children, left to their own devices by the continued breakup and fragmentation of the traditional family, might mount an offensive based on the generation gap. If anything, the gap has been widened by the hollowing out of their families. Even though youth are temporarily cowed by their dismal job prospects, and even though many of them appear to enjoy war as a spectator sport, the youth of the late 1980s and early 1990s cannot be written off as a lost generation. All things considered, the likelihood of another youth rebellion is very hard to assess.

Some resistance to corporate hegemony might be forthcoming from the aged. The young and the old are far more free from corporate domination than those in the middle of the age distribution, simply because the young and the old do not have to work for corporations. The youth rebellion of the 1960s had many complex causes, one of them being the very large number of youth in that decade. Sheer numbers do make a difference. So as the number of old people who have survived long enough to escape dependence on corporate career increases, the likelihood of a symbolic rebellion of the old people also increases. The aged have not resisted the main drift, but their response might be radically different if their Social Security benefits are drastically cut or if their corporate pensions are put in jeopardy by managerial malfeasance. The latter is more than just likely. Furthermore, as more old people struggle with redefining the meaning of their lives, new symbols, meanings, and values may be forthcoming that seriously challenge their traditional corporate and family lives.

Some resistance to corporate hegemony might be forthcoming from the nonevangelical churchmen and churchwomen, particularly the latter. The resistance may arise in reaction to the spectacle provided by the electronic evangelists. Religion has always had a degree of entertainment value to it. And religion has always had a bit of superstition as well. But the electronic evangelists inject very heavy doses of superstition and entertainment into their religion, cheapening it in the process. The other churchmen may join forces to censure their electronic brethren. And if they do, they may find themselves with a tiger by the tail. The evangelists will accuse them of everything from consorting with the devil to being Communist fifth-columnists. Their only option then will be to go toe to toe with the evangelists in a full scale attempt to redefine the role of religion in American life. The evangelists will hold fast to religion as personal salvation. The nonevangelists will have to hue out an alternative position for themselves.

If they move to reconstruct and revitalize the social gospel, as they must do to resist the evangelists, they will have to become a part of a corporate resistance. They will have to propogate new symbolic values and meanings to replace those usurped by the corporation. They will have to recapture the spiritual vitality of the civil rights movement. They will have to recapture the moral high ground of the peace movement, and they will have to pick up the call for women's liberation. Catholics should be able to give spiritual meaning and symbolism to the civil rights and peace movements, but they will have very real problems with the women's movement. For too many years and on too many issues Catholics have been backing themselves into a corner on the woman question. Fundamental change must be made in Catholic positions on abortion, birth control, divorce, family life, and woman's place in the church before the Catholic church can take a leadership position in the women's movement. The nonevangelical Protestants should encounter no fundamental theological barriers to spiritually invigorating all the movements—the civil rights, peace, and women's movements. But they will have problems reaching the vast numbers of unchurched Protestants. Jews have Zionism to deal with before they can link up with the civil rights and peace movements. So the likelihood of an effective resistance to the corporation's domination of American life is hard to assess.

Opposing institutions are in retreat. The state is scapegoated, the school vocationalized, the family truncated, and the churches confused. With unions seriously weakened, corporate hegemony faces no powerful challenger. At least for the time being, the corporation dominates the mainstream of American life. It is the new fountainhead.

Conclusion

WHERE ARE WE GOING?

Fascism in the United States?

We are a nation of hirelings. We used to be pioneers. Our traditional values, beliefs, and meanings are those of a bygone era, of a bygone culture. That era—that culture—was of frontier individualism. Our era—our culture—is of corporate careerism. We are only now coming to realize the difference, but vaguely and with great reluctance. We are only now beginning to formulate the fruitful questions. As the anvil of free will, as the source of enlightened human character, pluralism made us construct and reconstruct our own selves from a rich collage of conflicting, reinforcing, and overlapping roles played in different and autonomous institutions. What will become of our free will now that our institutions are losing their differences and autonomy to the rising corporation and now that our roles are coalescing into one overwhelming role—that of corporate careerist? Can we do our own thing when our career requires us to do someone else's? Can we question authority when we are hemmed in by it at every turn? What are the impacts on the person—on the American character, if you will—of the rise to power of the conglomerate corporation? What are the cultural changes occurring as a result of corporate careerism? Is the United States becoming a fascist nation?[1]

In its classic form, as manifested by Nazi Germany, fascism is based on a dominant political party. It is racist, imperialist, and xenophobic. Its economic base is capitalism and its religion, Christianity. In its scapegoating it is extraordinarily brutal and conspicuously irrational. It is a particularly nasty form of hegemony. But what we are coming down with in the United States is not quite fascism, at least not in its classic form. What we are getting is probably worse, because it is far more insidious. What we are coming down with is corporate hegemony rather than classic fascism. Two simple slogans will illustrate the difference: under fascism, the slogan is *all power to the party*; under corporate hegemony, the slogan is *all power to the corporation*.

But in either case, the real trick to exercising power is to deny possessing it in the first place. Since managerial processes are intimate and private while political processes are formal and public, power based on managerial manipulation is more secure than power based on direct political action. When you exercise power as a politician, it is often hard to deny that you do so. But when you exercise power through others, including politicians, as corporate leaders do, denying it is easy. So corporate leaders are the most powerful stratum in the United States today. They can make or break politicians. Furthermore, since the corporation has become the foremost institution in our culture, I have focused my attention on it and its cultural impacts rather than on the state and its political machinations. The Vietnam War, Watergate, Iran-Contragate, and the decades of reactionary abuse heaped on the welfare state and civil servants have taken their toll: in the United States, the institution of the state is held in contempt. Civil servant has become a synonym for scheming empire builder or lazy shirker, and politicians are regarded as low-life fixers and bagmen. With the state held in such low esteem, men and women lusting for big money, real power, and high status seek them in the corporation, not in the state. Of course, they also seek to control the state, but the important game is now played in the corporation. Therefore, what the United States is coming down with is better described as corporate hegemony rather than as classic fascism. This should give us no grounds for complacency, however. For the former shows every promise of being even worse than the latter.

The corporation has grown to such prominence as an institution, and we have shrunk to such insignificance as individuals, because we quite simply depend upon the corporation to hire us. The corporation deserves far more attention in the literature of dissent than it is getting. Capitalism comes in for its share of criticism, but the preeminent capitalist institution needs attention as well. The corporation is institutionalized capitalism, capitalism in its purest and most powerful form. The corporation is not only organized to maximize its own profit and growth at others' expense, it is also organized to shape our values, influence our beliefs, and give meaning to our lives at the expense of the fading values, beliefs, and meanings of other spheres of life.

Degenerate Pragmatism

The question here is, what do hirelings value? What do kept men want? Why, to be well kept, of course. However, more is involved than just that. This nation of hirelings is a nation of pragmatists, but we are degenerate pragmatists rather than democratic pragmatists. Our pragmatism is not to be confused with John Dewey's pragmatism. To Dewey and other democratic pragmatists, the learning process is the essence of pragmatism. Learning requires active participation in the formulation and reformulation of new means in the attempted realization of new ends. To democratic pragmatists, man is a learning being who learns by participating and communicating, by creating and recreating means and ends in a continuing process. "The only social organization adequate to his nature," according to Raymond Williams, "is a participating democracy, in which all of us, as unique individuals, learn, communicate and control."[2] According to John Dewey, "The keynote of democracy as a way of life [is] the necessity for the participation of every mature human being in formation of the values that regulate the living of men together: which is necessary from the standpoint of both the general social welfare and the full development of human beings as individuals."[3] So democratic pragmatism is a participatory process of determining ends, devising means to achieve them, and reformulating both in the light of experience. It involves a cooperative and iterative process of give and take and of trial and error as we devise and redevise more workable means to achieve more proper ends. Pluralism thrives in democratic pragmatism because in the give and take and the trial and error of the democratic process, the means and ends of each different sphere of life are allowed to grow and coexist without dominating the other spheres of life and without being dominated by them. That is, the means and ends of church life do not come to dominate the means and ends of school life; the means and ends of economic life do not dominate the means and ends of family life, and so on.

At the close of the twentieth century our pragmatism is of the degenerate rather than democratic variety, however. We have allowed one end to dominate the others. The one end is career success, and we have allowed it to turn our family life, our school, our church, and even our state into mere means to satisfy that one all-absorbing end. Pluralism dies in degenerate pragmatism. It is dying for us because the other major institutions are bending to serve the corporation's end. In a hegemonic means-ends continuum, the church, the family, the school, and the state are becoming means to satisfy corporate ends. This is the sense in which the corporation is a jealous institution. It is the end and the other institutions are its means. The corporation has become the new golden calf; the corporadoes have become the new idolaters; and their families, schools, churches, and state have become the new sacrificial lambs. Democratic pragmatism results in mutual affirmation and organic unity, in the kinds of relations between people that cannot be paid for. Degenerate pragmatism results in using each other and mechanical unity, in the kinds of relations between people that must be paid for. The first kind of unity is of feeling and experience. It arises from cooperation and sharing between equals. The second kind of unity is of contract and gain. It arises from bargaining and the threat of physical or legal sanction between competitors.

Under the sway of degenerate pragmatism, personal and communal relations break down into means to individual ends. Friendship and community stop being ends that are meaningful by themselves. Instead, they become means to pursuing some other end; and take on the value and meaning of that other end. The other end, of course, is career success. The former personal-communal ends are now turned to corporate account in a degenerate means-ends continuum. The corporate sphere of life provides the ends, all the other spheres of life serve as the means. In the degenerate gatherings of hirelings perpetually on the make, sweetness and light are the orders of the day. (Corporadoes do not party, they network.) Everyone is as polite and courteous as can be. They act as if their very happiness is dependent upon the comfort and ease of others. Their personal relations are always correct and often as ceremonially elaborate as a traditional Japanese tea ceremony. But their personal relations are also something other than what they appear to be. Americans on the make spend little time bowing to each other, it is true. Nevertheless, their hospitality and politeness are all feigned, all carefully measured out and turned to account. Every politeness, courtesy, and personal favor is duly recorded, and a politeness, courtesy, or personal favor of equal or greater magnitude is always expected in return. In this way, personal-communal relations become a form of accounting for the debits and credits of life on the make, and all pleasantries rendered become investments in the personal portfolio, held for future returns. Pleasantries rendered by these new corporate courtesans, these new managerial mandarins, are booked into the general ledger as accounts receivable; while pleasantries received are booked as accounts payable.

Japanese Reflections

Personal-communal relations among American corporadoes are coming to resemble commercialized oriental ceremonies, and for good reason. Japan has led the way in the establishment of aggressive, all-embracing corporate organizations; Japan, Inc., foreshadows much that lies in store for us. In the early 1980s, American interest in Japanese management and organization reached the intensity of a fad. It has subsequently declined to a more rational level, but continues to be very serious. What we are witnessing is a foreboding case of organizational convergence. The American corporate world is converging with the more highly developed corporate world of Japan. Organization evolution has been much faster in Japan than in America because the Japanese have carried little of the excess cultural baggage we carried. The South Koreans, even freer than the Japanese from the excess baggage carried by Americans, have been able to develop new organizational forms and processes very rapidly and mount a mini-invasion of America similar to that of the Japanese. While many American manufacturers are moving their production abroad to take advantage of low wages, the South Koreans are following the Japanese pioneers by moving their production facilities to the United States.[4] In spite of American wage rates, the Japanese and South Koreans think that the managerial methods they have been able to develop more rapidly in an oriental environment will enable them to thrive in the newly evolving American environment.

Their organizational forms and processes have developed much faster than ours because they entered the age of corporate capitalism directly from entrenched feudalism, without much of an intervening period. The United States, on the other hand, evolved by an indirect route. On our way to corporate capitalism from feudalism, we first passed through an intervening period of institutional instability characterized by pluralism and individualism—the Enlightenment. The baggage we picked up during the age of the Enlightenment is excess in the sense that it now slows down our development of newer, more effective organizational forms and processes in the age of the corporation. Although the Japanese and South Koreans obviously entered the corporate age after we did, they have adapted to it much faster than we have.[5] Because of our roundabout way of getting here, America now suffers from a curious kind of cultural lag. William G. Ouchi, an authority on American and Japanese managerial practices, states the following: "Our [American] technological advance seems to no longer fit our social structure: in a sense, the Japanese can better cope with modern industrialism. While Americans still busily protect our rather extreme form of individualism, the Japanese hold their individualism in check and emphasize cooperation."[6]

At least that is the way Ouchi, who is not only an academic authority but also a corporate consultant, sees it. But an interesting contrast can be drawn between Ouchi's Japanese view of American culture and Veblen's American view of Japanese culture. Veblen summarized his analysis of Japan as follows: "It is in this unique combination of a high-wrought spirit of feudalistic fealty and chivalric honor with the material efficiency given by the modern technology that the strength of the Japanese nation lies.[7]

The Japanese have grafted modern technology directly onto feudal tradition, and the result is a hearty hybrid—the hegemonic corporation. Japanese management of this hybrid—the so-called Theory Z management—is characterized by (1) anticipatory socialization, based on (2) personal fealty, (3) group-think, and (4) intimate embrace. These are the four new corporate characteristics developed so quickly by the Japanese and the South Koreans that have also been developed, but more slowly, by leading American corporations. These are the characteristics of corporate hegemony.

The first characteristic resembles participatory management but is actually a very sophisticated form of anticipatory socialization. As production workers are drawn into quality circles and new managers are assigned the task of formulating new policies in Type Z organizations, they are not really empowered to make decisions on their own. That is, they are not really given new powers through participatory management; rather, they are taught new values through anticipatory socialization. For example, through a story provided by a friend, Ouchi describes anticipatory socialization at a major Japanese bank. The process is really quite subtle. When an important decision is to be made at the bank, an alternative is proposed and the task of writing up the formal proposal is given to the newest managerial trainee. The trainee then "tries like heck to figure out" from the more experienced managers "what the boss wants." The trainee includes his own thoughts in his formal proposal, of course.[8] But in framing it, he must anticipate what higher management expects and wants in the first place. The successful trainee is said to have participated in decisionmaking. But the trainee only thinks he has participated in decisionmaking. He has actually participated in his own socialization. He was tricked into socializing himself, into accepting the values and beliefs of his superiors so that some day he may rise into their ranks. This very subtle socialization method also yields a dividend to higher management in the form of new ideas that have been pre-shaped to fit their needs. The same is true of quality circles for production workers—they appear to involve participatory management but actually involve more anticipatory socialization than anything else.

The second characteristic of so-called Type Z corporations is the personal fealty they draw on and inculcate in their employees. Here, the Japanese have a very big head start over the Americans because personal fealty was the cement that held feudal Japan together, even into the twentieth century.[9] Fealty is the absolute loyalty of a feudal knight to his lord (European feudalism) and of a samurai to his daimyo (Japanese feudalism). Fealty is an intense relation based on the personal allegiance of fighting men to their warrior chieftain. The allegiance is a mutual one, but also an unequal and servile one. It is not really a formal or explicit contract but a set of personal obligations. In Japanese corporations, and in American ones trying to develop similar ties, the personal obligations are between an employee and an organization rather than between a vassal and a lord. In large Japanese corporations the employee is obligated to be personally loyal to the organization while the organization is obligated to provide employment for the subservient employee till he reaches age 55. The obligations definitely are not equal, however. The employee receives a lump-sum payment at age 55 but no pension of any kind. Furthermore, the properly loyal employee has assurances of a regular job until he is 55, but no assurances of a regular income during that period. Only about half of the employee's usual income is paid to him regularly, so if the corporation encounters difficulty, the other half of the employee's usual income can be held back and paid only at the discretion of the corporation. Of course, when the other portion is paid, it is called a "bonus" and the loyal employee is taught to be properly thankful for it. But the facts of the case are simply that the loyal employees are obliged to accept much of the risk of their employers. In good times, all is well. But in bad times or in the event of corporate miscalculations, the Japanese corporation pushes the burden of its declining financial position onto the backs of its loyal employees by not paying them their so-called bonuses. The "bonus" is not a bonus at all, but a loan from the workers' wage fund to the corporation's working capital fund. So the reciprocal trust in Japanese corporations between employee and employer that many American corporations would like to cash in on is really very unequal fealty, not trust at all.

The third characteristic of the Type Z corporation resembles the subtle relations one finds among friends who care about each other's feelings. However, as exemplified by the more advanced Japanese practices, the subtlety of managerial relations is a case of group-think. Managerial subtlety is not based on caring for other's feelings. Rather, it is based on a contrived consensus of beliefs and values. Management trainees move up into positions of real decision-making after undergoing successful anticipatory socialization. That is, the managerial initiate must first make the values and beliefs of upper management his values and beliefs. Only after he internalizes them can he move into the higher circles, because only then has he become properly trustworthy and personally responsible. Then he can be counted on to pursue the corporate purpose with the expected single-mindedness and in the expected ways. His personal fealty assured and his socialization completed, he needs only the subtlest of hints and prods to do what is expected, when it is expected, and how it is expected. Clearly this results in a very subtle managerial system where direction and supervision are nearly absent, but it is based on homogenized group thinking. Such subtlety is highly efficient because it allows people to be managed with little effort. After pre-programming, people perform well without additional outside input. Supervising them is easy and inexpensive.

In Japan, the pre-programming is made possible by the value placed on personal fealty and career success. In America, the pre-programming is made possible by the value placed on personal status and career success. In both countries, the values serve as buttons or strings that those above can push or pull to get the desired response from those below. In both countries, the buttons and strings used by those above are installed in those below during the educational process. The Japanese have become very adept at the installation, having developed the most savagely competitive and inhumanly rigorous educational system in the world. Children of ambitious Japanese families start at an early age to attend after-school cram courses designed to increase their scores on crucial exams. Pressure to score high on entrance exams in order to get into the most prestigious universities is intense. A degree from Kyoto, Tokyo, Waseda, or Keio University is even more important to the budding young Japanese careerist than a degree from their Ivy League counterparts is to a budding young American careerist. In Japan, according to Naohiro Amaya, a member of a national advisory council on education, colleges and universities "have become in effect subcontractors for the major companies."[10] In education, we may be behind Japan in the 1980s, but we Americans are struggling mightily to catch up.

The fourth characteristic of the Type Z corporation is the intimacy of its style. We all need intimacy, but with others of our own choice. When we choose a job we do not really choose to be subjected to this new managerial intimacy with its extreme pressure to believe and behave as expected by those above us. With a corporate job, we get much more than we bargain for. We get a set of shared meanings, beliefs, and values that we too are expected to share. We get an intimate organizational culture, of sorts, when all we wanted was a job. According to Ouchi, "The organizational culture consists of a set of symbols, ceremonies and myths that communicate the underlying values and beliefs of that organization to its employees."[11] As the new worker-manager learns his job he also learns something else: "slowly individual preferences give way to collective consensus."[12] He learns to submerge his own individuality into the corporate collectivity. And he is aided in this learning process by the intimacy of the relationship prefabricated for him in his new corporate family. Other, noncorporate relations and commitments decline in intimacy and importance in his life. If he joins the corporate family as a trained professional, even his commitments to his profession and his relations to outside professionals decline in significance to him. Ouchi explains, "Every Type Z organization that I know experiences some loss of professionalism. Whether it is a financial analyst, a salesperson, a personnel specialist, or an engineer, a Type Z company manifests a lower level of professionalism."[13] The intimate corporation is a jealous organization. In its fully developed form, it tolerates no rivals to its intimate embrace—not professional, not familial, not even spiritual. In its fully developed form, manifested so clearly in corporate Japan and envied so strongly in corporate America, it is a hegemonic institution.

Further Inklings of Hegemony

In Japanese reflections we can see ourselves, but only dimly. We need to look more closely at ourselves. Our values are those of corporate careerists—

corporadoes. We value status. So we give fealty to those above us, in hopes they will promote us. We value career success, so we forsake all other values to pursue success. We turn all other values (ends) into means. So our corporate values are impoverishing us rather than enriching us because we have begun to sacrifice everything else to them. Our degenerate pragmatism has enslaved us. Our values are those of hirelings. We value that which is useful to value—useful to those who hire us, that is. We sacrifice our democratic traditions in education to turn the school into a career-primer. We (male careerists) sacrifice time with our family to time for our career and, in a classic case of double-think, rationalize the sacrifice by saying we did it for our family. Then, double-think not enough, we blame working women by applying the old double standard to them when they too begin to sacrifice more and more to their own career success. In a rear-guard, misdirected lashing out, we (the Moral Majority types) blame feminists and abortionists for the disintegration of the family and try to place a heavy burden of guilt on women who have abortions or careers instead of children.

When we look more closely at ourselves, we see a rising intolerance accompanying an increasingly competitive conformity. Our rising intolerance manifests itself in many dimensions, all of which relate in one way or another to our central dimension—career. The rising intolerance toward feminists clearly is related to the spread of aggressive careerism among working women. Feminists are identified with abortion, with critical attitudes towards housewives, and with a lack of appreciation for traditional family values. So the feminist movement is seen increasingly as a threat to a traditional life-style, even though the real threat comes from somewhere else—from corporate career. The rising intolerance toward abortion is similar in origin and composition to the rising intolerance against feminism. Those who oppose abortion also oppose feminism, and both are opposed as threats to a traditional family life-style, while the real threat to that life-style is the growing attraction and compulsion of corporate career. The fears for traditional family life-style are real but the enemies imaginary. Nonetheless, never underestimate the importance of fear and confusion in stirring up man's intolerance.

Neither should the force of competitive conformity be underestimated. Small-town businessmen in the United States have been competitively conformist for generations. Small towns breed true. The practiced normalcy in personal attitudes and aggressive averageness in the social behavior of business boosters have given a notably parochial tone to small-town life, and the small-town surveillance of personal practices has enforced that parochial tone effectively enough. The narrow-mindedness of the small town has been a major form of social control in the United States. With regard to "un-American" values and beliefs, the small town has provided its inhabitants with a remarkably resilient intolerance. Babbittry is not a new disciplinary force. However, the surveillance of career *is* a new disciplinary force. A few secret or discreet nonconformists could exist even among the businessmen of Babbitt's small town. They were often lonely, isolated figures, it is true. Nonetheless, nonconformists could survive in the nooks and crannies of the unorganized and informal system of social control that made up the small-town business world.[14] Now, their survival in the formally tighter and hierarchically organized world of the corporate career has become far more difficult. The discipline of the small town was informal and unorganized. That of the corporate career is formal and organized.

In spite of the declining hold of the small town on the national character, most of us are in no danger of deviating from our conformity and intolerance into individuality and liberality. The system is holding, even solidifying. The social-control function once performed somewhat loosely by the small town is being taken over by the corporate career. So the small town has passed the burden of social control on to the corporation. The small town functioned amicably within the remnants of a haphazard pluralism, while the corporation functions efficiently within the tightening bonds of an emergent hegemony. Furthermore, while the small town tended to coexist with or reinforce the values, beliefs, and meanings of traditional spiritual and familial life, the corporate career is tending to overwhelm them, to literally incorporate them into its own cultural hegemony.

Hegemonic Culture

Hegemonic culture, along the lines of modern oriental despotism—Japan, Inc.—is where we are going, but not because of classical fascism. Instead, just like the small town left its cultural mark of intolerance and conformity on the national character, the corporate career is leaving a similar mark. Corporate career, however, cuts much deeper and broader than the small town. The corporation has become the dominant institutional force shaping U.S. culture and character. It has reached this preeminent position through its own attraction and the default of other, opposing institutions. The petty mindlessness and narrow conformity of the small-town booster are giving way to the organized irresponsibility and anxiety-driven sameness of the corporate careerist. The small-town boosters can no longer match the salaries and perquisities of the corporate careerists. Large gains are made occasionally by the boosters with their shady real estate deals and minor wheelings and dealings. But the big money is now in the corporate world. So that is where the ambitious go today. And the corporate world is absorbing even the wheelings and dealings of the boosters, as real estate businesses are either bought out by corporate conglomerates or franchised by same, and as hinterland banks, insurance companies, newspapers, TV and radio stations, and even restaurants are bought out or franchised out. And now the once independent physicians are being hemmed in by growing hospital bureaucracies and squeezed by expanding HMOs—health maintenance organizations. There is no room left; no place to make a stand. Not even the family farmers can hold out against the agribusiness of corporate farmers allied with the high interest rates of corporate bankers.

In short, the economic and cultural bases of formerly independent businessmen and farmers have eroded away, leaving them exposed to the corporate onslaught. As they are ground down, they either join the corporate world or become marginalized. Little real occupational choice is left for a youth on the make. Sports and rock and roll provide chances to only a few. The ministry is no fun. Teaching is low-pay and low-status drudgery. Government service is disreputable. Medicine is still promising, but very expensive to enter. Law and journalism are overcrowded. That leaves the corporate career, or crime.

The End

In sum, we are moving, more or less willingly, into a system of corporate hegemony. To explain how we got into this predicament, I have constructed an institutional analysis of the American case. My analysis has relied heavily on the processes of contamination, emulation, subordination, and mystification to explain why most of our institutions are being hollowed out and why our lives are being sped up by the demands of corporate career. The roles we play and the institutions in which we play them are being turned to account for a system of corporate hegemony. The outlines of that system are only barely visible at this stage, so I have sketched them out with a heavy hand, and I have explained corporate hegemony as if it were already fully operational, even though it is still in its infancy. I have done this, the better for us all to see what lies ahead and to take the appropriate steps to make our own future.

If pluralism is to be in that future, we must take steps now to put it there. We must defend noncorporate institutions from corporate hegemony. We must make it possible for the school to mean something more than vocational education. We must make it possible for the family to mean more than a foundation for a successful career. We must make it possible for young and old, white people and people of color, to come together in real, meaningful communities. We must make it possible for our spiritual lives to grow from a narrow concern with individual salvation to a broad concern with the social gospel. We must eliminate class inequalities to allow tolerance to take permanent root in our cultural soil. We must make it possible for a real labor movement to develop in the United States, one with a strong political party and a solid base of affiliated unions. We must make it possible for a real patriotism to emerge in this country, a patriotism that takes pride in honest, caring government rather than in conquest and domination.

We must not merely help noncorporate institutions adjust to the evolution of corporate hegemony. Institutional adjustment is not what we need. We do not want to adjust to the new corporate dispensation. Instead, we want a new set of rights. We want the right to a meaningful family, whether we are gay or straight, black or white, rich or poor. We want the right to a meaningful union. We want the right to a meaningful education, and to meaningful community, spirituality, and nationality. We do not want these basic institutions to be hollowed out. We do not want to lose our rights in them only to find ourselves ever more dependent upon, ever more involved in, ever more sped up by the corporation. Instead, we want to enlarge our rights in these basic institutions so that we can grow as independent human beings, as creatures of the Enlightenment. To enlarge our rights in these basic institutions requires that we take action in each institutional realm.

In institutions, meaning follows function. If an institution loses its function to other institutions, it will also lose its meaning—it will be hollowed out. So, if we strengthen and enlarge the independent functions of the family, say, then we make the family more meaningful to those who participate in its ongoing activities. The same is true of the other noncorporate institutions. If their independent functioning were strengthened and protected, they too would become far more meaningful counterbalances to corporate hegemony.

In the realm of the family, we need state and federal legislation recognizing the rights of gay people to marry and form their own families. Family life needs to be cultivated in all its richness and diversity. A revitalized commune and/or kibbutz movement would be very fruitful. We need state and federal task forces to deal with the problems of child abuse and battered spouses. Children and spouses have the right to a nonviolent home. We need generous, universal child allowances, based neither on income nor on any kind of work requirement. We need generous paid leaves for birthing, for both parents—six months at full pay should be written on our banner. We need a whole series of new public housing programs, including a more effective fair housing program. We need to eliminate mandatory overtime, not just for employees currently covered by federal labor standards, but for exempt employees as well. Executives, like everyone else, should go home after forty hours on the job. The other members of their family have a right to demand it of them. We need federal, state, and local task forces to deal with the problems of the single parent. Along with much else, single parents need generous financial allowances and programs built on genuine human kindness rather than on the desire to control and/or punish the one-parent family. If we did all these things, and more, because we really considered children a joy and families a necessity, abortion would be much less frequent than it is today and family life would be a far more meaningful counterbalance to the demands of work and career.

The institution in most need of strengthening and enlarging is the union. The capitalists have their institution for effective collective action. It is the corporation, and it is on the rise. But the workers' institution for collective action, the union, is in decline. The union, where it exists, has little influence outside of strictly bread-and-butter issues. So it does not provide an effective social counterbalance to the corporation. Substantial internal change is called for in the labor movement. The social functions of the union need to be enlarged. Union hierarchies need to be reformed and democratized. The labor movement needs a socialist-oriented labor party to give the movement political meaning. The corporations have their political party with its capitalist orientation. (It is the Republican party, with its me-too Democratic wing.) The workers need their own party too. The first thing their party needs to do is eliminate so-called right-to-work laws. Then, the first thing the unions need to do is organize the white-collar worker.

A vital labor movement with a vital labor party would help bring new life to the nation's government. A socialist-oriented labor party would help reverse the privatization and deregulation trends that have been stripping government in the United States of function and meaning. If the labor movement succeeded in organizing most government workers, a significant increase in wages and salaries could help improve the morale and integrity of public servants. A vital labor party would also help reduce the new patriotism's emphasis on conquest and domination in international affairs. No miracles or utopian transformations should be expected, however. After all, the labor movement and the labor party in the United Kingdom did a poor job of resisting the march of Thatcherism in Britain.

But the nation-state need not depend entirely on its party system for revitalization. New voting registration laws—on-site registration—and new voting practices—proportional representation—would help considerably. Demilitarization and peace would too, as would reform of campaign financing. All of these improvements are needed for each of us to realize fully our right to vote and our more inclusive right to participate in the democratic process. New voting registration laws and voting practices could increase the participation of the poor and the excluded. Reform of campaign financing could give their spokespersons a better chance to get their messages across. Demilitarization and peace could reduce the pressure for covert actions against state enemies and weaken the justifications for state secrecy. The windows of the state would be opened to some badly needed fresh air.

Perhaps a revitalized spirituality could blow a gust of the social gospel through the windows of the state, if the electronic evangelists can be driven from the airwaves in disgrace, and if the spirit of the civil rights and peace movements can infuse America's mainline denominations with a sense of social urgency. Bringing about such a transformation would require America's white churches to borrow heavily from her black ones. Such a borrowing is possible, if not likely. At least it took place once before, in music. Perhaps the Reverend Jesse Jackson and the Rainbow Coalition will lead the way. Jackson's 1988 presidential campaign was far more successful than anyone thought it would be.[15]

And perhaps our concern for America's schools will strengthen them, making them independent institutions of learning rather than dependent centers for vocational education. Students have a right to more than a vocational education. They have a right to full participation in their cultural heritage and a right to know other cultures as well. The greatest heritage of all, one in which students have rights as full citizens, is the heritage of free inquiry. So in addition to more financial support, particularly at the head-start, grade school, middle school, and high school levels, students must be free to learn and teachers free to teach—free from self-appointed censors and administrative hierarchies.

The community could be strengthened as well, for quite often resistance to corporate power breaks out at the community level. Sweeping new community environmental rights should be enacted that make it easier for local communities to bring class action suits against corporate polluters. Such laws should include treble damages and provisions for making parent corporations liable for the harm done by their subsidiaries. Federal environmental controls need to be strengthened, and when state or local controls are stricter than the corresponding federal ones, the state or local controls take precedent. Sweeping new community plant-closing laws should also be enacted to make corporations liable for the damage to communities caused by improperly announced plant closings. Not only should corporations give due notice to employees when a plant is closed, but also to the communities affected by the closing. Furthermore, action must be taken to protect communities from themselves by strictly limiting state and local governments from competing with each other for new corporate investment by offering corporate investors tax incentives and other inducements to locate in their community instead of in someone else's.

To emphasize the importance of corporate hegemony, I have written as if it were already an accomplished fact. But it is not, not quite. Life is still left in opposing institutions. From the grass roots of the country continue to come demands for rights. In those demands lie hope, for the demands could strengthen noncorporate institutions against the corporation.

To realize our hope for a true pluralism, the retreat of opposing institutions must be stopped along a wide front. Privatization must be reversed. Instead of selling off bits and pieces of the state to the highest bidder, we must restructure and improve the state. Instead of knee-jerk, fearful reaction from the pulpit, religious leaders must reconstruct a social gospel that takes the moral high ground and deals with social issues rather than personal salvation. Instead of vocation, we want education in the school. Instead of truncated families, we should protect ourselves from our own ambition by limiting time and energy spent on career. A truncated family is one from which the adults are essentially absent—they are at work. Furthermore, instead of the old patriarchy, a far richer and more diverse family life is possible in which more than one set of family roles is practiced. Instead of a commercialized communications media stuck in a rut that maximizes advertising revenue while minimizing challenge and controversy, we need a vitalized "noncommercial" media focused on social, moral, and aesthetic issues. In sum, instead of a trivialized culture, we need a vibrant culture with independent institutions, all posing important issues and challenges, all forcing us to make choices, take stands, and defend ourselves. We need a culture in which individual human character is the single most important value. But the corporation stands in our way, and the corporation is a most powerful institution.[16]

Notes

CHAPTER 1

1. A more thorough discussion of the issues and characteristics involved is in Hans Gerth and C. Wright Mills, *Character and Social Structure* (New York: Harcourt, Brace, Jovanovich, 1953).

2. For a detailed, fascinating, and sweeping account, see the five-volume series, Robert Coles, *Children of Crisis* (Boston: Little, Brown and Company, 1977).

3. Two histories of the Nazis are William L. Shirer, *The Rise and Fall of the Third Reich* (New York: Simon and Schuster, 1959); and Alan Bullock, *Hitler: A Study in Tyranny*, rev. ed. (New York: Harper and Row, 1964).

4. David Riesman with Nathan Glazer and Reuel Denny, *The Lonely Crowd* (1950; Garden City, N.Y.: Doubleday, 1956); C. Wright Mills, *White Collar* (New York: Oxford University Press, 1951); William H. Whyte, Jr., *The Organization Man* (Garden City, N.Y.: Doubleday, 1957); Michael Maccoby, *The Gamesman* (New York: Bantam Books, 1978).

5. Mills, *White Collar*, p. 110.

6. Maccoby, *The Gamesman*, p. 100.

7. Ibid., p. 164.

8. Michael Maccoby, *The Leader* (New York: Simon and Schuster, 1981).

9. Ibid., p. 202. See also pp. 184–207.

10. For further discussion in a much broader context, see Erich Fromm, *The Anatomy of Human Destructiveness* (New York: Holt, Rinehart and Winston, 1973); and Christopher Lasch, *The Culture of Narcissism* (New York: W. W. Norton, 1978).

11. The school-based form of hegemony is qualified with "perhaps" because no clear historical examples of it come to mind. Nevertheless, the leaders of the Moral Majority deeply fear it. What they fear most of all is secular humanism. See Jerry Falwell, *Listen, America!* (Garden City, N.Y.: Doubleday, 1980). A second concerned group—Accuracy in Academia—also fears some kind of totalitarian mind control in America's colleges and universities. The Accuracy in Academia people have tried to cultivate a network of snitches from among concerned college students to help ferret out pernicious professors who secretly teach free thought and free inquiry (secular humanism again).

12. My general theory of hegemony is different from, but draws upon, that of Antonio Gramsci, *Selections from the Prison Notebooks,* edited and translated by Quintin Hoare and Geoffrey Nowell Smith (New York: International Publishers, 1971).

13. See also C. E. Ayres, *The Theory of Economic Progress,* 2d ed. (New York: Schocken Books, 1962); Fernand Braudel, *Capitalism and Material Life, 1400–1800,* translated by Miriam Kochan (New York: Harper and Row, 1973); Douglas F. Dowd, *The Twisted Dream,* 2d ed. (Cambridge, Mass.: Winthrop Publishers, 1977); and R. H. Tawney, *The Agrarian Problem in the Sixteenth Century* (1912; New York: Harper and Row, 1967).

14. See Tamar Lewin, "Some Assert S.E.C. Pushes Law Too Far," *New York Times* (July 21, 1986); Nathaniel C. Nash, "They Who 'Delivered' Boesky Are Perplexed," *New York Times* (Jan. 2, 1987); and Stratford P. Sherman, "Drexel Sweats the SEC Probe," *Fortune* (March 16, 1987).

15. For the early evolution of the corporate form see John P. Davis, *Corporations,* edited by Abram Chayes (1905; New York: Capricorn Books, 1961); and Tom Hadden, *Company Law and Capitalism* (London: Weidenfeld and Nicolson, 1972). See also the classic, Adolf A. Berle and Gardiner C. Means, *The Modern Corporation and Private Property,* rev. ed. (New York: Harcourt, Brace and World, 1968).

16. An interesting insider's account is by Harold S. Geneen, "Why Directors Can't Protect the Stockholders," *Fortune* (Oct. 15, 1984).

17. On this point see Samuel Bowles, David M. Gordon, and Thomas E. Weisskopf, *Beyond the Wasteland* (Garden City, N.Y.: Anchor Press/Doubleday, 1983) pp. 122–78; Seymour Melman, *Profits without Production* (New York: Alfred A. Knopf, 1983); and William M. Dugger, *An Alternative to Economic Retrenchment* (Princeton, N.J.: Petrocelli Books, 1984), pp. 100–131.

18. The first and so far the only major academic study of this general area is Marshall B. Clinard and Peter C. Yeager, with Ruth Blackburn Clinard, *Corporate Crime* (New York: Free Press, 1980).

19. In academic terms, this section has dealt with the debate between the methodological individualists and the methodological collectivists. To put the debate in its context, see William M. Dugger, "Two Twists in Economic Methodology: Positivism and Subjectivism," *American Journal of Economics and Sociology* 42 (Jan. 1983): 75–91.

20. This section is adapted from my article, William M. Dugger, "The Shortcomings of Concentration Ratios in the Conglomerate Age: New Sources and Uses of Corporate Power," *Journal of Economic Issues* 19 (June 1985): 343–53.

21. An excellent history of how corporate administration has been replacing market haggling is Alfred D. Chandler, Jr., *The Visible Hand: The Managerial Revolution in American Business* (Cambridge, Mass.: Belknap Press of Harvard University Press, 1971).

22. John Kenneth Galbraith, *The New Industrial State* (Boston: Houghton Mifflin, 1967).

23. The classic on economic concentration is John M. Blair, *Economic Concentration* (New York: Harcourt, Brace, Jovanovich, 1972).

24. Bureau of the Census, *1972 Census of Manufactures* (Washington, D.C.: Government Printing Office, 1976).

25. Bureau of the Census, *1977 Census of Manufactures* (Washington, D.C.: Government Printing Office, 1981).

26. Bureau of the Census, *Statistical Abstract of the United States, 1985* (Washington, D.C.: Government Printing Office, 1986), p. 524.

27. Ibid., p. 522, and *Statistical Abstract, 1984* (Washington, D.C.: Government Printing Office, 1985), p. 538.

28. The Census Bureau's "multiple-industry companies" include a few vertically integrated companies whose vertical integration takes them outside of their primary industry, as classified by the bureau. However, including such kinds of vertically integrated companies as conglomerates does not harm the argument advanced here, for whether classified as vertically integrated or conglomerate, such multiple-industry companies possess a size and degree of power that single-industry companies generally do not.

29. Bureau of the Census, *Enterprise Statistics: General Report* (Washington, D.C.: Government Printing Office, various years).

30. Willard F. Mueller, "Conglomerates: A 'Nonindustry,'" p. 427, in Walter Adams, ed., *The Structure of American Industry*, 6th ed. (New York: Macmillan, 1982), pp. 427–74.

31. Mueller notes that the major meat packers had assembled vast enterprises that spanned many industries by as early as 1919. See ibid., p. 427. The Du Pont empire is another example of an early conglomerate.

32. The classic works on conglomerate power are Corwin D. Edwards, "Conglomerate Bigness as a Source of Power," in *Business Concentration and Price Policy* (Princeton, N.J.: Princeton University Press, 1955), pp. 331–59; and Mueller, "Conglomerates: A 'Nonindustry.'" See also John F. Winslow, *Conglomerates Unlimited* (Bloomington: Indiana University Press, 1973).

33. A brief discussion is in Ed Cray, *Chrome Colossus* (New York: (McGraw-Hill, 1980), pp. 389–92, 446.

34. The testimony of Harold Geneen is of particular interest. See pp. 129–33 in Winslow, *Conglomerates Unlimited*.

35. For a brief discussion of such behavior in gasoline retailing, see John M. Blair, *The Control of Oil* (New York: Pantheon Books, 1976), pp. 244–46.

36. Edwards, "Conglomerate Bigness as a Source of Power," p. 335.

37. Ibid., p. 335.

38. Ibid., p. 334.

39. Ibid., pp. 342–44.

40. These and other coordinating arrangements are discussed in John R. Munkirs, "Centralized Private Sector Planning: An Institutionalist's Perspective on the Con-

temporary U.S. Economy," *Journal of Economic Issues* 17 (Dec. 1983): pp. 931–67; and John R. Munkirs, *The Transformation of American Capitalism* (Armonk, N.Y.: M. E. Sharpe, 1985).

41. *New York Times* (July 3, 1984): 31.

42. Aloysius Ehrbar, "Have Takeovers Gone Too Far?" *Fortune* (May 27, 1985): 22.

43. Thorstein Veblen, *Absentee Ownership and Business Enterprise in Recent Times* (1923; New York: Augustus M. Kelley, 1964), pp. 374–94.

44. Ibid., pp. 385–86.

45. Samuel M. Loescher uses the term "plane of competition" in a slightly different way and traces it back to Henry Carter Adams. See Loescher's "Corporate Giantism, Degradation of the Plane of Competition, and Countervailance," *Journal of Economic Issues* 8 (June 1974): 329–51.

46. Further discussion of cash cows and corporate milking is in Dugger, *An Alternative to Economic Retrenchment,* pp. 62–63. See also Michael E. Porter, *Competitive Strategy* (New York: Free Press, 1980), pp. 361–67; and George S. Day, "Diagnosing the Product Portfolio," *Journal of Marketing* 41 (April 1977): 29–38. See also Barry Bluestone and Bennett Harrison, *The Deindustrialization of America* (New York: Basic Books, 1982). A fine case study is Michael F. Sheehan, "Corporate Control and the Decapitalization of Subsidiary Corporations: The Looting of the Bangor and Aroostook Railroad," *Journal of Economic Issues* 22 (Sept. 1988): 729–45.

47. See also Richard Edwards, *Contested Terrain* (New York: Basic Books, 1979).

48. See Walter Adams and James W. Brock, "Corporate Power and Economic Sabotage," *Journal of Economic Issues* 20 (Dec. 1986): 919–40; and Anthony Sampson, *The Sovereign State of ITT* (New York: Stein and Day, 1973).

49. See the local coverage of Jackie Koszczuk, "Film Recovery Officials Guilty" and "Film-lab Verdict: Corporate Notice," *The Daily Herald* (June 15 and 16, 1985).

CHAPTER 2

1. Walter Adams and James W. Brock, *The Bigness Complex* (New York: Pantheon, 1986).

2. See Alfred D. Chandler, Jr., *The Visible Hand: The Managerial Revolution in American Business* (Cambridge, Mass.: Belknap Press of Harvard University Press, 1977); and his *Strategy and Structure: Chapters in the History of the American Industrial Enterprise* (Cambridge, Mass.: MIT Press, 1962).

3. Some holding companies and trusts are also vehicles for concentrating and controlling family wealth. The Christiana Securities Company and the Wilmington Trust Company, for examples, have held the Du Pont family's wealth together for many years.

4. See Peter E. Earl, *The Corporate Imagination* (Armonk, N.Y.: M. E. Sharpe, 1984). See also Oliver E. Williamson, *Markets and Hierarchies* (New York: Free Press, 1975); and Oliver E. Williamson, "The Modern Corporation: Origins, Evolution, Attributes," *Journal of Economic Literature* 19 (Dec. 1981): 1537–68. Contrast Williamson with Charles R. Spruill, *Conglomerates and the Evolution of Capitalism* (Carbondale: Southern Illinois University Press, 1982); and with William M. Dugger,

"The Transaction Cost Analysis of Oliver E. Williamson: A New Synthesis?" *Journal of Economic Issues* 17 (March 1983): 95–114.

5. See Morty Lefkoe, "Why So Many Mergers Fail," *Fortune* (July 20, 1987).

6. David Halberstam, *The Reckoning* (New York: William Morrow, 1986).

7. William G. Ouchi, *Theory Z* (Reading, Mass.: Addison-Wesley, 1981).

8. Further discussion is in Thomas J. Peters and Robert H. Waterman, Jr., *In Search of Excellence* (New York: Harper and Row, 1982).

9. Terrence E. Deal and Allan A. Kennedy, *Corporate Cultures* (Reading, Mass.: Addison-Wesley, 1982), p. 7.

10. Lefkoe, "Why So Many Mergers Fail." See also Richard Pascale, "Fitting New Employees into the Company Culture," *Fortune* (May 28, 1984).

11. See Bro Uttal, "The Corporate Culture Vultures," *Fortune* (Oct. 17, 1983).

12. Barry Bluestone and Bennett Harrison, *The Deindustrialization of America* (New York: Basic Books, 1982).

13. For a recent misinterpretation see Stewart Toy, "Splitting Up," *Business Week* (July 1, 1985). For the empirical evidence, see William M. Dugger, "Centralization, Diversification, and Administrative Burden in U.S. Enterprises," *Journal of Economic Issues* 19 (Sept. 1985): 687–701.

14. The need for organizational unity, and the difficulty of achieving it in M-form corporations, is referred to as the "indecomposability problem" in the technical literature. See Earl, *Corporate Imagination,* pp. 162–72.

15. Allan Cox, *The Cox Report on the American Corporation* (New York: Delacorte Press, 1982), p. 144.

16. Administrative Management Society, *Thirteenth Annual Guide to Management Compensation* (Willow Grove, Pa.: AMS, 1985).

17. John P. Steinbrink and William B. Friedeman, *Executive Compensation: Dartnell's 14th Biennial Survey* (Chicago: Dartnell Press, 1982).

18. Bureau of the Census, *Statistical Abstract of the United States, 1984* (Washington, D.C.: Government Printing Office, 1984).

19. Thorstein Veblen was the first to explore in depth the issues and processes involved in his *The Higher Learning in America* (1918; New York: Augustus M. Kelley, 1965). See also William M. Dugger, "Corporate Bureaucracy," *Journal of Economic Issues* 14 (June 1980): 399–409; idem, "Power: An Institutional Framework of Analysis," *Journal of Economic Issues* 14 (Dec. 1980): 897–907; and idem, "The Continued Evolution of Corporate Power," *Review of Social Economy* 43 (April 1985): pp. 1–13. Parts of this section were first presented in my paper, "Power and Values in Economics," at the Midwest Economics Association's March 1985 meetings in Cincinnati. Stephen T. Worland made helpful comments.

20. In addition to his *Higher Learning in America,* see Thorstein Veblen, *The Instinct of Workmanship* (1914; New York: Augustus M. Kelley, 1964); and *Absentee Ownership and Business Ownership in Recent Times* (1923; New York: Augustus M. Kelley, 1964). Michael Maccoby has also explored craftsmanship in his *The Gamesman* (New York: Bantam Books, 1978).

21. Maccoby, *The Gamesman,* pp. 98–123.

22. Further discussion of women in dual-career families is in Jacqueline B. Stanfield, "Research on Wife/Mother Role Strain in Dual Career Families," *American Journal of Economics and Sociology* 44 (July 1985): 355–63.

23. Ralph Nader and William Taylor, *The Big Boys* (New York: Pantheon, 1986).

24. John Brooks, *Showing Off in America* (Boston: Little, Brown and Company, 1979), p. 195.

25. Thorstein Veblen, *The Theory of the Leisure Class* (1899; New York: New American Library, 1953).

26. Although the article fails to draw the obvious conclusions, see the following description of a Chicago-based women's network: Grant Pick, "When Women Mean Business," *Chicago* (May 1985).

27. Robert B. Avery, Gregory E. Elliehausen, Glenn B. Canner, and Thomas A Gustafson, "Survey of Consumer Finances, 1983," *Federal Reserve Bulletin* 70 (Sept. 1984): 679–92. See also by the same authors, "Survey of Consumer Finances, 1983: A Second Report," *Federal Reserve Bulletin* 70 (Dec. 1984): 857–68.

28. Avery et al., "Survey of Consumer Finances, 1983," p. 686.

29. Ibid., p. 683.

30. Avery et al., "Survey of Consumer Finances, 1983: A Second Report," p. 863.

31. Ibid., p. 862.

32. Cox, *The Cox Report*, p. 271.

33. Strongly influenced by Veblen, C. Wright Mills was an exception to the myopia of U.S. intellectuals. See his *White Collar* (New York: Oxford University Press, 1951).

34. Adolf A. Berle and Gardiner C. Means, *The Modern Corporation and Private Property*, rev. ed. (New York: Harcourt, Brace and World, 1968); John Kenneth Galbraith, *The New Industrial State* (Boston: Houghton Mifflin, 1967).

35. See Robin Marris, *The Economic Theory of "Managerial Capitalism"* (New York: Basic Books, 1964); and Edith T. Penrose, *The Theory of the Growth of the Firm* (1959; White Plains, N.Y.: M. E. Sharpe, 1980).

36. Edward S. Herman, *Corporate Control, Corporate Power* (Cambridge: Cambridge University Press, 1981), pp. 112–13.

37. Marc R. Tool, *The Discretionary Economy* (Santa Monica, Calif.: Goodyear, 1979), p. 143.

38. Frederick Winslow Taylor, *Scientific Management* (1911; New York: Harper and Brothers, 1947). Nothing here is to imply that Taylor and his followers were cruel men. For their human side see Frank B. Gilbreth, Jr., and Ernestine Gilbreth Carey, *Cheaper by the Dozen* (New York: Thomas Y. Crowell, 1948).

39. Elton Mayo, *The Social Problems of an Industrial Civilization* (Boston: Harvard University Press, 1945).

40. For more extensive treatments see Harry Braverman, *Labor and Monopoly Capital* (New York: Monthly Review Press, 1974); and Richard Edwards, *Contested Terrain* (New York: Basic Books, 1979).

41. This is not necessarily so for managers in the public sector.

42. Harold Geneen with Alvin Moscow, *Managing* (Garden City, N.Y.: Doubleday, 1984), p. 131.

43. Chester I. Barnard, *The Functions of the Executive* (1938; Cambridge, Mass.: Harvard University Press, 1968).

44. Geneen, *Managing*, p. 47.

45. Anthony Sampson, *The Sovereign State of ITT* (New York: Stein and Day, 1973).

46. Geneen, *Managing*, p. 33 (italics and capitalization in original).

47. Sampson, *The Sovereign State of ITT*, pp. 189–228.

48. But see Robert Tressell, *The Ragged Trousered Philanthropists* (1914; New York: Monthly Review Press, 1962).

CHAPTER 3

1. Upton Sinclair, *The Goose Step: A Study of American Education*; rev. ed. (Los Angeles: Upton Sinclair, 1923), p. 331.

2. Although it slights Voltaire, the following is a good introduction: Isaiah Berlin, *The Age of Enlightenment* (New York: New American Library, 1956).

3. See John Dewey, *Democracy and Education* (1916; New York: Macmillan, 1961).

4. John Dewey, *Intelligence in the Modern World*; edited by Joseph Ratner (New York: Random House, 1939), pp. 724, 429.

5. Ibid., p. 422.

6. See Thorstein Veblen, *The Higher Learning in America* (1918; New York: Augustus M. Kelley, 1965); and Sinclair, *The Goose Step*.

7. For an excellent case study, see Ronnie Dugger, *Our Invaded Universities* (New York: W. W. Norton, 1974). See also David Caute, *The Great Fear* (New York: Simon and Schuster, 1978), pp. 403–55.

8. See Robert Coles, *Privileged Ones,* (Boston: Little, Brown and Company, 1977), pp. 413–56.

9. Bureau of the Census, *Statistical Abstract, 1985* (Washington, D.C.: Government Printing Office, 1985), p. 137.

10. C. Wright Mills, *White Collar* (New York: Oxford University Press, 1951), p. 266.

11. Robert M. Hutchins, as quoted in Richard Hofstadter and Wilson Smith, eds., *American Higher Education: A Documentary History* (Chicago: University of Chicago Press, 1961), pp. 932–33.

12. Much of the following section is based on my experiences in the higher learning over the past nineteen years and on the experiences of many of my friends. However, I have been extraordinarily fortunate in my positions at the University of North Texas outside of Dallas and at DePaul University in the Chicago Loop. In fact, NT and DePaul are among the exceptions that prove the rule. A collaborating account can be found in Bertell Ollman, "Academic Freedom in America Today: A Marxist View," *Monthly Review* 35 (March 1984): 24–46.

13. For a description of the child's point of view in these little tragedies, see Coles, *Privileged Ones,* pp. 206–22.

14. C. Wright Mills was an exception to the radical tradition of more or less ignoring the middle class. His *White Collar* is a classic. See also Studs Terkel, *The Great Divide* (New York: Pantheon Books, 1988).

15. Bureau of the Census, *Statistical Abstract of the United States, 1988* (Washington, D.C.: Government Printing Office, 1988), p. 123.

16. Maureen Dowd, "Private-School Race Enters Climax," *New York Times* (Feb. 11, 1985).

17. Bureau of the Census, *Statistical Abstract of the United States, 1988,* p. 122.

18. Ibid., p. 125.

19. Ibid., p. 82.

20. Peter Cohen, *The Gospel According to the Harvard Business School* (New York: Penguin Books, 1974), p. 263.

21. Ibid., p. 67.

22. Ibid., p. 8.

23. Ibid., p. 169.

24. Peter Blau and Otis Dudley Duncan, *The American Occupational Structure* (New York: Wiley, 1967).

25. Christopher Jencks et al., *Inequality* (New York: Basic Books, 1972); and Christopher Jencks et al., *Who Gets Ahead?* (New York: Basic Books, 1977).

26. For further discussion, see Rosabeth Moss Kanter, *Men and Women of the Corporation* (New York: Basic Books, 1977).

27. For further discussion, see William M. Dugger, *An Alternative to Economic Retrenchment* (Princeton, N.J.: Petrocelli Books, 1984).

CHAPTER 4

1. For a brief account of early Puritan New England, see Edmund S. Morgan, *The Puritan Dilemma: The Story of John Winthrop* (Boston: Little, Brown and Company, 1958).

2. Jessie Bernard, *The Future of Marriage* (New York: Bantam Books, 1972), p. 123.

3. Two fine books on the history of the family are William J. Goode, *World Revolution and Family Patterns* (New York: Free Press, 1963); Michael Gordon, ed., *The American Family in Social-Historical Perspective* (New York: St. Martin's Press, 1973).

4. For further discussion see Oscar Handlin, *The Uprooted,* 2d ed. (Boston: Little, Brown and Company, 1973).

5. All data are from the Bureau of the Census, *Statistical Abstract of the United States* (Washington, D.C.: Government Printing Office, various years).

6. Quoted by William H. Whyte, Jr., in his "The Corporation and the Wife," *Fortune* (Nov. 1951): 111.

7. Ibid., p. 111.

8. Jessie Bernard, *Women, Wives, Mothers* (Chicago: Aldine, 1975), p. 232.

9. See Rosabeth Moss Kanter, *Work and Family in the United States* (New York: Russell Sage Foundation, 1977).

10. Bernard, *The Future of Marriage,* p. 53.

11. Ibid., pp. 56–57. See also Betty Friedan, *The Feminine Mystique* (New York: W. W. Norton, 1963); Kanter, *Work and Family,* pp. 37–38; and Hanna Papanek, "Men, Women, and Work: Reflections on the Two-Person Career," *American Journal of Sociology,* 78 (Jan. 1973): 852–72.

12. Whyte, "The Corporation and the Wife," p. 156.

13. See Kenneth Keniston and the Carnegie Council on Children, *All Our Children* (New York: Harcourt, Brace, Jovanovich, 1977); and the following, all by the same authors: Robert Rapoport and Rhona Rapoport, *Dual Career Families* (Baltimore: Penguin, 1971); *Dual Career Families Re-examined* (New York: Harper and Row, 1976); and (eds.), *Working Couples* (New York: Harper and Row, 1978).

14. A notable exception is Paul Goodman, *Growing Up Absurd* (New York: Random House, 1956).

15. See Emmett H. Buell, Jr., and Lee Sigelman, "Popular Support for the Moral Majority in 1980," *Social Science Quarterly* 66 (June 1985): 426–34.

16. See also Brigitte Berger and Peter L. Berger, *The War over the Family* (Garden City, N.Y.: Anchor Press/Doubleday, 1983).

17. See Ferdinand Lundberg, *The Rich and the Super-Rich* (New York: Bantam Books, 1968); G. William Domhoff, *Who Rules America Now?* (Englewood Cliffs, N.J.: Prentice-Hall, 1983); and Howard P. Tuckman, *The Economics of the Rich* (New York: Random House, 1973).

18. Bureau of the Census, *Statistical Abstract of the United States, 1988*, p. 65.

19. Bernard, *The Future of Marriage*, p. 66.

20. The most noteworthy exceptions are Kanter's *Work and Family* and the works of the Rapoports cited above.

21. See Max Weber, *The Protestant Ethic and the Spirit of Capitalism*, translated by Talcott Parsons (1920; New York: Charles Scribner's Sons, 1958).

CHAPTER 5

1. For the original gemeinschaft-gesselschaft distinction, see Ferdinand Tönnies, *Community and Society*, translated and edited by Charles P. Loomis (East Lansing: Michigan State University Press, 1957).

2. See John Kenneth Galbraith, *American Capitalism*, rev. ed. (Boston: Houghton Mifflin, 1956), pp. 114–17.

3. See David Caute, *The Great Fear* (New York: Simon and Schuster, 1978), pp. 352–59.

4. Richard B. Freeman and James L. Medoff, *What Do Unions Do?* (New York: Basic Books, 1984).

5. After considerable survey research, Stark and Glock concluded: "Concern for man-to-man ethics [social gospel] is for all practical purposes not a part of general Protestant religious commitment. Those whose religiousness does take an ethical form are not especially apt to exhibit other kinds of religious commitment, while those who show considerable man-to-God commitment [individual salvation] seem to have little interest in the traditional ethical component of their faith." Rodney Stark and Charles Y. Glock, *American Piety* (Berkeley and Los Angeles: University of California Press, 1970), pp. 181–82.

6. Herbert Wallace Schneider, *Religion in 20th Century America*, rev. ed. (New York: Atheneum, 1964), p. 113.

7. Quoted in Russel B. Nye, *Midwestern Progressive Politics* (New York: Harper and Row, 1965), p. 156.

8. See Dave Davis and Tim Peek, "Pittsburgh Pastor Rallies Victims of Hi-Tech Visions," *In These Times* (Dec. 19, 1984-Jan. 8, 1985).

9. Rodney Stark et al., "Ministers as Moral Guides: The Sounds of Silence," in Charles Y. Glock, ed., *Religion in Sociological Perspective* (Belmont, Calif.: Wadsworth, 1973): 163–86.

10. Ibid., pp. 182–86; and Phillip E. Hammond and Robert E. Mitchell, "Segmentation of Radicalism: The Case of the Protestant Campus Minister," in Glock ed., *Religion in Sociological Perspective*, pp. 136–48.

11. Cornel West, "Religion and the Left: An Introduction," *Monthly Review* (July-

Aug. 1984): 16. See also Sheila D. Collins, "The New Underground Railroad," *Monthly Review* (May 1986): 1–7.

12. Michael Harrington, *The Politics at God's Funeral* (New York: Holt, Rinehart and Winston, 1983), pp. 180–87.

13. Schneider, *Religion in 20th Century America,* p. 9.

14. Martin Luther King, Jr., *Where Do We Go from Here: Chaos or Community?* (Boston: Beacon Press, 1967), pp. 132, 133.

15. See Louis Wirth, "Urbanism as a Way of Life," *American Journal of Sociology* 44 (July 1938): 8–20.

16. Robert A. Nisbet, *Community and Power* (1953; New York: Oxford University Press, 1962), pp. 25–26.

17. Hunter S. Thompson, *Generation of Swine* (New York: Summit Books, 1988), p. 259.

18. Seymour Melman, *Profits without Production* (New York: Alfred A. Knopf, 1983), p. 151.

19. For fiscal years 1981–84, Council of Economic Advisers, *Economic Report of the President, 1985* (Washington, D.C.: Government Printing Office, 1985), p. 317.

20. All data from ibid., p. 317.

21. See John E. Schwarz, *America's Hidden Success,* rev. ed. (New York: W. W. Norton, 1988).

22. Further discussion is in David Halberstam, *The Powers That Be* (New York: Alfred A. Knopf, 1979); and A. J. Liebling, *The Press* (1975; New York: Pantheon Books, 1981).

23. Leary still believes in the liberating power of drugs. See Timothy Leary, *Flash Backs* (Los Angeles: J. P. Tarcher, 1983).

24. Halberstam, *The Powers That Be,* p. 202.

CHAPTER 6

1. G. William Domhoff, *Who Rules America Now?* (Englewood Cliffs, N.J.: Prentice-Hall, 1983). Discussion of the incompatibility of corporate capitalism and democracy is in Amitai Etzioni, *Capital Corruption* (New York: Harcourt, Brace, Jovanovich, 1984); and Charles E. Lindblom, *Politics and Markets* (New York: Basic Books, 1977). See also C. Wright Mills, *The Power Elite* (New York: Oxford University Press, 1956); and G. William Domhoff, *The Powers That Be* (New York: Random House, 1978). More recent discussion is in Robert Lekachman, *Visions and Nightmares* (New York: Collier Books, 1988).

2. Further discussion is in Seymour Melman, *The Permanent War Economy* (New York: Simon and Schuster, 1974).

3. Ferdinand Tönnies, *Community and Society,* translated and edited by Charles P. Loomis (East Lansing: Michigan State University, 1957), p. 119.

4. See A. J. Liebling, *The Press,* 2d ed. (1975; New York: Pantheon Books, 1981); and David Halberstam, *The Powers That Be* (New York: Alfred A. Knopf, 1979).

5. See Max Weber, *From Max Weber: Essays in Sociology,* translated and edited by H. H. Gerth and C. Wright Mills (New York: Oxford University Press, 1946), pp. 51–55 and pp. 196–264.

6. For the pluralist-dominationist debate at its best, see Domhoff, *Who Rules*

America Now? and Robert A. Dahl, *Who Governs?* (New Haven, Conn.: Yale University Press, 1961).

7. The Mentor edition is best because it includes an introduction by C. Wright Mills. Thorstein Veblen, *The Theory of the Leisure Class* (1899; New York: New American Library, 1953).

8. Further discussion of the major issues in Texas education, particularly higher education, is in Geoffrey Rips, "Higher Education and the Cult of Technology," *The Texas Observer* (Dec. 20, 1985).

9. See Domhoff, *Who Rules America Now?* pp. 103–5.

10. John Kenneth Galbraith, *Money* (Boston: Houghton Mifflin, 1975), pp. 22–23.

11. The best case study is of the giant University of Texas. See Ronnie Dugger, *Our Invaded Universities* (New York: W. W. Norton, 1974).

12. Bureau of the Census, *Statistical Abstract of the United States, 1985* (Washington, D.C.: Government Printing Office, 1985), p. 53.

13. Madalyn Murray O'Hare, *Freedom under Siege* (Los Angeles: J. P. Tarcher, 1974).

14. Further discussion of the leading right-wing evangelists is in Perry Deanne Young, *God's Bullies* (New York: Holt, Rinehart and Winston, 1982).

15. See Etzioni, *Capital Corruption.*

16. Samuel Bowles and Herbert Gintis, *Schooling in Capitalist America* (New York: Basic Books, 1976); Ira Katznelson and Margaret Weir, *Schooling for All* (New York: Basic Books, 1985).

17. For a sympathetic treatment of this thesis, see Morris Silver, *Affluence, Altruism, and Atrophy* (New York: New York University Press, 1980).

18. See Students for a Democratic Society, "Port Huron Statement," in Ronald Gross and Paul Osterman, ed., *Individualism: Man in Modern Society* (New York: Dell, 1971), pp. 233–40. See also James Miller, *Democracy Is in the Streets* (New York: Simon and Schuster, 1987), pp. 329–74.

19. The city-on-a-hill myth goes a long way toward explaining the peculiarly moral tone of American imperialism and war. See Loren Baritz, *Backfire* (New York: William Morrow, 1985).

20. See Seymour Melman, *Profits without Production* (New York: Alfred A. Knopf, 1983), pp. 207–22.

21. An excellent description of the politics of deregulation is Susan J. Tolchin and Martin Tolchin, *Dismantling America* (Boston: Houghton Mifflin Company, 1983). Excellent discussions of the economies of regulation are Harry M. Trebing, "The Chicago School versus Public Utility Regulation," *Journal of Economic Issues* 10 (March 1976): 97–126; and Larry Reynolds, "Foundations of an Institutional Theory of Regulation," *Journal of Economic Issues* 15 (Sept. 1981): 641–56.

22. See Lester C. Thurow, *Dangerous Currents: The State of Economics* (New York: Random House, 1983); and William M. Dugger, *An Alternative to Economic Retrenchment* (Princeton, N.J.: Petrocelli Books, 1984).

CHAPTER 7

1. Bertram Gross, *Friendly Fascism* (Boston: South End Press, 1980).

2. Raymond Williams, *The Long Revolution,* rev. ed. (New York: Harper and Row, 1966), p. 100.

3. John Dewey, *Intelligence in the Modern World,* edited by Joseph Ratner (New York: Random House, 1939), p. 400.

4. See Nicolas D. Kristof, "Management, Korean Style," *New York Times* (April 11, 1985).

5. For an earlier, similar case, see Thorstein Veblen, *Imperial Germany and the Industrial Revolution* (1915; New York: Augustus M. Kelley, 1964).

6. William G. Ouchi, *Theory Z* (Reading, Mass.: Addison-Wesley, 1981), p. 56.

7. Thorstein Veblen, "The Opportunity of Japan," in *Essays in Our Changing Order,* edited by Leon Ardzrooni (1934; New York: Augustus M. Kelley, 1964), p. 251.

8. Ouchi, *Theory Z,* pp. 36–39.

9. For an excellent brief description of Japanese feudalism, see Peter Duus, *Feudalism in Japan* (New York: Alfred A. Knopf, 1969).

10. Clyde Haberman, "Japan Schools, Graded, Get Some Hard Knocks," *New York Times* (July 12, 1985), p. 4.

11. Ouchi, *Theory Z,* p. 35.

12. Ibid., p. 35.

13. Ibid., p. 76.

14. See Robert S. Lynd and Helen Merrell Lynd, *Middletown* (1929; New York: Harcourt, Brace and World, 1956), pp. 471–95; and Thorstein Veblen, "The Country Town," in *What Veblen Taught,* edited by Wesley C. Mitchell (New York: Augustus M. Kelley, 1964), pp. 394–442. What Veblen said over fifty years ago about the country town now applies to the corporate career: "The country town is one of the great American institutions; perhaps the greatest, in the sense that it has had and continues to have a greater part than any other in shaping public sentiment and giving character to American culture" (p. 394).

15. See Sheila D. Collins, *The Rainbow Challenge* (New York: Monthly Review Press, 1986).

16. Further discussion of institutional analysis and of the rights dialogue is in William M. Dugger, ed., *Radical Institutionalism* (Westport, Conn.: Greenwood Press, 1989); and Samuel Bowles and Herbert Gintis, *Democracy and Capitalism* (New York: Basic Books, 1986). Further discussion of corporate power is in Wallace C. Peterson, ed., *Market Power and the Economy* (Boston: Kluwer Academic Publishers, 1988); and Warren J. Samuels and Arthur S. Miller, ed., *Corporations and Society* (Westport, Conn.: Greenwood Press, 1987).

Bibliographical Essay

Materials on the subject of corporate hegemony are voluminous and extremely wide-ranging, so I have grouped them into five broad areas: (1) the corporation proper, its origins, evolution, and present conglomerate structure; (2) the general theory of hegemony and its contemporary, corporate form; (3) the social control exercised by the corporation, and the corporation's own escape from the social control of other institutions; (4) the opposing institutions themselves, primarily the school, family, church, community, and state; and (5) the social processes of hegemony—contamination, subordination, emulation, mystification, speeding up, and hollowing out. The resulting bibliographical collection is badly needed and, as far as I know, unique. However, it is limited to materials in English.

THE CORPORATION

For historical perspectives on the changing roles played by the market and the corporation in the evolution of capitalism, see C. E. Ayres, *The Theory of Economic Progress,* 2d ed. (New York: Schocken Books, 1962); Fernand Braudel, *Capitalism and Material Life, 1400–1800,* translated by Miriam Kochan (New York: Harper and Row, 1973); Douglas F. Dowd, *The Twisted Dream* 2d ed. (Cambridge, Mass.: Winthrop Publishers, 1977); R. H. Tawney, *The Agrarian Problem in the Sixteenth Century* (1912; New York: Harper and Row, 1967); Karl Polanyi, *The Great Transformation* (Boston: Beacon Press, 1944); and Raymond Williams, *The Long Revo-*

lution, rev. ed. (New York: Harper and Row, 1966). Explanations of how corporate administration has been replacing market haggling are provided by Alfred D. Chandler, Jr., *The Visible Hand: The Managerial Revolution in American Business* (Cambridge, Mass.: Belknap Press of Harvard University Press, 1977); and Alfred D. Chandler, Jr., *Strategy and Structure: Chapters in the History of the American Industrial Enterprise* (Cambridge, Mass.: MIT Press, 1962).

For the early evolution of the corporate form, see John P. Davis, *Corporations,* edited by Abram Chayes (1905; New York: Capricorn Books, 1961); and Tom Hadden, *Company Law and Capitalism* (London: Weidenfeld and Nicolson, 1972). A classic is Adolf A. Berle and Gardiner C. Means, *The Modern Corporation and Private Property,* rev. ed. (New York: Harcourt, Brace and World, 1968). An attempt to bring the corporation under the umbrella of neoclassical theory is in Oliver E. Williamson, *Markets and Hierarchies* (New York: Free Press, 1975); and Oliver E. Williamson, "The Modern Corporation: Origins, Evolution, Attributes," *Journal of Economic Literature* 19 (Dec. 1981): 1537–68. Contrast Williamson with Charles R. Spruill, *Conglomerates and the Evolution of Capitalism* (Carbondale: Southern Illinois University Press, 1982); and with William M. Dugger, "The Transaction Cost Analysis of Oliver E. Williamson: A New Synthesis?" *Journal of Economic Issues* 17 (March 1983): 95–114. Of major significance is John Kenneth Galbraith, *The New Industrial State* (Boston: Houghton Mifflin, 1967). The classic on economic concentration and market deterioration is John M. Blair, *Economic Concentration* (New York: Harcourt, Brace, Jovanovich, 1972). More recent discussions of the U.S. corporate economy include Samuel Bowles, David M. Gordon, and Thomas E. Weisskopf, *Beyond the Wasteland* (Garden City, N.Y.: Anchor Press/Doubleday, 1983); Seymour Melman, *Profits without Production* (New York: Alfred A. Knopf, 1983); and William M. Dugger, *An Alternative to Economic Retrenchment* (Princeton, N.J.: Petrocelli Books, 1984). An interesting survey is found in Allan Cox, *The Cox Report on the American Corporation* (New York: Delacorte Press, 1982).

Excellent discussions of the conglomerate corporation are Willard F. Mueller, "Conglomerates: A 'Nonindustry,'" in Walter Adams, ed., *The Structure of American Industry,* 6th ed. (New York: Macmillan, 1982), pp. 427–74; John F. Winslow, *Conglomerates Unlimited* (Bloomington: Indiana University Press, 1973); Charles R. Spruill, *Conglomerates and the Evolution of Capitalism* (Carbondale: Southern Illinois University Press, 1982); and Corwin D. Edwards, "Conglomerate Bigness as a Source of Power," in *Business Concentration and Price Policy* (Princeton, N.J.: Princeton University Press, 1955), pp. 331–59. See also William M. Dugger, "The Shortcomings of Concentration Ratios in the Conglomerate Age: New Sources and Uses of Corporate Power," *Journal of Economic Issues* 19 (June 1985): 343–53; and William M. Dugger, "Centralization, Diversification, and Administrative Burden in U.S. Enterprises," *Journal of Economic Issues* 19 (Sept. 1985): 687–701. Coordinating arrangements not based on conglomerate ownership are discussed in John R. Munkirs, "Centralized Private Sector Planning: An Institutionalist's Perspective on the Contemporary U.S. Economy," *Journal of Economic Issues* 17 (Dec. 1983): 931–67; and John R. Munkirs, *The Transformation of American Capitalism* (Armonk, N.Y.: M. E. Sharpe, 1985).

Japanese comparisons are in David Halberstam, *The Reckoning* (New York: William Morrow, 1986); and William G. Ouchi, *Theory Z* (Reading, Mass.: Addison-Wesley, 1981). For an earlier international comparison, see Thorstein Veblen, *Im-*

perial Germany and the Industrial Revolution (1915; New York: Augustus M. Kelley, 1964); and Thorstein Veblen, "The Opportunity of Japan," in *Essays in Our Changing Order,* edited by Leon Ardzrooni (1934; New York: Augustus M. Kelley, 1964), pp. 248–66. For an excellent brief description of Japanese feudalism, see Peter Duus, *Feudalism in Japan* (New York: Alfred A. Knopf, 1969).

Basic theoretical contributions include Robin Marris, *The Economic Theory of "Managerial Capitalism"* (New York: Basic Books, 1964); Edith T. Penrose, *The Theory of the Growth of the Firm* (1959; White Plains, N.Y.: M. E. Sharpe, 1980); Alfred S. Eichner, *The Megacorp and Oligopoly* (White Plains, N.Y.: M. E. Sharpe, 1980); and Alfred S. Eichner, *The Macrodynamics of Advanced Market Economies* (Armonk, N.Y.: M. E. Sharpe, 1987). Also of interest are Peter E. Earl, *The Corporate Imagination* (Armonk, N.Y.: M. E. Sharpe, 1984); and Dennis C. Mueller, *The Modern Corporation* (Lincoln: University of Nebraska Press, 1986).

Additional works of substance in this area are Ed Cray, *Chrome Colossus* (New York: McGraw-Hill, 1980); John M. Blair, *The Control of Oil* (New York: Pantheon Books, 1976); Walter Adams and James W. Brock, *The Bigness Complex* (New York: Pantheon, 1986); Edward S. Herman, *Corporate Control, Corporate Power* (Cambridge: Cambridge University Press, 1981); John Kenneth Galbraith, *American Capitalism,* rev. ed. (Boston: Houghton Mifflin, 1956); and Warren J. Samuels and Arthur S. Miller, ed., *Corporations and Society* (Westport, Conn.: Greenwood Press, 1987). Further discussion of corporate economic power is in Wallace C. Peterson, ed., *Market Power and the Economy* (Boston: Kluwer Academic Publishers, 1988).

HEGEMONY AND ITS CORPORATE FORM

Theoretical works include Hans Gerth and C. Wright Mills, *Character and Social Structure* (New York: Harcourt, Brace, Jovanovich, 1953); C. Wright Mills, *The Power Elite* (New York: Oxford University Press, 1956); Antonio Gramsci, *Selections from the Prison Notebooks,* edited and translated by Quintin Hoare and Geoffrey Nowell Smith (New York: International Publishers, 1971); and Bertram Gross, *Friendly Fascism* (Boston: South End Press, 1980). Two histories of the Nazis are William L. Shirer, *The Rise and Fall of the Third Reich* (New York: Simon and Schuster, 1959); and Alan Bullock, *Hitler: A Study in Tyranny,* rev. ed. (New York: Harper and Row, 1964).

The question of whether the United States is pluralist or hegemonic is discussed in G. William Domhoff, *Who Rules America Now?* (Englewood Cliffs, N.J.: Prentice-Hall, 1983); G. William Domhoff, *The Powers That Be* (New York: Random House, 1978); and Robert A. Dahl, *Who Governs?* (New Haven, Conn.: Yale University Press, 1961). Veblen's institutional analysis is instructive. See Thorstein Veblen, *The Theory of the Leisure Class* (1899; New York: New American Library, 1953). Although Augustus M. Kelley has brought out a fine set of Veblen works, the Mentor edition of *Leisure Class* is best because it includes an introduction by C. Wright Mills. Further institutional analysis is in William M. Dugger, ed., *Radical Institutionalism* (Westport, Conn.: Greenwood Press, 1989); and Samuel Bowles and Herbert Gintis, *Democracy and Capitalism* (New York: Basic Books, 1986). Of related interest are Ferdinand Lundberg, *The Rich and the Super-Rich* (New York: Bantam Books, 1968); and Howard P. Tuckman, *The Economics of the Rich* (New York: Random House, 1973).

Discussion of the incompatibility of corporate capitalism and democracy is in Amitai Etzioni, *Capital Corruption* (New York: Harcourt, Brace, Jovanovich, 1984); and Charles E. Lindblom, *Politics and Markets* (New York: Basic Books, 1977). More recent discussion is in Robert Lekachman, *Visions and Nightmares* (New York: Collier Books, 1988). A manifesto of hope is in Students for a Democratic Society, "Port Huron Statement," in Ronald Gross and Paul Osterman, eds., *Individualism: Man in Modern Society* (New York: Dell, 1971); and James Miller, *Democracy Is in the Streets* (New York: Simon and Schuster, 1987). See also Marc R. Tool, *The Discretionary Economy* (Santa Monica, Calif.: Goodyear, 1979); and William M. Dugger, *An Alternative to Economic Retrenchment* (Princeton, N.J.: Petrocelli Books, 1984). The role of war and war spending is discussed in Seymour Melman, *The Permanent War Economy* (New York: Simon and Schuster, 1974). The city-on-a-hill myth goes a long way toward explaining the peculiarly moral tone of American imperialism and war. See Loren Baritz, *Backfire* (New York: William Morrow, 1985).

For the seminal role of the country town in the emerging U.S. hegemony, see Robert S. Lynd and Helen Merrell Lynd, *Middletown* (1929; New York: Harcourt, Brace and World, 1956); and Thorstein Veblen, "The Country Town," in *What Veblen Taught,* edited by Wesley C. Mitchell (New York: Augustus M. Kelley, 1964), pp. 394–442.

SOCIAL CONTROL

The social control of other institutions over the corporation is weakening. The major academic study of crimes committed by U.S. corporations is Marshall B. Clinard and Peter C. Yeager, with Ruth Blackburn Clinard, *Corporate Crime* (New York: Free Press, 1980). Of related interest is Paul Brodeur, *Outrageous Misconduct* (New York: Pantheon Books, 1985). Discussion of cash cows and corporate milking is in William M. Dugger, *An Alternative to Economic Retrenchment* (Princeton, N.J.: Petrocelli Books, 1984), pp. 62–63; Michael E. Porter, *Competitive Strategy* (New York: Free Press, 1980), pp. 361–67; and George S. Day, "Diagnosing the Product Portfolio," *Journal of Marketing* 41 (April 1977): 29–38. See also Barry Bluestone and Bennett Harrison, *The Deindustrialization of America* (New York: Basic Books, 1982). A fine case study is Michael F. Sheehan, "Corporate Control and the Decapitalization of Subsidiary Corporation: The Looting of the Bangor and Aroostook Railroad," *Journal of Economic Issues* 22 (Sept. 1988): 729–45. Walter Adams and James W. Brock, "Corporate Power and Economic Sabotage," *Journal of Economic Issues* 20 (Dec. 1986): 919–40; and Anthony Sampson, *The Sovereign State of ITT* (New York: Stein and Day, 1973).

The social control of the corporation over individuals is strengthening. Classic works include Thorstein Veblen, *Absentee Ownership and Business Enterprise in Recent Times* (1923; New York: Augustus M. Kelley, 1964); David Riesman with Nathan Glazer and Reuel Denny, *The Lonely Crowd* (1950; Garden City, N.Y.: Doubleday, 1956); C. Wright Mills, *White Collar* (New York: Oxford University Press, 1951); William H. Whyte, Jr., *The Organization Man* (Garden City, N.Y.: Doubleday, 1957); Michael Maccoby, *The Gamesman* (New York: Bantam Books, 1978). See also Ralph Nader and William Taylor, *The Big Boys* (New York: Pantheon, 1986); Michael Maccoby, *The Leader* (New York: Simon and Schuster, 1981); and Rosabeth Moss Kanter, *Men and Women of the Corporation* (New York: Basic Books, 1977).

For further discussion of human character in contemporary society, see Erich Fromm, *The Anatomy of Human Destructiveness* (New York: Holt, Rinehart and Winston, 1973); and Christopher Lasch, *The Culture of Narcissism* (New York: W. W. Norton, 1978). To put in context the debate between methodological individualists, who believe that individuals create their own values, and methodological collectivists, who believe that individuals acquire their values through interaction with others, see William M. Dugger, "Two Twists in Economic Methodology: Positivism and Subjectivism," *American Journal of Economics and Sociology* 42 (Jan. 1983): 75–91. Further discussion of corporate culture is in Thomas J. Peters and Robert H. Waterman, Jr., *In Search of Excellence* (New York: Harper and Row, 1982); and Terrence E. Deal and Allan A. Kennedy, *Corporate Cultures* (Reading, Mass.: Addison-Wesley, 1982).

Discussions of occupation, income, and social standing are in Peter Blau and Otis Dudley Duncan, *The American Occupational Structure* (New York: Wiley, 1967); Seymour Martin Lipset and Reinhard Bendix, *Social Mobility in Industrial Society* (Berkeley and Los Angeles: University of California Press, 1964); Richard P. Coleman and Lee Rainwater with Kent A. McClelland, *Social Standing in America* (New York: Basic Books, 1978); Christopher Jencks et al., *Inequality* (New York: Basic Books, 1972); and Christopher Jencks et al., *Who Gets Ahead?* (*New York: Basic Books, 1977).

THE OPPOSING INSTITUTIONS

The classic on higher education in the United States is Thorstein Veblen, *The Higher Learning in America* (1918, New York: Augustus M. Kelley, 1965). An excellent source is Richard Hofstadter and Wilson Smith, eds., *American Higher Education: A Documentary History* (Chicago: University of Chicago Press, 1961). Of more recent interest are Samuel Bowles and Herbert Gintis, *Schooling in Capitalist America* (New York: Basic Books, 1976); Ira Katznelson and Margaret Weir, *Schooling for All* (New York: Basic Books, 1985). For an excellent case study, see Ronnie Dugger, *Our Invaded Universities* (New York: W. W. Norton, 1974). On repression in education, see David Caute, *The Great Fear* (New York: Simon and Schuster, 1978); Upton Sinclair, *The Goose Step: A Study of American Education*; rev. ed. (Los Angeles: Upton Sinclair, 1923); Bertell Ollman, "Academic Freedom in America Today: A Marxist View," *Monthly Review* 35 (March 1984): 24–46. Although it slights Voltaire, the following is a good introduction to the underlying values on which education in the West is based: Isaiah Berlin, *The Age of Enlightenment* (New York: New American Library, 1956). See also John Dewey, *Democracy and Education* (1916; New York: Macmillan, 1961); and John Dewey, *Intelligence in the Modern World*; edited by Joseph Ratner (New York: Random House, 1939). Critical views of the contemporary scene are Peter Cohen, *The Gospel According to the Harvard Business School* (New York: Penguin Books, 1974); and J. Paul Mark, *The Empire Builders: Power, Money and Ethics Inside the Harvard Business School* (New York: William Morrow, 1987). For a detailed, fascinating, and sweeping account, see the five-volume series, Robert Coles, *Children of Crisis* (Boston: Little, Brown and Company, 1977).

Materials on the family abound. For a brief account of early Puritan New England, see Edmund S. Morgan, *The Puritan Dilemma: The Story of John Winthrop* (Boston:

Little, Brown and Company, 1958). The following are very helpful: Jessie Bernard, *Women, Wives, Mothers* (Chicago: Aldine, 1975); Jessie Bernard, *The Future of Marriage* (New York: Bantam Books, 1972); Rosabeth Moss Kanter, *Work and Family in the United States* (New York: Russell Sage Foundation, 1977); Betty Friedan, *The Feminine Mystique* (New York: W. W. Norton, 1963); and Hanna Papanek, "Men, Women, and Work: Reflections on the Two-Person Career," *American Journal of Sociology* 78 (Jan. 1973): 852–72. See also Kenneth Keniston and the Carnegie Council on Children, *All Our Children* (New York: Harcourt, Brace, Jovanovich, 1977); and the following, all by the same authors: Robert Rapoport and Rhona Rapoport, *Dual Career Families* (Baltimore: Penguin, 1971); *Dual Career Families Re-examined* (New York: Harper and Row, 1976); and (ed.), *Working Couples* (New York: Harper and Row, 1978). Discussion of women in dual-career families is in Jacqueline B. Stanfield, "Research on Wife/Mother Role Strain in Dual Career Families," *American Journal of Economics and Sociology* 44 (July 1985): 355–63. Paul Goodman is profound in *Growing Up Absurd* (New York: Random House, 1956). See also Brigitte Berger and Peter L. Berger, *The War over the Family* (Garden City, N.Y.: Anchor Press/Doubleday, 1983). On the history of the family, see William J. Goode, *World Revolution and Family Patterns* (New York: Free Press, 1963); and Michael Gordon, ed., *The American Family in Social-Historical Perspective* (New York: St. Martin's Press, 1973).

For the original gemeinschaft-gesselschaft distinction on which much of the analysis of community is based, see Ferdinand Tönnies, *Community and Society,* translated and edited by Charles P. Loomis (East Lansing: Michigan State University Press, 1957). For a continuation of the Tönnies-type theory of community, see Louis Wirth, "Urbanism as a Way of Life," *American Journal of Sociology* 44 (July 1938): 8–20; and Robert A. Nisbet, *Community and Power* (1953; New York: Oxford University Press, 1962). Also see Oscar Handlin, *The Uprooted,* 2d ed. (Boston: Little, Brown and Company, 1973). For community destruction, see Barry Bluestone and Bennett Harrison, *The Deindustrialization of America* (New York: Basic Books, 1982). Excellent oral history is in Studs Terkel, *The Great Divide* (New York: Pantheon Books, 1988).

On the church in the United States, see Jerry Falwell, *Listen, America!* (Garden City, N.Y.: Doubleday, 1980). Contrast Falwell with Madalyn Murray O'Hare, *Freedom under Siege* (Los Angeles: J. P. Tarcher, 1974). Less controversial sources are Emmett H. Buell, Jr., and Lee Sigelman, "Popular Support for the Moral Majority in 1980," *Social Science Quarterly* 66 (June 1985): 426–34; Max Weber, *The Protestant Ethic and the Spirit of Capitalism*, translated by Talcott Parsons (1920; New York: Charles Scribner's Sons, 1958). On the social gospel and the social relevance of religious belief, see Rodney Stark and Charles Y. Glock, *American Piety* (Berkeley and Los Angeles: University of California Press, 1970); Herbert Wallace Schneider, *Religion in 20th Century America,* rev. ed. (New York: Atheneum, 1964); Charles Y. Glock, ed., *Religion in Sociological Perspective* (Belmont, Calif.: Wadsworth, 1973); Michael Harrington, *The Politics at God's Funeral* (New York: Holt, Rinehart and Winston, 1983). Also of interest along these lines is Cornel West, "Religion and the Left: An Introduction," *Monthly Review* (July-Aug. 1984): 9–19; and Sheila D. Collins, "The New Underground Railroad," *Monthly Review* (May 1986): 1–7. Still relevant is Martin Luther King, Jr., *Where Do We Go from Here: Chaos or Community?* (Boston: Beacon Press, 1967). Popular issues are addressed in Perry Deane Young,

God's Bullies (New York: Holt, Rinehart and Winston, 1982); and Larry Martz, *Ministry of Greed* (New York: Weidenfeld and Nicolson, 1988).

The decline of the state in the United States is taking place primarily through deregulation. The politics of deregulation are described in Susan J. Tolchin and Martin Tolchin, *Dismantling America* (Boston: Houghton Mifflin Company, 1983). The economics of regulation are covered in Harry M. Trebing, "The Chicago School versus Pubic Utility Regulation," *Journal of Economic Issues* 10 (March 1976): 97–126; and Larry Reynolds, "Foundations of an Institutional Theory of Regulation," *Journal of Economic Issues* 15 (Sept. 1981): 641–56. For a broader discussion of the politics of economic theory, see Lester C. Thurow, *Dangerous Currents: The State of Economics* (New York: Random House, 1983). Also of interest are Russel B. Nye, *Midwestern Progressive Politics* (New York: Harper and Row, 1965); John E. Schwarz, *America's Hidden Success,* rev. ed. (New York: W. W. Norton, 1988); and Sheila D. Collins, *The Rainbow Challenge* (New York: Monthly Review Press, 1986).

The labor union and the news media are also significant institutions within the structure of corporate hegemony. See Richard Edwards, *Contested Terrain* (New York: Basic Books, 1979); Richard B Freeman and James L. Medoff, *What Do Unions Do?* (New York: Basic Books, 1984); Mitchell Stephens, *A History of News* (New York: Viking, 1988); David Halberstam, *The Powers That Be* (New York: Alfred A. Knopf, 1979); and A. J. Liebling, *The Press* (1975; New York: Pantheon Books, 1981).

THE SOCIAL PROCESSES OF HEGEMONY

Thorstein Veblen was an early analyst of the social processes of hegemony. See his *The Higher Learning in America* (1918; New York: Augustus M. Kelley, 1965). C. Wright Mills was strongly influenced by Veblen. See C. Wright Mills, *White Collar* (New York: Oxford University Press, 1951). See also William M. Dugger, "Corporate Bureaucracy," *Journal of Economic Issues* 14 (June 1980): 399–409; idem, "Power: An Institutional Framework of Analysis," *Journal of Economic Issues* 14 (Dec. 1980): 897–907; idem, "The Continued Evolution of Corporate Power," *Review of Social Economy* 43 (April 1985): 1–13; and idem, "An Institutional Analysis of Corporate Power," *Journal of Economic Issues* 22 (March 1988): 79–111.

An early literary study of contamination is in Robert Tressell, *The Ragged Trousered Philanthropists* (1914; New York: Monthly Review Press, 1962). In addition to his *Higher Learning in America,* see Thorstein Veblen, *The Instinct of Workmanship* (1914; New York: Augustus M. Kelley, 1964); and *Absentee Ownership and Business Ownership in Recent Times* (1923; New York: Augustus M. Kelley, 1964). Michael Maccoby has also explored contamination, but through his concept of craftsmanship in *The Gamesman* (New York: Bantam Books, 1978).

Different aspects of emulation are discussed and described in John Brooks, *Showing Off in America* (Boston: Little, Brown and Company, 1979); Thorstein Veblen, *The Theory of the Leisure Class* (1899; New York: New American Library, 1953); Robert B. Avery, Gregory E. Elliehausen, Glenn B. Canner, and Thomas A. Gustafson, "Survey of Consumer Finances, 1983," *Federal Reserve Bulletin* 70 (Sept. 1984): 679–92; and, by the same authors, "Survey of Consumer Finances, 1983: A Second Report," *Federal Reserve Bulletin* 70 (Dec. 1984): 857–68. Rather sensationalist treatments of mystification are to be found in Hunter S. Thompson, *Generation of Swine*

(New York: Summit Books, 1988); and Timothy Leary, *Flash Backs* (Los Angeles: J. P. Tarcher, 1983).

For accounts of pioneers in speeding up, see Frederick Winslow Taylor, *Scientific Managment* (1911; New York: Harper and Brothers, 1947); Elton Mayo, *The Social Problems of an Industrial Civilization* (Boston: Harvard University Press, 1945); and Harold Geneen with Alvin Moscow, *Managing* (Garden City, N.Y.: Doubleday, 1984). Nothing here is to imply that Taylor and his followers were cruel men. For their human side see Frank B. Gilbreth, Jr., and Ernestine Gilbreth Carey, *Cheaper by the Dozen* (New York: Thomas Y. Crowell, 1948). For more extensive treatments see Harry Braverman, *Labor and Monopoly Capital* (New York: Monthly Review Press, 1974); and Richard Edwards, *Contested Terrain* (New York: Basic Books, 1979). Also of interest is Chester I. Barnard, *The Functions of the Executive* (1938; Cambridge, Mass.: Harvard University Press, 1968).

Index

ing, 174; subordination of community values, 42; in U.S., xv, 130
Company: holding, 10, 32; joint-stock, 12; single-industry, 17–18, 20, 35–36
Compartmentalization, 99–100
Compensation, executive, 38
Competition: career, 75; international, xi; learning to compete in school, 63; plane of, 21–23; price of, 19–20
Computers, in education, 105
Concentration: conglomerate, 22; economic, 16–18; ratios, 16–17, 22
Conformity, 2–4; competitive, 169; corporate career, 170; in corporate life, 5–6; and emulation, 43; in graduate school, 66; small town, 169–70
Conglomerate, 18–21; defined, 17; go-go versus imperial, 18–19; growth, 17–18; imperial, 20–24, 32; as institutionalized greed, 52; merger, 10, 16; and separation of ownership from control, 50
Conglomerates Unlimited (Winslow), 19
Congress, xi
Congress of Industrial Organizations (CIO), 107–8
Conservatives, in the Democratic party, 123
Consulting, 34
Consumption, conspicuous, 44–45
Contamination, 39, 144–49; artisan, 41; church, 145–47; defined, 40, 136; family, 147–48; school, 144–45; state, 148–49
Continuum, means-ends, 163–64
Contractors, defense, xi, 132
Contracts, ability to make, 10
Control, separation of, from ownership, 48–52
Control, social, 33, 39; by the career, 170; of the corporation, 37; emulation, 43; in Japan, 167–68; of managers, 38; by the small town, 169–70
Convergence, of the U.S. and Japan, 165–68
Cooptation, 46, 56
Corporado, xv, 79–80, 100, 164; faith of, 115

Corporation: blocking progress, 175; characteristics of, 9–12; contradictory nature of, 15–16; as dominant institution, xiii, 9; as prime mover, ix; purpose of, xiii–xiv, 13
Corruption, 148
Counterbalancing institutions, xv–xvii
Counterculture, 1–2
Counterrevolution, xvi–xvii
Courtesy, 164
Cox, Allan, 38, 46
Craft, 40–41
Creationism, 135, 152
Creativity, 23, 57
Credentials, 73–74
Crozier, Michel, 1
Culture, 14; and control of management, 50, 54; corporate, 33–34, 38; cultural lag, 165; defined, 47; trivialization of, 135 Curran, Joe, 108

Darrow, Clarence, 154
Dealing, reciprocal, 19–21
Decentralization, 30
Deficit: balance of payments, xi; budget, xi–xiii
Deindustrialization, xii–xiii, 23, 35, 85
The Deindustrialization of America (Bluestone and Harrison), 35
DeLorean, John, 75
Demand, ix, xi, xiii; for college graduates, 72
Democracy, 163
Democrats, xvi, 122–23, 173
Department, functional, 29–30
Depreciation, 35
Deregulation, xvi, 156, 158
Desperado, 79–80
Detox centers, 139–40
Dewey, John, 56, 69, 150, 163
Diaspora, of the American mind and conscience, 67
Diem, Ngo Dinh, 119
Directors, boards of, 12–13, 21
Discipline, classroom, 74
Dispensation, new, 21–25
Dissertation, doctoral, 66
Dissidents, 57, 83

Thoreau, Henry David, 138
Tolerance, 1–2, 4, 171
Tönnies, Ferdinand, 81
Tool, Marc R., 51
Totalitarianism, xvii, 4–5, 101
Town, small, xv–xvi
Toyota, xiii, 20
Trade, balance of, xi
Trading, insider, x
Transfer, 104
Trial, by committee, 66
Trivialization, 132, 135
Truncation, 132, 134
Trustees, board of, 68–69, 76
Turner, Ted, 126

U-form organization, 29–30
Unemployment, x, 73–74, 145; "natural rate," 22–23
Union, 107–11; business, 129; as counterbalancing institution, 173; strengthening, 172–73; teachers, 64
United Motor Corporation, 20
Unity, 164
University, 59
Urbanization, 84–85
U.S. Steel Corp., x, xii
Utilities, 155–56

Values: career, 167; change in, 39–40, 106; contamination of, 40–41; corporate, xv, 5–7, 167–69; in culture, 47, 104; in hegemony, 4–5, 47; inculcated, 15; in Japan, 167; and the labor movement, 107; in pluralism, 1–2, 47; Puritan, 83; religious, 111–17; U.S., 168–69
Veblen, Thorstein, 21, 54; on education, 56; on emulation, 43, 138; on invaluation processes, 39; on Japan, 165; on the line of competition, 22
Venture, joint, xii–xiii, 21
Vietnam. *See* South Vietnam
The Village Voice, 125
Vocation, xvi, 132; vocational educa-

tion, xvi, 133–34, 141; vocationalism, 145, 151
Volcker, Paul, xi Voting, 123, 173
Vouchers, educational, 62, 133–34

Wagner Act, 107
Walden, 138
Wallace, Henry, 108
War: expensive junk, 155; in the media, 134; and pluralism, 1; privatization of, 132; profiteering, 121–22, 132; Second World War, 7; U.S. Civil War, 83; Wars of the Roses, 8
Washington Post, 124
Watergate, 123, 126, 134
Wealth, 95–96, 138
Weber, Max, 136
Welfare, 152
West, Cornel, 115
West, the, 9
Westmoreland, William C., 126
White Collar (Mills), 5
White-collar work, 109–10, 173
White Knight, 11
Whyte, William H., Jr., 5, 90
Wife: burden of, 98; career, 99; family role, 89–93; and the Moral Majority, 93–94
Will, 2–3, 40
Williams, Raymond, 131, 163
Winslow, John F., 19
Winthrop, John, 154
Wives, subordination of, 42
Women: women's liberation, 44, 90, 94, 113, 129, 143–44, 152; in the work force, 109. *See also* Misogyny
Workmanship. *See* Artisanship
World Council of Churches, 114

Yippies (Youth International Party), 46
Youth: gullible, 120; revolt of, 70, 153, 158–59; speeding up, 70–75
Yuppies (young urban professionals), 46, 63; song of, 79

Zionism, 159

ABOUT THE AUTHOR

WILLIAM M. DUGGER is Professor of Economics at DePaul University, Chicago. His publications include *Radical Institutionalism* (Greenwood Press, 1989), *An Alternative to Economic Retrenchment*, as well as articles in *Journal of Economic Issues*, *Review of Social Economy*, and other scholarly journals.

HD2785
D84
1989

MAY 2 2 1990

IAFHS401 02/27/90 AILL